Macromedia Generator and Flash Demystified

The Official Guide to Using Generator with Flash

MIKE CHAMBERS
PHILLIP M. TORRONE
CHRISTOPHER L. WIGGINS

macromedia®
PRESS

Macromedia Generator and Flash Demystified

The Official Guide to Using Generator with Flash

Mike Chambers, Phillip M. Torrone & Christopher L. Wiggins

 Published by Peachpit Press, a division of Addison Wesley Longman, in association with Macromedia Press.

Peachpit Press
1249 Eighth Street
Berkeley, CA 94710
510/524-2178 • 800-283-9444
510/524-2221 (fax)

Find us on the World Wide Web at: **http://www.peachpit.com**
http://www.macromedia.com

Find the Flash and Generator Demystified Web site at: **http://www.demystified.com**

Copyright © 2001 by Mike Chambers, Phillip M. Torrone & Christopher L. Wiggins

Editors: Jill Marts Lodwig and Corbin Collins
Copy Editor: Jill Simonson
Macromedia Tech Readers: David Adams, Colin Cherot, Gina Chin, Jonathan Duran,
Gayle Pietras, Chris Roomian, and Denise Seymour
Interior Design: Mimi Heft
Production Coordinator: Lisa Brazieal
Compositor: David Van Ness
Cover Design/Layout: Wolken Communica; **Concept:** Design Hovie Studios
Index: Emily Glossbrenner

ISBN 0-201-72584-3

9 8 7 6 5 4 3 2 1

Printed and bound in the United States of America

ACKNOWLEDGMENTS

The authors would like to thank the following people: Our editors and friends at Peachpit Press who made the impossible possible: Nancy, Marjorie, Jill, Corbin, Lisa, David, and Gary-Paul; our friends at Macromedia: Rob, Kevin, Tom, Eric, Jeremy, Linda, Shalini, Gayle, Mike, Steve, Brian, Karen, Anna Marie, Suzanne, Jerry, Julie and Troy; and our friends at Fallon: Pat, Rob, David, Anne, Mark, Paul, Kevin, Brooke, Jim, Tom and Christian. Finally, thanks to our community and friends: Margaret, Annie, Stewart, Lynda, Colin, Josh, Branden, Yugo, Sam, Todd, Natalie, Randy, Leo, Jim, Jason, Dan, Kevin, Glenn and Erin.

First and foremost I would like to thank my wife, Cathy, for putting up with all of my late nights of playing around with Generator and Flash. Without her patience, my contribution to this project would not have been possible.

I would also like to thank the Flash and Generator communities for providing the best resource on Flash and Generator anywhere, and for being a constant source of inspiration.

Finally, I would like to thank my family, Christian Cantrell, Har'el Romans-Murray, Paul Arce, Robb Corrigan, John Orme and everyone on the Generator team at Macromedia.

—Mike Chambers

This is for my mother, who has always been there for me. I'd also like to thank the people who have stuck with me on this crazy ride. Creativity and innovation cannot be developed in ease and quiet. Only through experience and hard work with our friends can our ambitions be inspired and success achieved.

—Phillip M. Torrone

Thanks to all my close friends who inspire me when I need it and who help me not take it all too seriously when I don't. And of course thanks to my parents, to whom I owe pretty much everything.

—Chris Wiggins

CONTENTS AT A GLANCE

TABLE OF CONTENTS

PART 2: USING GENERATOR

Chapter 6: Meet the Generator Objects   87

Chapter 7: Generator Data Sources   177

Chapter 8: Using Middleware with Generator   205

Part 3: Deployment

Chapter 9: Generator Offline   241

Chapter 10: The Generator Administration
Servlet and Caching 263

Chapter 13: Generator for Video   331

PART 4: ADVANCED TOPICS

APPENDIXES

INTRODUCTION

IF YOU'RE A PROFESSIONAL DESIGNER OR DEVELOPER USING MACROMEDIA Flash, chances are Macromedia Generator should be or already is part of your tool kit. Although Flash is great for delivering sophisticated vector-based animations and interactive movies over the Web, it isn't powerful enough to create the kind of on-demand content that large corporate sites and applications often require.

For example, say you wanted to redesign a corporate financial site using beautiful vector-based stock charts calculated and drawn on the fly. Or perhaps your goal is to let visitors personalize your site's content. In the past, you would have had to rely on traditional HTML or Java applets; Flash simply wasn't up to the job—that is, not until the advent of Generator.

With Generator—a data-driven solution that processes dynamic content in Flash movies—you can perform such disparate tasks as automating daily news updates (and their accompanying graphics) for large Flash sites and delivering secure and personalized bank account information within a dynamic Flash interface. You can even use Generator to create *non*-Flash assets—for example, you can use it to deliver content on the fly to Palm devices or Web-based phones. Imagine a portal site created entirely within Flash that serves up personalized data like sports scores and stock prices, which users can download to their PDAs each time they synchronize with their PCs!

High-end developers responsible for big-budget corporate projects will likely be easily seduced by all the possibilities that Generator affords. But creators of smaller-scale projects have reason to get excited, too. Because Generator is able to separate content from design, every project is easier to execute, regardless of scope. That means last-minute content changes from the client are much simpler to incorporate. And personal Flash sites can be updated more easily and frequently.

DESIGNER OR PROGRAMMER TOOL?

Because Generator is not a stand-alone authoring application like other Macromedia products, it's difficult to categorize. First, Generator comprises two very different components, the authoring extensions and the server. To further complicate matters, it's available in two versions, or what we call "flavors," Generator 2 Developer Edition and Generator 2 Enterprise Edition. There's even a quasi-flavor: The authoring extensions are included as an add-on with Flash 5, allowing just a portion of the program to be used.

One way to think of Generator is as a bridge between the Flash front-end application and the back-end source of dynamic data. The authoring extensions enhance the Flash authoring environment by providing additional panels and the ability to export to a new format. It's the server, however, that does the bulk of the work: Once designers or developers have inserted placeholders indicating where dynamic content should be delivered, the server substitutes the dynamic content from a database or other data source and serves up the result as a standard Flash movie.

So is Generator intended for programmers or designers? The answer is *both*. One of Generator's greatest strengths, in fact, is that it promotes collaboration among people with *different* skill sets. Some users are Flash designers who know a lot about design principles and interface creation in Flash but almost nothing about programming, databases, or Java classes. Other Generator users are experienced developers with strong technical backgrounds but little or no creative training. Still others fall somewhere in between. This book is written with all of these audiences in mind.

Platforms and requirements

Because Generator has two components—the authoring extensions and the server—system requirements are more complex than usual. For the authoring extensions, system requirements are identical to those of the Flash authoring environment:

Windows

- 133-MHz or faster Pentium or compatible processor
- Windows 95, 98, NT 4.0 or later, or Windows 2000
- 32 MB of free RAM

Macintosh

- PowerPC processor
- Mac OS 8.5 or later
- 32 MB of free RAM

Cross-platform

- 40 MB free disk space
- 800 x 600 color monitor
- CD-ROM drive
- Microsoft Internet Explorer 4.0 or later, or Netscape Navigator 4.0 or later

For the server-side component, system requirements differ depending on which Generator edition you use—Developer or Enterprise. Chapter 1 includes an exhaustive list of the system requirements for each.

WHAT YOU'LL LEARN FROM THIS BOOK

As Web designers and developers, we've been using Flash with Generator to create corporate intranets, Web sites, and Web applications for a range of corporate clients since Generator first appeared. Along the way, we've learned a lot about these products' strengths and weaknesses—knowledge we're now ready to pass on to you.

Whether you're a designer or a programmer, our goal is to provide all the information you need to get up and running with Generator as quickly as possible. This book is intended as both tutorial and reference—something to keep handy and refer back to when building Flash sites with dynamic content. We'll warn you about pitfalls and provide tips that can shave hours from projects. We'll also answer common questions and address typical concerns (for example, "When is it better to use Generator with Flash than Flash by itself?").

Designers will learn everything they need to know about the tools and panels Generator adds to the Flash authoring environment, as well as how to use them to create Flash movies with dynamic content. We'll also share some tricks for formatting and animating real-time content, even though the content isn't actually inside the Flash movie.

Programmers and systems integrators, on the other hand, will get the low-down on the server side of the equation, including the differences between the Developer and Enterprise Editions and what makes one better than the other for a given project. We'll show you how to choose the correct edition for your project, install it, and optimize it—everything you need to know to successfully deploy a Generator solution.

GENERATOR: BETTER LIVING THROUGH BETTER INTERFACES

When Flash made its debut as FutureSplash, it wasn't much more than a fun, albeit primitive, tool for delivering simple vector-based animation to a limited number of viewers. After Macromedia acquired the program in 1996, however, it began to change dramatically. The company added feature upon feature and jump-started its adoption by way of the Flash Player plug-in. As a result, the number of Flash-enabled viewers grew exponentially, and Flash evolved into the Web designer's tool of choice in the entertainment industry. The combination of high-quality, fully animated vector graphics and quick download times made it extremely attractive for Web-based animations, short cartoons, and similar content. Not coincidentally, as the number of Flash users grew, so did developers' interest in bringing Flash into more sophisticated corporate projects.

Flash's appeal is obvious: Well-designed Flash interfaces download quickly and provide a richer, more enjoyable user experience than can be achieved through the traditional HTML-based interfaces. Today, over a quarter of a billion Web surfers are able to view Flash content via the Flash plug-in on their browsers, making it more readily viewable than Java applets and almost as universally viewable as HTML. As a result, entire site interfaces and even complex online applications are being created in Flash today.

Yet Flash has not forgotten its roots: Judging from the number of talented animators who use the program today, Flash remains the best tool for creating cartoon-like Web content.

One of Generator's best features is the power it brings to interface design for sophisticated corporate Web-based projects. Thanks to Generator, Flash is deployed today in situations where it wouldn't even have been considered in the past: corporate intranets, business-to-business and e-commerce sites, personalized Web portals, even online banks.

But why is this a good thing? After all, Generator isn't bringing any new functionality to the Web; it merely lets us use existing functionality inside Flash. The following are just a few of the advantages of creating interfaces entirely in Flash for sites that demand real-time content.

Flash provides more bang for the bandwidth buck. Because Flash is vector based, you can give users either a more graphically rich interface for the same bandwidth price as a traditional bitmap-based site or the same degree of graphic richness in a faster-loading interface. The choice is yours, but either way users win.

USABANCSHARES.COM: The first 100 percent Flash-based, Generator-driven online bank.

And because Flash movies can load other Flash movies, it's possible to run entire sites from within a single Flash movie embedded in just one HTML page—an approach that allows you to further decrease download time and provide users with a more seamless experience. For example, the main interface can be loaded first, and after that, each request the user makes requires a wait only for the loading of a tiny vector-based file into the main file. The speed advantage this brings, especially over the course of an entire session, is tremendous when compared to traditional HTML.

Flash reduces platform and browser compatibility problems. This is one of the most overlooked advantages of using Flash as the entire interface. Web designers and developers are accustomed to struggling to make their interfaces look and function properly across all browsers and platforms—a problem that nearly vanishes when you use a *single* plug-in (rather than the browser itself) as the client. When you use Flash with Generator, you control both server and the client, which means better compatibility.

Flash offers better display options for dynamic content. Because Generator lets you use Flash to render dynamic content, you can use the same custom antialiased fonts and animated interface elements that you've employed for other Flash projects. Although there are other ways to dynamically generate a chart for the Web, Generator charts are scalable, antialiased, and as picture-perfect as you want them to be. And even though the content is dynamically generated, you can still control its appearance using Flash's familiar display options.

Flash opens the door for sophisticated navigation. Flash offers plenty of ways to create sophisticated but corporate-friendly navigation throughout a site. Hierarchical drop-down menus, sliding menus, and other schemes can be executed much more elegantly using Flash than with HTML or DHTML. Familiar draggable windows become an interface option with Flash, introducing even more possibilities.

THE BEST OF BOTH WORLDS:
Flash and Generator offer total control over the display and naviagation of data-driven Web sites.

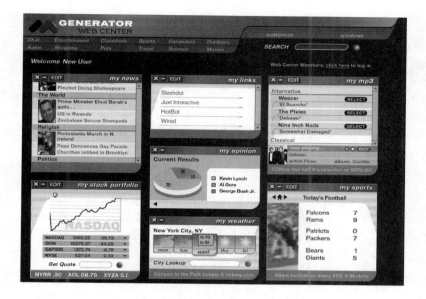

There are lots of reasons to offer up your dynamic content from within Flash. However, Generator can also update *any* graphic content—not just content developed in Flash. Say you already have Generator pumping out dynamic Flash content at your site and you want to get the same dynamic content into a format that is PDA friendly. Generator can generate GIF and JPG files as easily as it can generate Flash files, saving you lots of development time. Once you've done the necessary work with the data sources, you can then have Generator dynamically create the content for Flash sites on the Web, PDAs, cell phones, and various other Web-enabled devices. In addition, Generator lets you create multiple versions of your Flash site for international users simply by changing the data sources. With a little planning, you can avoid most reediting of the Flash source files.

HOW TO USE THIS BOOK

This book covers a lot of material and is intended for a wide variety of readers. If you're new to Generator and need to get up to speed as quickly as possible, you can read it front to back and participate in all the tutorials in order. If you're already familiar with Generator, you'll probably want to use this book as a handy reference, referring back to it when you need to be reminded how to do something.

We've used icons to flag chapters and sections of the book that are of particular interest to certain types of users.

From the Designer's perspective. Most designers will be interested primarily in learning how the new features in the Generator authoring extensions will add to the familiar Flash interface. You'll see the Designer icon beside sections of the book that discuss new panels, inspectors, and an on-stage element called Generator objects, all of which are part of the authoring extensions component. You'll also find the Designer icon next to sections that discuss idiosyncrasies in the way Generator formats dynamic content. And just as traditional Web designers need to understand HTML so that they can avoid impractical design decisions, Flash-with-Generator designers need a rough understanding of the way Generator works to avoid designs that aren't well suited to this program. For that reason we've also used the Designer icon to flag areas that discuss the program's inner workings.

From the Techie's perspective. The system integrator or technical developer is usually less interested in getting Generator to format content in beautiful ways than in learning how to get various data sources to work with Generator. Their questions include the following: What sorts of data sources can Generator work with? How does the data need to be formatted? Can you use ODBC, JDBC, Java classes, and XML? What is the application layer all about? Can you create your own Generator objects? How can you use caching to improve performance and manage content? These are the issues likely to be of interest to system integrators, and we'll discuss them and more in the chapters and sections marked with the System Integrator icon.

At many studios, the designer and techie roles are sometimes blurred. When the Designer and System Integrator icons appear together, the discussion applies to both types of users.

In addition to the Designer and System Integrator icons, we also use the following icons to call attention to special sections:

This indicates a helpful suggestion—not something you necessarily have to pay attention to but advice that will help you get the most out of Generator or Flash.

The Key Concept icon means pay attention; this is important stuff!

The CD icon indicates that the accompanying CD includes an example of what you're reading about. You can use the CD example to follow along yourself.

The Try icon indicates another idea you might want to try in addition to the main point we're making.

The See Elsewhere arrow points you to related sections of the book where the same topic is discussed in more detail.

This symbol warns you of problems you may encounter if you're not careful.

The CD-ROM component

The accompanying CD-ROM includes all the tools and examples we wish had been available to us over the last few years as we were developing large-scale projects using Flash and Generator. Many of the files and applications demonstrated on the CD-ROM are from live, working projects.

PART 1:
GETTING STARTED

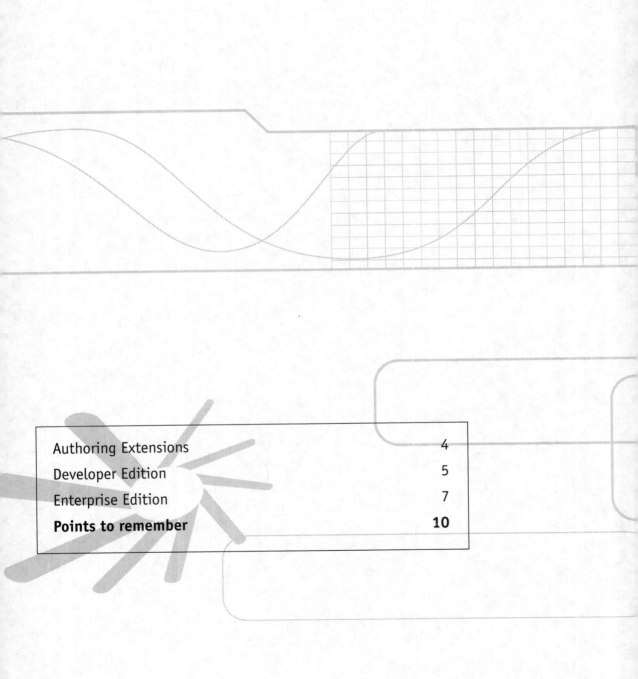

CHAPTER 1

THE FLAVORS OF GENERATOR

AN UNUSUAL FEATURE OF GENERATOR IS THAT IT'S AVAILABLE IN TWO QUITE different versions—a fact that can cause confusion at first. You see, usually when developers talk about versions of software, they're referring to differences between older and newer versions of the same program. In the case of Generator, however, they could well be talking about two equally up-to-date versions, each with its own unique feature set. Thus, instead of using the word *versions* when we talk about Generator; we prefer to use the word *flavors*.

Generator is offered in two flavors so that users can purchase just the amount of power they need: For low-transaction-volume sites that require regular updates and personalized content, Generator Developer Edition is the right choice. However, for large-scale projects that require mission-critical, real-time information, Generator Enterprise Edition (the more powerful flavor) is the more appropriate package. Finally, if you count the Generator Authoring extensions included with Flash 5, there are actually *three* Generator flavors. This quasi-flavor is all you need if you're only looking for a slightly easier way to make infrequent changes to your Flash site.

AUTHORING EXTENSIONS

With no server-side component, the Generator Authoring extensions represent only the authoring side of the program—the side with which designers interact. They contain only the raw basics: just the enhancements to the Flash authoring software.

Some of the things you can do with the authoring extensions include the following:

Take Generator for a test drive. The extensions contain everything you need to create, preview, and test Flash movies with Generator content—perfect for helping you determine which of the true Generator flavors is right for your project.

Update your Flash sites more easily. With the extensions installed, you can update the content of your Flash movie simply by replacing sections of text or graphics with placeholders. Using a placeholder isolates the content from its formatting, allowing you to change copy inside text blocks, or replace graphics simply by editing a text file and re-exporting the movie.

Automate production. By using the authoring extensions, non-Flash experts can easily update your Flash site's content because the updates can be made without actually editing the Flash movie.

The authoring extensions are included on the Flash 5 CD. Once you've installed the extensions, your Flash interface will include all of the Generator panels and inspectors, as well as Generator objects. You can also download a fully functional version of the Generator Authoring Extensions for free from Macromedia's Web site—and it's not just a 30-day trial version!

Keep in mind, however, that by themselves, the authoring extensions don't really fulfill Generator's main purpose—that is, to serve up dynamic content through Flash. For that, you'll need the Developer or Enterprise Edition.

Authoring-extensions platforms and requirements

Windows

Flash for Windows (Version 4 or later)

133-MHz Pentium processor

Windows 95, 98, 2000, NT 4, or later

32 MB RAM (64 MB RAM recommended)

20 MB available hard disk space

Macintosh

Flash for Macintosh (Version 4 or later)

Power Macintosh

Mac OS 8 or later

32 MB RAM (64 MB RAM recommended)

20 MB available disk space

DEVELOPER EDITION

The first of the two true Generator flavors is the Developer Edition, a data-driven solution for automatically updating Flash and graphical content. This edition includes a version of the server component as well as the authoring extensions. For coders who want to create their own custom Generator objects, it also includes a software development kit (SDK) and an open application programming interface (API).

Ideal for sites that need to be automatically updated at regular intervals (rather than in real time), the Developer Edition is appropriate for the majority of Generator projects. It would work well, for example, on a site that included news and images that needed to be automatically updated nightly. Updates to catalogs, press releases, and graphic content for mobile devices are all examples of tasks this flavor can easily accommodate.

Often, the developers of sites that incorporate this type of content will also create a Web-based tool for the administrator so that updates are easy to perform. In such cases, the server-side component to Generator is run only when the administrator makes a change to the site. Since Generator isn't being run every time a user comes to the site, the implementation doesn't need to be as powerful—another instance in which Generator Developer Edition provides the perfect solution. People also like to use this flavor with common scheduling applications (for example, Windows Task Manager or Cron for Unix systems), which update content automatically.

The Developer Edition does have some limitations, however. Because it processes requests one at a time, it's not useful for projects that require real-time generation of dynamic content. For example, you couldn't use this flavor on a site that served up real-time data, such as an online bank. It also doesn't scale across multiple processors.

Developer Edition platforms and requirements

Windows NT 4.0 (with Service Pack 5.0 or higher installed) or Windows 2000

64 MB RAM

48 MB available disk space

64 MB available disk swap space

200-MHz Pentium processor or faster recommended

Windows 95, 98, or 2000

32 MB RAM (64 MB Recommended)

48 MB available disk space

200-MHz Pentium processor or faster recommended

Sun Solaris 2.6, 2.7 or 2.8

64 MB RAM

128 MB available disk swap space

80 MB available disk storage space

SPARC processor (Intel version of Solaris is not supported)

Red Hat 6.1 Linux

64 MB RAM

128 MB available disk swap space

80 MB available disk storage space

ENTERPRISE EDITION

Generator Enterprise Edition is the heavy-hitter of the Generator flavors. It allows mission-critical, real-time information to be viewed by large numbers of users, and it can still scale based on your needs. Like the Developer Edition, it includes the authoring extensions. However, in addition to offering all of the capabilities of the Developer Edition, this flavor also offers a number of much more powerful features such as caching and a browser-based administration servlet. It also includes the Generator SDK for creating custom objects. Generator Enterprise Edition also supports multiprocessor systems, which are a prerequisite on sites with very high-volume traffic.

Not surprisingly, this flavor is also the more expensive; however, if you're deploying enterprise-class Generator projects, this is the application you want. Say you need real-time display of information based on data that changes frequently, or you're updating graphics that need to be part of a Flash interface. Real-time financial information such as charts and tickers needs to take advantage of real-time serving of content. Personalized Web sites that allow the user to view content in real time based on the user's choices, such as Flash-based portals, benefit from the Enterprise Edition as well. Large Flash-based Web sites with enterprise-level server loads also require the caching, content management, and performance of Generator Enterprise Edition.

The SDK included with all versions of Generator allows developers to extend the functionality of Generator by creating their own objects. For example, if a company needed custom graphics, the developer could easily create the objects in Java and then add them to the Generator Object Panel, where other designers and developers could make use of them. The developer could also create a custom object that always pulls the appropriate data from the database and displays it as a certain type of scrolling list.

Then, the designer could simply drag an object off the Generator Object Panel without even entering a data source. Sample objects and source, such as boxes, buttons, URL actions, data sources, and extrude objects, are shipped with all versions of Generator.

Enterprise Edition platforms and requirements

Generator Enterprise Edition runs on the following operating systems: Windows NT 4.0, Windows 2000, Solaris 2.6/2.7/2.8, and Red Hat Linux 6.1. It supports the following Web servers: IIS, 4.0/5.0 (Windows 2000), iPlanet Web Server 4.0/4.1, Apache version1.3 or later.

For any real-time generation of content, a dual processor server is recommended for Generator Enterprise Edition.

Windows NT 4.0 (with Service Pack 5.0 or higher installed) or Windows 2000

64 MB RAM

48 MB available disk space

64 MB available disk swap space

200-MHz Pentium processor or faster recommended

For online generation:

Internet Information Server 4.0

Internet Information Server 5.0 (Windows 2000 only)

Personal Web Server 4.0

iPlanet Web Server, Enterprise Edition 4.0 or 4.1

Dual-processor server recommended

Windows 95, 98, or 2000

32 MB RAM (64 MB recommended)

48 MB available disk space

200-MHz Pentium processor or faster recommended

For online generation:

Personal Web Server 4.0

Dual-processor server recommended (Windows 2000)

Sun Solaris 2.6, 2.7 or 2.8

64 MB RAM

128 MB available disk swap space

80 MB available disk storage space

SPARC processor (Intel version of Solaris is not supported)

For online generation:

Apache HTTP server 1.3 or later

Netscape Enterprise Server 3.5 and 3.6

iPlanet Web Server, Enterprise Edition 4.0 or 4.1

Dual-processor server recommended for Generator Enterprise Edition

Red Hat 6.1 Linux

64 MB RAM

128 MB available disk swap space

80 MB available disk storage space

For online generation:

Apache HTTP server 1.3.9 or greater

Dual-processor server recommended for Generator Enterprise Edition

Points to Remember

Here's are a few key concepts to take away from what we've covered so far:

- Generator comes in two flavors, Developer Edition and Enterprise Edition—three if you count the authoring extensions as a flavor.

- The authoring extensions serve as Generator's user interface, allowing developers to test-drive Generator, create data-driven content locally, and automate production.

- Generator Developer Edition is designed primarily for use on projects that need to automatically update their graphics workflow or have low transaction volumes or require real-time and personalized content.

- Generator Enterprise Edition allows mission-critical, real-time information to be displayed to very large numbers of users, and it can still scale based on your needs.

- All the Flash templates you create work on both flavors of Generator.

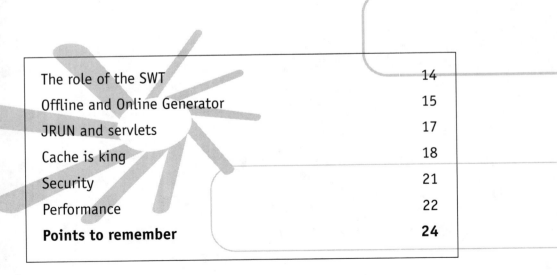

CHAPTER 2

GENERATOR UNDER THE HOOD

BEFORE YOU PUSH UP YOUR SLEEVES AND START CREATING DATA-DRIVEN Flash content, let's take a look at how Generator works, as well as what effect it will have on performance and security. In this chapter, we examine the individual components that make up Generator and describe in detail a recent and important addition to the Generator product line: caching.

THE ROLE OF THE SWT

To put Generator in perspective, let's take a look at how Flash content is typically requested and served. When Generator isn't involved, a client computer requests a Flash movie— also known as a SWF (pronounced *swiff*) file—which the Web server immediately delivers. The Flash player—typically a plug-in that resides inside the Web browser— then plays the movie. The browser displays *exactly* what resides on the Web server, which means that all users see precisely the same content.

Serving up content the traditional way.

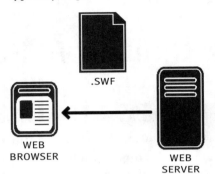

WEB BROWSER

.SWF

WEB SERVER

When a Flash movie's content needs to be generated dynamically, it's time for Generator to enter the picture. As you might expect, things become a bit more complex at this point.

So how do we introduce the kind of dynamic content and design that require Generator? Through Flash! Flash is the *front-end interface*, or authoring tool, of Generator. The Generator authoring extensions (which are installed along with Flash unless you specify otherwise) enable you to create not only SWF files but also SWT (pronounced *swit*) files. (SWTs are also sometimes called Generator templates.) If you've installed the authoring extensions, you can create SWT files; you don't need the server-side component of Generator running on your system to do this. Conversely, developers don't need Flash on the Web server to serve SWTs. The templates, which must be placed on the server, are what Generator uses to wed data and content.

Once the extensions are installed, SWTs can be created and uploaded to the Web server.

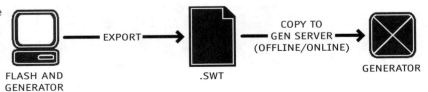

FLASH AND GENERATOR

EXPORT

.SWT

COPY TO GEN SERVER (OFFLINE/ONLINE)

GENERATOR

OFFLINE AND ONLINE GENERATOR

Both the Developer and Enterprise Editions of Generator can be run in either online or offline mode. Although the mode you select will not affect the process of serving dynamic content, it will determine how often Generator runs and, consequently, how personalized or up to date the information contained in your Flash movie will be.

In either mode, Generator uses a .SWT file (the Generator template) and its associated data sources to produce and serve a standard SWF movie. In offline mode, Generator runs less frequently—perhaps according to an arbitrary schedule set by an administrator—and the SWFs it produces are served no differently than SWFs produced in Flash without Generator. In online mode, in contrast, SWFs are generated on the fly every time an end user makes a request to the server: This means that the movie doesn't actually exist until a user requests it, allowing its content to be extremely personalized and up to date.

Offline mode

Although for certain tasks there's no substitute for online mode, the majority of Generator projects do just fine in offline mode: They simply don't require the more robust (and server-intensive) capabilities of online mode. A good example of a project well suited for Generator offline mode would be a site that needed to be regularly updated by a site administrator. If that site included blocks of time-sensitive text (for example, press releases, news headlines, and so on), it would be too labor-intensive to require a designer to update the text inside the Flash authoring environment and then re-export the SWFs daily. However, with Generator offline mode, you can automate the tasks a designer would be performing in the Publish settings of Flash.

How it works

Offline mode relies on the executable component of Generator, called Generate. For PC users, this is basically a DOS application (generate.exe) that can run directly from the MS-DOS command line or from a batch or scripting environment such as an MS-DOS batch file. For UNIX folks, Offline Generator can be invoked from the command line in a shell or from a Perl script.

The generator application is invoked and generates a file that is added to the file system.

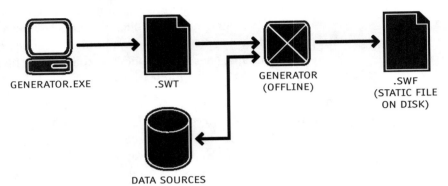

GENERATOR.EXE   .SWT   GENERATOR (OFFLINE)   .SWF (STATIC FILE ON DISK)

DATA SOURCES

Like most command-line applications, Offline Generator has several options (command-line switches) for modifying the program's default operation (for example, you can specify the file output type or the message debug level). It's also important to note that it does not require a Web server to run, and you can use it to output to a number of formats (not just SWF). You can also employ Offline Generator to create JPGs, GIFs, PNGs, QuickTime movies, image maps, and text files.

Offline Generator differs from Online Generator in several ways:

LET'S TALK OFFLINE:
For a comprehensive look at Offline Generator, see Chapter 9.

- Offline Generator is executed from the command line as opposed to online Generator, which is run through a Web server.

- Offline Generator saves the file it creates to the file system. Online Generator sends the generated file to what ever requested it (usually a Web browser) and does not save it to the file system.

- Offline Generator can create image maps and Mac and Windows Flash projectors.

Online mode

Although Offline Generator is the right tool for many jobs, it's not suitable for all. What if, say, your project needed to serve dynamic information so time-sensitive that even 10-minute-old data wasn't current enough? In cases like this, there's no substitute for online mode: It's what to use when you need highly personalized or time-sensitive information dynamically delivered inside Flash.

In online mode, Generator cooks up a custom Flash movie on the fly—*when the user requests it*—and then delivers it. As a result, this mode is far more taxing on the server and typically requires more robust hardware. It also works better with the more powerful version of Generator: Enterprise Edition.

It's important to remember that in online mode, a SWT is always being called in real time to produce developer-specified or user-requested output. It's also worth pointing out that all templates created in Flash will run on both the Enterprise and the Developer Editions, which means that designers can create their Generator templates without knowing (or caring) which edition will be used to serve the finished files.

How it works

When Online Generator is given a request for a custom Flash file, it marries the data from the data source with the SWT by passing the request to an instance of a Java servlet, an object used to process server-side requests and generate responses for the application or client that made the request. Just as offline mode uses Generate (the executable component of Generator) to do the work, Online Generator uses servlets.

Generator installs a servlet engine when it is installed. In most cases this is Macromedia JRun, although it will also work with other servlet engines, such as iPlanet.

Because Generator uses a high-performance architecture, more than one instance of the servlet can be executed. After the servlet has completed its task the instance is destroyed.

JRUN AND SERVLETS

Java servlets are similar to CGI applications, allowing developers to extend the functionality of their Web servers. However, unlike CGI applications which must be started each time they are needed, Java servlets remain in memory. This means that Java servlets are very fast and can handle high levels of traffic.

Generator's servlet engine

When you install Generator, you're also installing the JRun application server from Macromedia. JRun is the servlet engine that allows Generator to pass information to and from the Web server via the Java servlet protocol. Because JRun is preconfigured, it's unlikely that you'll ever have to do more than start or restart the service.

GOT SERVLETS?
Generator can be used with other servlet engines; see Chapter 15.

If you're using iPlanet, JRun is not installed; the iPlanet servlet engine is used instead. The online server component requires JRun or iPlanet as the application server; it also requires a Generator-supported Web server. One of the benefits of this architecture—and we speak from experience here—is that it allows you to develop applications on NT, Linux, or Solaris and then deploy them in other environments without modifying server-side code—a huge plus for developers because it allows them to meet a wide range of client needs by supporting a myriad of systems.

CACHE IS KING

As already mentioned, Generator Enterprise Edition's new caching feature provides some amazing performance gains by allowing content to be processed, saved to disk or memory cache, and then served repeatedly without having to be retrieved again. This allows you to reduce the load on the server and increase the response time for Generator.

The caching process

Let's say you have a financial hub that updates financial information every 20 minutes. In this case, you would set the cache to expire every 20 minutes. The manner in which you configure the caching feature will depend on your Web server's capabilities, your free disk space, and the type of files being processed. (And we can't stress enough how much good it does to run a server with a lot of disk space and RAM.) Generator caching is a powerful tool that can automate the process of updating media and become an important part of your organization's content management system—if not the content management system *itself*. However, caching can also increase the danger of serving stale or out-of-date data if you don't configure template expiration times properly.

If you're using Generator Enterprise Edition in online mode, you can specify to have a template cached as soon as it has been created—a capability that allows Generator to process information faster by storing frequently requested information for reuse. This can improve performance anywhere from to 30 to 200-plus percent!

All requests from the cache will be served from the cache until either the

The user requests the SWT; Generator marries the data with content; and then it checks the cache and serves the content accordingly.

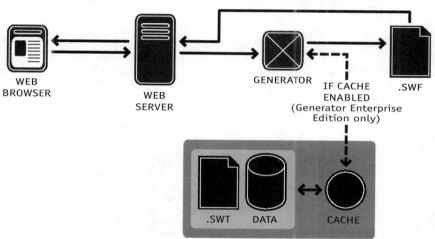

cache is updated or its settings are changed. You can make cache and expiration settings unique to each file; you can apply them globally; or you can put them in the URL string.

Types of caching

Generator Enterprise Edition uses three memory caches: request, media, and font. It also uses one disk cache (file). The settings on the Global Cache Settings panel apply to all of the caches. Although you configure each cache separately, they work together in a hierarchical manner to process requests; the *way* they work together depends on which configuration you choose.

Generator processes server templates based on two criteria: whether each cache is enabled, and whether the requested data is in the cache or must be fetched from the source.

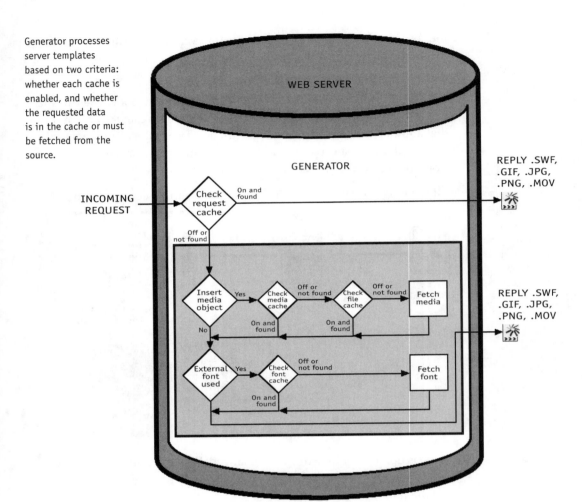

Generator's caching features are only available in the Enterprise Edition and can be controlled via the Administration Servlet, which is also only available in the Enterprise Edition. The Administration Servlet provides a browser-based user interface for viewing Generator information and modifying the Generator configuration. Because the Administration Servlet user interface is browser based, you can administer Generator and the caching feature from either a local or remote machine.

Caching and performance

By using Generator's caching capabilities with the Enterprise Edition, you can significantly improve a single machine's throughput when the application's caching features *are not* enabled. The number and types of extensions used, the caching features deployed, and the way the caching features are configured will all affect the magnitude of that improvement.

Request caching—in which the request cache captures the generated output in memory and then reuses it for subsequent requests—will produce the most dramatic performance increases. When a request arrives for the cached template, Generator returns the cached output rather than process the request from scratch. The primary drawback of request caching is that the output is not generated per request, a fact that makes it less suitable for personalized applications. However, the request cache can be refreshed or expired at regular intervals (one second, for example) to "freshen" the data being delivered from the cache.

Font caching improves performance in two ways: It reduces the size of each template file by the size of the font data that would have been included with the template. And it caches and shares data across all the templates that use it. The reduction in overall template file size means that Generator template files can be loaded much more quickly. In cases in which multiple, complex fonts have been used, the time savings can be significant.

When Generator caches fonts, the external font data is loaded once into memory and used for any template that references that data. By reducing load time for each template and sharing redundant data, Generator is able to process template files more efficiently: It increases throughput and response time without sacrificing any of Generator's dynamic capabilities. For most projects, font caching can be easily implemented to improve performance because font data is generally static.

SECURITY

As we've already explained, Generator provides a way to include dynamic data within Flash movies. Dynamic data, however, often means personal, sensitive information; thus, the question, How secure is Flash with

Generator? The answer is *exactly as secure as any other method of delivering data over the Web.* This is because Generator works in conjunction with whatever security model the Web server employs to encode sensitive data (for example, bank account information) that passes between you and the server. For example, one model—the industry-standard Secure Sockets Layer (SSL)—works by creating a temporary shared "key" that lets only the client and the server on either end of a transmission scramble and unscramble information. To everyone else—including all the servers that may relay the message—the SSL transmission is indecipherable.

PERFORMANCE

A meeting with a client eager to use Generator for a given project is usually followed by another round of meetings that include representatives from the client's IT staff. Arm yourself: Sometimes the hardest part of a Generator project is convincing these folks that the program is up to the task. The first question they're likely to ask is, "Can Generator handle the intense traffic and data volumes of large corporate Web sites, intranets, and extranets?" They're also likely to be reluctant to use Generator if they're unfamiliar with JRun, application servers, and so on.

What you need to make these IT staffers understand is that Generator is hands-down the fastest, most robust, heaviest-duty compositing engine on the market. To help with that task we've included on the enclosed CD a white paper analyzing Generator's performance characteristics, as determined for Macromedia by third-party testing. We encourage you to check it out: Armed with this document and a string of successful projects, we've turned a fair number of nonbelievers into Generator devotees.

Mode and performance

Generator in online mode can deliver thousands of GIFs, JPGs, animated GIFs, MOVs, and Flash Movies (SWFs) to hundreds of simultaneous users (depending on template construction, networks, and hardware configurations). As good as Generator is at delivering content in online mode, we recommend that you take a hard look at your project to determine whether you can get away with using offline mode. Many projects that at first glance seem to require real-time data can actually be executed perfectly in offline mode. And offline generation poses far fewer performance constraints than online generation because of its batched nature.

Offline generation can take place on a machine other than the Web server, and the resulting files can be placed on the Web server(s) to be served up as static files. By allocating resources this way, files can be updated on a regular schedule without imposing the performance constraints of online mode on the Web serving environment.

Another thing to keep in mind is that offline generation can be performed on the same hardware as that used by the Web serving environment. This has little affect on performance because generation only takes place at the frequency set by the administrator. In contrast, online (or real-time) generation enables you to create content that's generated every time a user requests a Generator template. Although online mode poses significant performance constraints, remember that caching can come to the rescue: With some type or combination of caching enabled, you can boost performance by as much as 200 percent.

POINTS TO REMEMBER

- When serving a static Flash movie, or SWF, from a Web server, the browser displays exactly what resides on the Web server, and all users see precisely the same content. You don't need Generator to serve a static Flash movie—it's much like embedding graphics into HTML pages.

- Generator's authoring extensions serve as the program's front end. Once installed, placeholders for data driven content can be created when the Flash template is generated.

- Generator offline mode relies on the executable component of Generator, called Generate. It allows Flash movies to be generated via batch processing. Generator Offline does not require a Web server to run.

- You can use offline mode to output to a number of formats, including SWF, JPG, GIF, PNG, QuickTime, image maps, and text files.

- In online mode, Flash templates are called in real time to generate developer-specified or user-requested output.

- By enabling some type or combination of caching in Generator Enterprise Edition, you can boost performance by as much as 200 percent.

- When you install Generator, you're also installing the JRun application server. JRun is the servlet engine that allows Generator to pass information to and from the Web server via the Java servlet protocol.

- You can use other servlet engines with Generator; see Chapter 15 for details.

- Generator works in conjunction with the security model used by the Web server, which means that Flash with Generator is exactly as secure as any other method of delivering data via the Web.

PART 2:
USING
GENERATOR

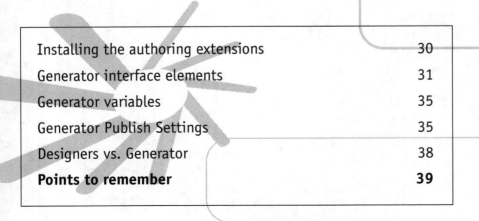

CHAPTER 3

GENERATOR'S AUTHORING ENVIRONMENT

RATHER THAN REQUIRE DEVELOPERS TO LEARN A BRAND-NEW STAND-ALONE interface, Macromedia has done us all a favor by piggybacking Generator's interface on the already established interface of Flash itself—a practical approach since Generator is used primarily to place dynamic content within Flash movies. All Generator template creation takes place inside what amounts to an enhanced version of Flash—i.e., Flash with the Generator authoring extensions installed.

In this chapter, we'll acquaint you with the additions and alterations that the Generator authoring extensions bring to your familiar Flash authoring environment (many of which we'll describe in greater detail in later chapters). It's important to note, however, that this chapter is not intended as a Flash tutorial; that program has far too much depth for us to adequately cover here in a single chapter. If you have little or no familiarity with Flash, we urge you to take advantage of the many great resources available for learning it. See Chapter 17 for more information on where to look for good information on Flash.

INSTALLING THE AUTHORING EXTENSIONS

To transform Flash into a powerful Generator authoring tool, you must install the Generator authoring extensions. These extensions are nothing more than some additional files that augment your copy of Flash 5 with Generator's authoring tools. They are included on the Flash 5 CD, and you are given the option to install them while running the Flash 5 installer.

THE GENERATOR
AUTHORING INTERFACE.

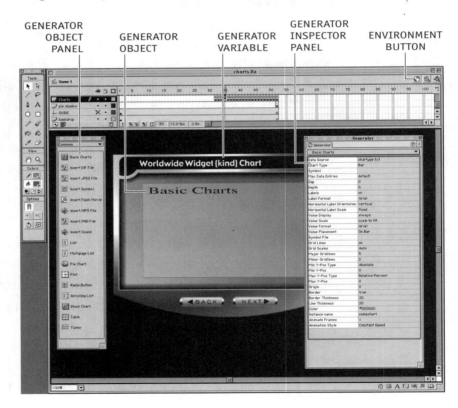

GENERATOR INTERFACE ELEMENTS

Once you've installed the authoring extensions, you're ready to start creating your own Generator templates. Launch Flash, and you'll notice that it now contains some new and unfamiliar elements. The following provides a tour of these elements and explains their functions.

Generator objects

Generator uses a new type of stage element, called a Generator object, to specify where and how dynamic content should appear within Flash movies. Generator objects serve as placeholders for various types of dynamic content; you can place them on stage and manipulate them just as you would other types of symbols. However, because they are merely placeholders for content to come, Generator objects appear on stage as generic-looking, semi-transparent gray boxes with the object's type identified in the upper right corner.

You can think of Generator objects as a special kind of movie clip because, in many respects, that's how they behave. You can drag them onto the stage and position, scale, rotate, and animate them. In most cases, you can even assign instance names to Generator objects so that you can change their properties (_alpha, _x, _y, and so on) via ActionScript just as you would with a movie clip. Generator objects cannot, however, be edited—at least not in the way movie clips are edited.

Although the included predefined objects are likely to be all you'll need, you can also create custom Generator objects or use objects that others have created.

Generator Objects panel

The first step in creating any Generator template is to get an object into the movie; this menu is where you do so. Think of the Generator Objects panel as Generator's toolbox. All of the predefined objects are listed here, and you can drag an object from this panel directly onto the stage or into a symbol. Alternatively, you can double-click a menu item to put the selected item in the center of the stage. The objects themselves are simply nondescript boxes that show you where the content they produce will appear in the movie

Each button represents a different type of Generator object with a unique function. Although the objects are listed alphabetically in this menu, it's useful to think of them in groups.

Chart objects

Generator's powerful chart objects can produce some of the most beautiful, legible charts on the Web. What's more, they're your only option for including familiar charts and graphs (for example, bar, line, area, pie, and stock) in your movie.

Insert-bitmap objects

You can use this type of object to dynamically place bitmap images into your movie. Insert-bitmap objects, such as Insert GIF File, Insert JPG, and Insert PNG, are useful for bringing advertising content or catalog items into your Flash interface (especially Insert GIF and Insert JPG).

Insert Flash objects

Objects such as Insert Symbol and Insert Flash Movie enable you to dynamically bring Flash assets (in the form of symbols or entire SWFs) into your movie. These powerful objects are among the most commonly used.

Insert-sound objects

Generator also gives you a way to dynamically bring sounds into your Flash movies. Among other things, these objects make it possible for users to request audio news reports or design personalized music play lists for Flash jukeboxes. Examples include Insert Sound and Insert MP3.

Dynamic-text objects

It's important to be able to bring dynamic text into Flash, and Generator provides several ways of doing so in the form of List, Scrolling List, Multi-Page List, and Ticker objects. (As you'll learn later, there are also ways of doing this—for example, using Generator variables—that don't involve Generator objects).

Other objects

Objects such as Table, Radio Button, and Plot don't really fit into any of the above groups; however, each is useful in its own way. You could use the Table object, for example, to format dynamically generated items in an e-commerce catalog or the Radio Button object to dynamically create radio button–based interface elements. And with the powerful Plot object, you can create all kinds of on-the-fly graphics (for example, personalized graphic weather maps).

Generator panel

GENERATOR PANEL.

Generator objects provide users with a fair amount of flexibility in terms of behavior and the way dynamic data is rendered in a published movie. Each object has its own set of user-definable properties, which users can edit in the Generator panel.

The panel will remain empty until you select a Generator object; once you do that, the panel will display the editable properties for the selected object. Keep in mind that each object's list of editable characteristics will be different. For example, the Basic Chart's properties lets you control things like where the chart gets its data, what type of chart to draw, how many grid lines to draw, whether to include labels, and so on.

You can even use the Generator panel to change the type of object the on-stage instance represents. However, you cannot preview Inspector panel settings, which means that the changes you make in the panel will make

The Inspector panel settings for every type of Generator object are described in detail in Chapter 6.

no visible difference to the object as it appears on the stage. The good news is that with the authoring templates installed, you can preview dynamic Generator content through Flash's Test Movie command (Control > Test Movie). Thus, if your data sources are local (recommended practice during the design phase), you'll be able to see how your objects will look when published and served at the time you test your movie.

Generator Environment button

One of the more visually subtle changes that the Generator authoring extensions bring to Flash's interface is a new button on the upper right corner of the timeline. You use this button—called the Generator Environment button—to attach data sources to your timelines. Each time-line in your movie will get its own Generator Environment button so that it can have its own data source.

ENVIRONMENT
BUTTON

GENERATOR ENVIRONMENT VARIABLE BUTTON.

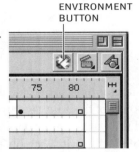

Clicking this button produces a dialog box where you enter your data source. Each timeline (i.e., movie clip) in a Flash movie can have its own data source—a feature that proves useful when dealing with Generator variables (another type of placeholder; see below).

SETTING THE ENVIRONMENT DATA SOURCE.

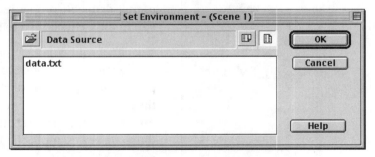

GENERATOR VARIABLES

See Chapter 4 for a complete discussion of Generator variables.

The authoring extensions also allow Flash to make use of Generator variables. Once a data source has been assigned to a timeline via the Generator Environment button, text anywhere in the timeline can be turned into a placeholder for the real content that will be swapped in from the data source. This is accomplished through the use of Generator variables—special words surrounded by braces. A generator variable looks like this:

{myVariable}

These variables can appear on the stage as visible text, or you can place them inside Object properties fields, ActionScript, or frame labels. Placing them in this way means that the data source determines not only the content that appears inside the object but also every changeable property of that object. And since Generator variables can be used inside ActionScript, you can even let the data in the data source affect the way the movie plays.

GENERATOR PUBLISH SETTINGS

The final stop on our tour of the Generator-enhanced version of Flash is the Publish Settings dialog box (File > Publish Settings). When you installed the authoring extensions, two changes were made to the Publish Settings dialog box: A SWT output format option was added to the Formats tab, and a Generator tab was added.

As we mentioned in Chapter 2, your Generator-enhanced copy of Flash is now capable of exporting a new type of file: a Generator template, or SWT file, which is used in place of SWFs when working with Generator. Instead of embedding a .SWF into an HTML document, you'll now be embedding a SWT.

When you work with source files that include Generator objects or variables, you need to be sure to check the SWT option on the Formats tab of the Publish Settings dialog box. If you don't check this option, the SWT file will not be created, which means that none of Generator's placeholders will be substituted with dynamic content when the flash file is played. Even the Test Movie preview will not work unless this export option has been enabled. Forgetting or not knowing to do this is one of the most common mistakes made by Generator beginners—and sometimes even experts!

A NEW PUBLISHING
FORMAT: THE GENERATOR
TEMPLATE, OR .SWT.

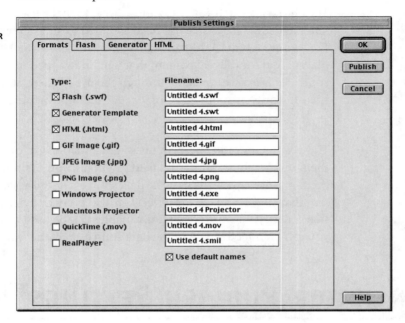

GENERATOR PUBLISH
SETTINGS WINDOW.

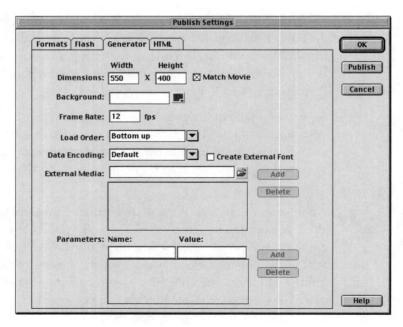

The Generator tab on the Publish Settings dialog box includes many new settings that affect the Generator Template's features when the file is exported:

Width and Height. You use these settings when you're exporting to a file using offline mode. In most cases, these dimensions will be identical to those of the movie (leaving the Match Movie option checked is usually appropriate).

Background. This rarely used setting lets you override the background color specified in the Modify Movies dialog box.

Frame Rate. This is important. The exported SWT file will use this fps setting and ignore the fps setting in the Modify Movies dialog box. Thus, if your movie requires a certain frame rate, you need to make sure you set that frame rate here before exporting your template.

Load Order. This setting is identical to the Load Order setting in the Flash tab of the Publish Settings dialog box. However, as with the Frame Rate, it is this setting that will be used when the template is exported. Thus, if load order is important to your Generator project, make sure this is where you set it.

Data Encoding. This setting specifies the type of encoding you wish to use for your data sources.

Create External Font Files. This setting is most useful with the Enterprise edition. If it's selected, Generator will create font files for all the fonts used in the template.

External Media. In this setting you can specify the location of a Generator template that includes a library of symbols. Through this setting, your template will be able to access that library as if it were in the original movie itself.

Parameters. This setting permits you to define variables and their values. You will use it primarily for debugging your templates; it's discussed in more detail in Chapter 6.

DESIGNERS VS. GENERATOR

 It's not surprising that Generator's authoring environment is fairly user-friendly since it's really just an enhanced version of Flash. As such, the additional elements feel very Flash-like in their use and manipulation. For this reason, Flash designers should have little trouble formatting, laying out, coloring, and animating Generator content (though there will certainly be times when a system integrator type needs to tweak the source Flash file, most likely to adjust export settings or data source assignments). And because the authoring extensions can test dynamic movies locally (using local text files as data sources), designers are able to see the results of their work almost immediately.

POINTS TO REMEMBER

- The Generator authoring extensions are the front-end user interface to Generator, and they are included with the Flash 5 CD.

- Generator objects serve as placeholders for various types of dynamic content that can be placed on stage and manipulated just like other types of symbols.

- Each object has its own set of user-definable properties, and the Generator panel is the place where you edit those properties.

- The Generator Environment button is where you specify your data source to the main timeline or a movie clip's timeline.

- A Generator variable is a placeholder for data-driven content.

- The Generator tab on the Publish Settings dialog box contains settings that affect the Generator templates' features when the file is exported.

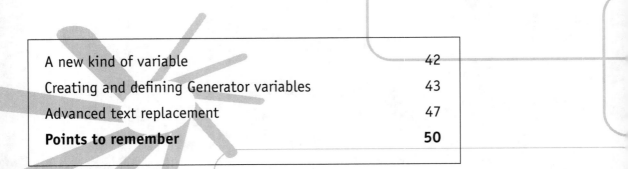

CHAPTER 4

GENERATOR VARIABLES

NOW THAT OUR TOUR OF GENERATOR AND FLASH BASICS IS COMPLETE AND you know something about the nuts and bolts of these powerful tools, it's time to start working with Generator. To get started, we'll create some examples that make use of the more common features of Generator as well as what may be the program's most powerful capability: dynamic text replacement.

You've already learned that Generator replaces text through the use of Generator variables—placeholders for values supplied to Generator by a data source. Although you don't need to know a lot about data sources to reap the benefit of the following exercises, we will explore their use as the exercises become more sophisticated.

We'll show you how and where you can replace text in your dynamic Flash movies using Generator's dynamic text replacement feature. We'll also create a simple Generator template, assign a basic data source, and allow you to view your work. Finally, we'll discuss some advanced techniques that you can use in your project and which will also prepare you for some of the more sophisticated material to come in this book.

A NEW KIND OF VARIABLE

Most readers are likely to be familiar with one type of Flash variable already: ActionScript variables. Now comes a new type: Generator variables. Although the two variable types share some similarities, they also differ in important ways in terms of behavior and function. For example, while ActionScript variables work on the client side (like JavaScript in HTML), Generator variables work on the server side (like ASP, ColdFusion, and JSP).

And—if you feel comfortable skipping ahead—take a look at Part IV of this book, which includes a lengthy discussion of when and where it's appropriate to use Flash as well as when and where it's appropriate to use Generator.

How Generator variables work

The most common use of Generator variables—the building blocks of most Generator projects—is to replace text, especially when that text comprises frequently updated information such as news, stocks, or product prices. Generator variables function as placeholders, which means that you use them to hold positions where you want to insert "string literal" (text string) for values to be assigned later (when the Generator template is processed). You supply the values for these variables through data sources you create. Keep in mind, however, that you're not limited to visible text on the stage: You can also use Generator variables inside ActionScript; you can even use them within other Generator objects.

Where to use Generator variables

You can define Generator variables in the following places:

- **Text blocks on the stage.** Allowing you to dynamically insert text into the movie.

- **Parameters and arguments to Flash actions and instance names.** Allows you to essentially create ActionScript on the fly.

- **Properties for Generator objects.** This allows you to dynamically specify properties for Generator objects at run time. This is a very powerful technique that allows you to customize the functionality of the object for each user.

- **Frame labels.** This allows you to dynamically name and target frame labels.

- Just about anywhere else that you can type in the Flash environment.

In this chapter, we'll focus on the use of Generator variables for the first two items on the above list: text blocks on the stage and parameters to Flash actions.

CREATING AND DEFINING GENERATOR VARIABLES

The best way to learn how Generator variables operate is to create a Generator template that uses them. Remember that for this exercise (and for creating *any* Generator templates) you need to install the Generator extensions when you install Flash. Let's start a new Flash movie.

1. *Set the stage dimensions at 300 x 300 and the background color to white.*

2. *Now let's set up some layers (starting at the bottom of the layer stack and working our way up):*

GenVars, FlashVars, Actions

3. *From the toolbox, select the Text tool and create a text box on the stage on the GenVars layer.*

Choose whatever font you like and then position the pointer where you want the text to start and drag the box to the desired width.

4. *Type the variable name into the text block and enclose it in curly braces.*

For our example we'll use {lastname}. Make sure you extend the text box by pulling the square, fixed text-block handle. This will determine the point at which the text will wrap to the next line.

Remember, the curly braces { } indicate a Generator variable, and everything between the braces is counted as the variable's name. The variable can consist of any alphanumeric characters, but it cannot contain spaces and it's not case sensitive.

Because the text that will be substituted will almost certainly be longer than the variable name, it's important that you make sure your text blocks are large enough to accommodate the data being passed into Generator. Unlike Flash variables, Generator variables will not expand dynamic- or input-text blocks to accommodate larger chunks of text.

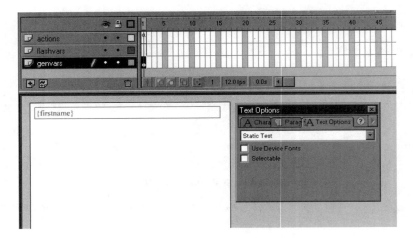

5. *Click the Generator Environment Variable button to define a data source for our variable.*

6. *Type the actual data source data in the Generator Environment Variable Edit area to store the data directly within the template.*

Although the Generator Environment Variable Edit area is generally intended for use as a reference to an external data source, you can also type the data directly into this space, as seen here: This is known as using a native data source—useful when you want to test your movie with temporary data. This way, you're spared managing a separate text-file data source that would serve the same purpose. If we were to specify a text file or other data source, it would look similar to the native data source but would not include the pound (#) sign. If you type the data source directly into the Data Source window, you must begin the declaration with a pound sign, as in:

```
#name, value
"lastname", "aerator"
```

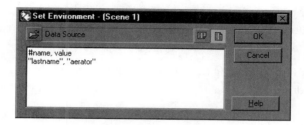

It's not a good idea to name a variable {var} because in ActionScript, *var* is a reserved word, which means it cannot be specified as a variable name. Because Generator and ActionScript variables can be mixed together, this might be confusing.

The column names "name, value" are required. Each row is a separate line within the file; commas separate column values. Under the Name column, specify the variable names; our variable name is "lastname." Under the Value column, specify the variable values; our value is "aerator." You can assign only one value to each variable. If you accidentally end up with multiple columns that have the same name but include different variables, Generator will use the last value it received. If you do not specify a value for a variable, Generator will leave it blank.

Quotation marks ("") enclosing the values are optional as long as the value does not contain any embedded commas. Generally, it's a good idea to enclose values within quotation marks to make sure they're fully encapsulated and treated as a single value. It is also necessary if your data contains quotes. See Chapter 7 for more information on formatting data for Generator.

7. **Click OK when you've filled out the data source as described.**

8. **Choose File > Publish Settings and check the Generator Template (.swt) box.**

9. **Name this file TextTest.fla and save (File > Save) it to a location on your hard drive.**

Since you'll be using this file a lot, you should put it somewhere that you can refer to quickly.

10. Now, let's test our movie (Control > Test Movie).

Congratulations, you've just used a powerful tool for the first time! If the value you specified is not generated, set the debug level in the Options window to Verbose. This will give you more information as well as help you troubleshoot the movie.

If you're still having trouble, open up the file on the CD in the Chapter 4 folder called text.fla and compare it with what you've created.

11. Add another variable in the text field, then double-click the text block and add {firstname} (in the text block).

Make sure you extend the text box by pulling the square, fixed text-block handle.

12. In our data source we've specified the Generator Environment Edit area. Now let's add another value to make it look like the following:

```
#name, value
"lastname", "Aerator"
"firstname", "Jen"
```

13. Test the movie (Control > Test Movie) to see the results.

As you can see, Generator substituted the variable name with the text from the data source you typed—it's as simple as that! Notice that the text from the second variable begins where the text from the first variable ends.

You may, however, be wondering how Generator decides which character, number, and punctuation outline information to include in the file to produce that nice anti-aliased text block. Because the Flash template created contains all of the font outlines for the font used for the Generator variable, the Flash template file is larger than the Flash movie produced with Generator or when publishing. However, the good news is that the newly created .SWF (which is generated based on the SWT) will only contain the outline information for the characters used in the Flash movie.

Feel free to experiment with adding more variables and data-source values before moving onto the next section.

ADVANCED TEXT REPLACEMENT

Now that you've used Generator variables to create dynamic text, let's look at ways you can control the look and functionality of that text dynamically—an important capability since most Generator projects bring large amounts of data-driven text into Flash (think of, say, a large corporate intranet site that includes job listings that need to be updated on a regular basis by a not-very-technical, non-Flash developer).

By tagging the text with a small set of familiar HTML tags in the data source or by creating a database that tags the text automatically, the Flash movie can contain bold and italic as well as multiple fonts, sizes, and links inside the dynamic text.

Using Flash and Generator variables together

Let's return to our TextTest.fla file (which contains the Generator variables we created) and add some Flash variables to which we'll pass data via Generator variables.

1. *From the toolbox, select the Text tool and create a text box on the stage on the FlashVars layer.*

Choose whatever font you wish, then position the pointer where you want the text to start and drag the box to the desired width.

2. *In the Text Options panel (Windows > Panels > Text Options), click the Text Type pull-down list and select Dynamic Text.*

From the Line Type pull-down list select Single Line. In the Variable field, type the name of the variable; for our example, we'll use the Flash variable name boldtext. Keep in mind that this is a Flash variable, so you don't need curly braces.

3. *Check off the HTML checkbox and make sure Border/Bg and Selectable are not checked.*

4. Click the first frame in the Action layer's timeline and open up the Actions panel (Windows > Actions).

Because we're creating frame actions, the Actions panel will be called Frame Actions.

5. Add a set-variable frame action by doing one of the following:

- Double-click the set-variable action in the Basics Actions category.

- Drag the set-variable action from the Basic Actions category on the left to the Actions list on the right side of the panel.

- Click the Add (+) button and choose the set-variable action from the pop-up menu.

- Use the keyboard shortcut you've defined for the set-variable command.

6. In the Variable field in the Frame Actions panel, name your variable boldtext (also the name of our dynamic text block on the stage).

7. In the Value field, type the following HTML:

```
<b>bold text inside a text field variable</b>
```

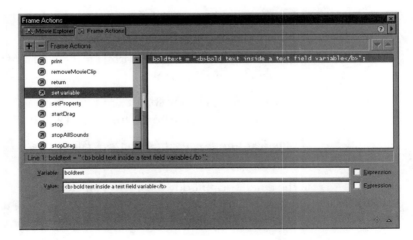

8. Test your movie (Control > Test Movie).

You'll notice that our movie contains text that is not antialiased (in contrast to our Generator variable, which *is* antialiased). If you wanted the Flash variable text to be antialiased, you would simply click one of the

Embed Fonts buttons in the Text Options panel, depending on what type of font outline you wanted to include. For our example it's not necessary.

Let's now turn our ActionScript variable into a Generator variable. Sound confusing? It won't be once you've done it a few times.

9. In the Frame Actions panel, replace the value (the HTML we specified) of the variable boldtext with a Generator variable. We'll call our Generator variable {gboldtext}.

When using Generator variables in ActionScript all data is treated as a string. Thus you must always surround the Generator variable with double quotes like this:

```
"{gBoldText}"
```

10. Click the Generator Environment Variable button to define a value for our Generator variable.

```
#name, value
"lastname", "aerator"
"firstname", "jen"
"gboldtext", "<b>bold text inside a textfield variable</b>"
```

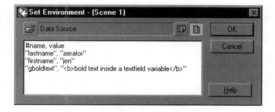

You can resize the Generator Environment Variable Edit area by placing the mouse pointer over any side or corner of the Set Environment window and then clicking and dragging.

11. Test the movie (Control > Test Movie).

You've now created a Flash movie that uses Generator variables as ActionScript variable values!

POINTS TO REMEMBER

- The Generator Environment Variable window allows native data sources for quick editing and testing.

- Generator and Flash variables can be used together to create extremely customizable, data-driven text manipulation.

CHAPTER 5

GENERATOR COMMANDS

GENERATOR COMMANDS ARE USED TO MODIFY SYMBOL INSTANCES WHEN A template is processed. Although at first glance it may appear that many of the tasks performed by Generator commands can also be accomplished via plain, old ActionScript, you'll soon see that there are many cases where you'll want to handle much of the heavy lifting on the server side—and that means using Generator commands.

In this chapter we'll explore how and when to use these commands (which are also sometimes referred to as *dynamically modifying instances*) as well as when you can use ActionScript to perform a similar function. We'll also explain how to use all of the Generator commands together by employing *symbol nesting*.

Using the symbol commands you can dynamically insert, replace, and modify properties of a symbol when the template is processed, and before it is sent to the client.

GENERATED GRAPHIC
DISPLAYED ON A **PDA**.

For example, if you were creating a stock chart graphic for a handheld device that needed to show whether a particular market lost or gained, you could change the symbols from a red down-arrow to a green up-arrow—something you couldn't accomplish via ActionScript because the delivery is a static graphic (for example, a JPG or a GIF) rather than a Flash movie.

Symbol commands are applied to instances of symbols that have already been placed in the movie. In order to access the symbol commands, first select an instance of a symbol and then select the command to apply on that symbol from the Generator panel.

THE COMMANDS

Let's take a quick tour of the commands.

THE GENERATOR
COMMANDS.

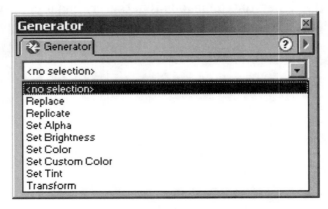

- Set Alpha. Sets the transparency of the selected symbol instance.

- Set Brightness. Adjusts the brightness percentage of the selected symbol instance.

- Set Tint. Applies a tint to all colors within the selected symbol instance.

- Set Custom Color. Enables you to specify a custom color for the selected symbol instance.

- Set Color. Similar to Set Custom Color except that you can specify a color name or value.

- Transform. Scales, rotates, and offsets the position of a selected symbol instance.

- Replace. Replaces selected symbol instances with other symbols from the library.

- Replicate. Displays movie clips or graphics sequentially for each row of data in a data source.

GENERATOR COMMANDS VS. ACTIONSCRIPT

ActionScript—especially with the introduction of Flash 5—can perform many of the same tasks as Generator, though that doesn't mean the two programs are interchangeable. By using Generator, you can avoid burdening the client with processing and business logic. Take, for example, a shopping cart: Just as you wouldn't use JavaScript to handle all of the pricing, tax, shipping, and sales information, you wouldn't use Flash to deal with that information either. Instead, you would want your server and middleware to handle that sort of heavy lifting—not only for security reasons but also for stability and ease of updating. There are times, however, when Flash offers advantages over Generator. Thus, when planning a project, you should always determine how best to separate client- and server-side functionality.

As we explore each type of Generator command, we'll also demonstrate the corresponding ActionScript (when there is one) to give you an idea of when and where to use Generator commands. Unlike Generator variables, you can't use Generator commands with ActionScript. Think of them, instead, as a means of modifying instances on the server side or when the template is processed.

Nondesigners may want to read the introductory paragraph to each of the following examples to familiarize themselves with the design terms used. Designers, on the other hand, may want to skip ahead to the examples themselves. Either way, it's important to go through the following examples in order because later examples build on earlier ones.

As you go through the following lessons, you may notice that using Generator commands is much like using the Effect panel in Flash.

THE EFFECT PANEL.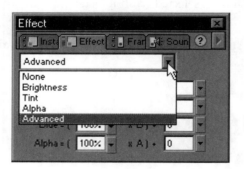

The main differences between Generator commands and the Effect panel are as follows:

- You must set the Effect panel manually from within the authoring environment; it's not data-driven.

- If you use the Generator commands, you may need to employ Generator to see the results (depending on what you want your delivery to be).

- You can produce data-driven GIFs, JPGs, MOVs, PNGs, and Flash movies using the Generator commands—something you can't accomplish via the Effect panel.

Now let's build!

SET ALPHA

A portion of the data in every computer graphic is reserved for transparency information. Thirty-two-bit graphics systems contain four channels: three 8-bit channels for red, green, and blue (RGB) and one 8-bit alpha channel. The alpha channel acts much like a mask, specifying how one pixel's colors should be merged with another's when the two are overlaid.

In most applications (Flash included), you define the alpha channel on a per-object rather than a pixel-by-pixel basis. The level of transparency you apply to an object will depend on whether you want the background or other objects to show through.

But why, you ask, would you use a database rather than Flash itself to manage an object's alpha channel? The answer is simple: There are times when we've found Generator commands to be extremely useful. Take, for example, the case of a developer using Flash to create user-customizable greeting cards or mini-applications: He or she might want to create an executable file that's sent to the user. By using Flash to send the real-time alpha values that the user will be modifying via an ActionScript-driven interface, Generator can create a stand-alone file that contains the user-specified value.

Generator commands can also be used to achieve greater control over projects that need to be delivered on an older version of the Flash plug-in—say, a set-top box, such as WebTV, that supports only Flash 3 and earlier. If you're building an application that will be deployed on devices with previous versions of Flash, you can use Generator commands to create Flash 3-and-lower-compatible files for which you can still control object properties dynamically. Since these earlier versions of Flash are unable to modify instance properties through ActionScript, you can think of Generator commands as a way to perform limited server-side ActionScripting when needed!

In our example, we're going to create a circle and use Set Alpha with a data source. Then we'll create a similar modification using ActionScript.

Let's start a new Flash movie:

1. *Set the frame rate to 12 fps, Modify > Movie.*

2. *Set the stage dimensions to 500 x 300 and the background color to white.*

3. *Set up some layers (starting from the bottom and going up):*

GenCommand, FlashModify, Actions

4. *Choose Insert > New Symbol, then choose Movie Clip. Name the symbol "circle."*

5. *From the toolbox, select the Oval tool and create an oval on the stage. The oval can be any color; however, for our example we're going to use blue with a black outline.*

6. *Go back to our main timeline and pull up the library. Drag the circle movie clip from the library (Window > Library) onto the stage. You don't need to specify an instance name.*

7. *Using the Arrow tool, select the symbol instance "circle" and pull up the Generator panel (Windows > Panels > Generator).*

8. *In the Generator panel, choose Set Alpha from the pop-up menu.*

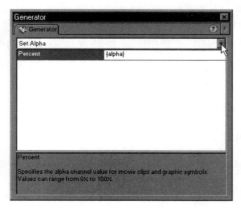

9. *You can specify a variable for Percent using the {variableName} syntax, or you can specify a value from 0 to 100. For this example, type 50 in the percent field.*

10. *Save your work before testing. Also, make sure the Generator checkbox is selected in the Publish settings.*

11. *Test the movie by selecting Control > Test Movie.*

If your circle is not 50 percent transparent now, you may want to look on the CD-ROM in the Chapter 5 folder to make sure you followed the instructions correctly.

You can also use variables defined in a data source to modify the alpha transparency of movie clips, buttons, and graphic symbols.

Instead of typing *50* in the Percent field, type *{alpha}*. Click the Generator Environment Variable button to define a data source for our variable {alpha}. Type the actual data source data in the Generator Environment Variable Edit area. It should look like this:

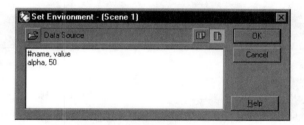

Test the movie (Control -> Test Movie) to see your data-driven results from the native data source.

Setting alpha with ActionScript

In the past you've probably set a movie clip's alpha properties by using SetProperty or by setting a Flash variable with the value modifying the movie-clip instance. As you read this section, it's important to note that you *cannot* use ActionScript to modify buttons or graphic symbols unless they're contained within a movie clip.

Now let's revisit our Flash movie: Drag another instance of the circle from the library to the stage and name that instance "flashcircle" (Window > Panels > Instance). In the Actions layer, click the first frame and pull up the Actions panel (Window > Actions); then insert the following script:

```
setProperty ("flashcircle", _alpha, "10");
```

You can also set alpha properties by using the MovieClip object method with the clip's instance name and property. The following statement sets the alpha property of the movie-clip instance flashcircle.

```
flashcircle._alpha = 50;
```

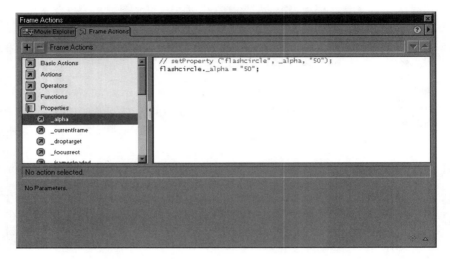

Statements written using the MovieClip object methods tend to be quicker because they don't require the tellTarget action. Use of the tellTarget action is discouraged because it is not compatible with the ECMA-262 standard on which ActionScript is based.

The European Computers Manufacturers Association (ECMA) wrote a document called ECMA-262 that was derived from JavaScript to serve as the international standard for the JavaScript language. ActionScript is based on the ECMA-262 specification. Flash's use of worldwide-recognized standards will not only provide effective interchange of information but will also help to remove some of the technical barriers to learning, creating, and deploying advanced applications built with Flash.

SET BRIGHTNESS

The Set Brightness command allows you to dynamically specify the brightness of a symbol. Valid values range from -100 to 100 with higher values making the symbol brighter. A value of 0 means that there will be no change to the brightness level.

To set the brightness of an instance:

1. *Select the movie-clip instance in the GenCommand layer on the stage.*

2. *Make sure the Generator panel is displayed by choosing Window > Panels > Generator.*

3. *Select the symbol instance in the GenCommand layer.*

4. *In the Generator panel, choose Set Brightness from the pop-up menu.*

5. *Type in a value or specify a variable for the percent using the {variableName} syntax or specify a value from -100 to 100.*

6. *For our example, type -50. This will make the circle darker.*

7. *Save your work before testing. Also, make sure the Generator checkbox is selected in the Publish Settings window.*

8. *Test the movie by selecting Control > Test Movie.*

If your circle is not 50 percent darker now, you may want to look on the CD-ROM in the Chapter 5 folder (design_commands.fla) to make sure you followed the instructions correctly.

Try other values to get a good sense of the ranges and results. Also, try using variable names and creating a native data source to try out the values.

Interestingly, this is one property that can only be controlled dynamically via a Generator command. There's no direct way to change the brightness of an element programmatically using ActionScript. You can only modify this property via the authoring environment's Effect panel (Window > Panels > Effect) or with Generator.

SET TINT

Just as variables defined in a data source may be used with Set Alpha and Set Brightness, they can also be used to modify the tint of movie clips, buttons, and graphic symbols. Back in the old days of film, tints were created by dipping film in a bath of chemicals to get a dominant tone. Setting tint with a Generator command is much like dipping your Flash file in data that creates a new color.

For example, if you needed to create a car configurator and wanted to manage the color of the available cars using a database, you might want to allow users to create their own tints and save them for subsequent visits to the site. As with other Generator commands that modify the way an instance is displayed, the Set Tint command doesn't offer the multitude of uses that other Generator objects do. Still, at some point you're likely to need to use this command for a project.

You specify a percentage (from 0 to 100) and an integer value (from 0 to 255) for red, green, and blue, with the new values applying to all colors of a symbol instance. The red, green, and blue values specify tint color, while the percentage value governs the degree of tint applied.

If you want to change an object to a solid color, you can use Set Tint by specifying the RGB color values and setting the percent value to 100.

To set an instance's tint:

1. *Select the movie-clip instance we created in the GenCommand layer on the stage.*

2. *Make sure the Generator panel is displayed by choosing Window > Panels > Generator.*

3. *In the Generator panel, choose Set Tint from the pop-up menu.*

4. *Specify either a variable or a value for the Percent, Red, Green, and Blue options.*

5. *For this example, let's turn our blue circle into a purple circle by entering the following values:*

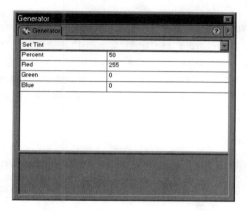

6. *Save your work before testing. Also, make sure the Generator checkbox is selected in the Publish settings.*

7. *Test the movie by selecting Control > Test Movie.*

If your circle does not turn purple, you may want to look on the CD-ROM in the Chapter 5 folder (design_commands.fla) to make sure you followed the instructions correctly.

Try using other values to create tints until you feel comfortable moving to the next section. Also, try using variable names and creating a native data source to try out the values.

There's no direct way to change the tint of an element programmatically using ActionScript. You can, of course, apply tint within the authoring environment using the Effect panel (Window > Panels > Effect).

Set Custom Color

The flexible and powerful Set Custom Color command specifies new color values for a symbol, based on percentages and offsets of the symbol's current RGB and alpha values. You could use it, for example, to create data-driven demographic maps containing geographical areas that changed color based on database returns. You could even update the colors in the map's legend in this fashion.

It's important to remember that once you've created a data-driven Flash movie, you can generate data-driven GIFs, JPGs, MOVs, and PNGs as well. The same Generator work that produces the Flash movie can just as easily produce these other types of media. Thus, no matter what your project demands of data-driven graphics, Generator will likely be able to handle the task.

To specify a custom color:

1. *Select the movie-clip instance in the GenCommand layer on the stage.*

2. *Make sure the Generator panel is displayed by choosing Window > Panels > Generator.*

3. *Select the movie-clip instance in the GenCommand layer on the stage.*

4. *In the Generator panel, choose Set Custom Color from the pop-up menu.*

5. *For our example we want to change the color to green. To do so, enter the following values:*

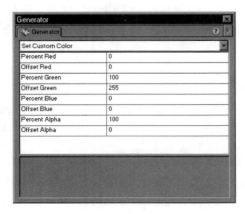

Set Custom Color	
Percent Red	0
Offset Red	0
Percent Green	100
Offset Green	255
Percent Blue	0
Offset Blue	0
Percent Alpha	100
Offset Alpha	0

Percent Red, Percent Green, Percent Blue, and Percent Alpha specify the percentage of the symbol's red, green, blue, and alpha values to use in the new color value. (Accepted ranges are -100 to 100.) Because we want the blue circle to turn green when we process the template, we need to set the Green value to 255 by adding 153. To get rid of the Blue value, we added a negative 204 (-204), making the Blue value 0.

Offset Red, Offset Green, Offset Blue, and Offset Alpha specify how much to increase or decrease the respective channel values. Because in this case we don't want to increase or decrease the colors, we set the offsets to 0.

Now let's take a closer look: The Percentage setting changes the color of a symbol by multiplying the percentage by the values in the channel. The Offset setting adds or subtracts the offset value from the channel as a whole. The overall calculation for the new color can be expressed as follows:

```
Percentage x Current Value + Offset = New Color Value
```

Our Movie Clip object has an RGB of (RGB 0, 102, 204). Here's a look at the formula and the resulting custom color:

```
Percent Red (0) x current value (0) + offset (0) = 0
Percent Green (0) x current value (102) + offset (255) = 255
Percent Blue (0) x current value (204) + offset (0) = 0
```

6. ***Save your work before testing. Also, make sure the Generator checkbox is selected in the Publish settings.***

7. ***Test the movie by selecting Control > Test Movie.***

If your circle does not turn green, you may want to look on the CD-ROM in the Chapter 5 folder (design-commands.fla) to make sure you followed the instructions correctly.

Try other values to get a good feel for ranges and results. Also, try using variable names and creating a native data source to try out the values.

You should use Set Tint rather than Set Custom Color to change an object's color to a solid color because Set Tint applies the tint to all colors of an instance, whereas Set Custom Color modifies the RGB values of the symbol instances. A percentage value of 0 sets the original color value for a channel to 0. By placing the RGB values for the desired color in the offset fields for each channel, you're specifying that every object in the channel be assigned that color. It's both easier and more efficient to use Set Tint for this purpose.

Setting RGB with ActionScript

Typically, when you want to set the color of your movie clips, you'll use ActionScript: It allows you to set and retrieve a movie clip's RGB color value via the Color object. Keep in mind, however, that only Flash 5 and later versions of Flash Player support the Color object.

To use the Color object, you must use the constructor new Color() to create an instance of the Color object before calling the methods of the Color object.

Constructors are functions you use to define the properties and methods of a class, and *classes* are data types you create to define a new type of object. To define a class of object, you create a constructor function. Methods are functions assigned to an object. After a function is assigned, it can be called a method of that object.

Let's use the setRGB command to change the color of a circle.

1. **In our example we're going to place a new instance of the circle Movie Clip on the stage and turn the circle red.**

2. **Drag the circle symbol we created from the library to the stage on the FlashModify layer and name the instance "'MyCircle" in the Instance panel (Windows > Panel > Instance).**

3. **In the first frame in the Actions layer we're going to set a variable called MyCircle. In the Value field we're going to use the constructor new Color() to create an instance of the Color object before we call on the method setRGB. The method specifies a RGB color for the Color object.**

    ```
    MyCircle = new Color(MyCircle);
    ```

4. **Use the Evaluate action if you're in normal mode; otherwise just type the expression in expert mode. Enter the following:**

    ```
    MyCircle.setRGB(0xFF0000)
    ```

When you use setRGB, "0xRRGGBB" is the hexadecimal representation of the color to be set. RR, GG, and BB each consist of two hexadecimal digits specifying the offset of the color component.

In our case we wanted red, so we used FF0000.

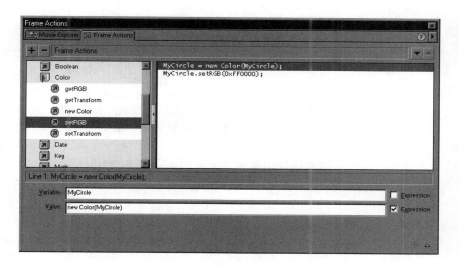

5. **Save your work before testing.**

6. **Test the movie by selecting Control > Test Movie.**

If your circle didn't turn red, you may want to look on the CD-ROM in the Chapter 5 folder (design-commands.fla) to make sure you followed the instructions correctly.

SET COLOR

The Set Color command works exactly like the set Custom Color command except that you can specify color names instead of color values.

Valid color values include Web-safe color names (blue), Web hexadecimal value (#000000), and regular hexadecimal values (0x000000).

Because most other Generator objects specify colors in these formats, the Set Color command is generally easier to use than the Set Custom Color command. This also makes the command very useful in creating items such as chart legends.

If you do not see the Set Color command in your Generator panel, then you need to make sure that you have downloaded the latest patch from Generator:

http://www.macromedia.com/generator/

TRANSFORM

The Transform command lets you transform movie clips and graphic symbols by scaling them, rotating them, and offsetting their positions. The command is especially useful if you're creating lots of data-driven graphics—say for data-heavy applications such as those used by financial and scientific institutions. You can use the Transform command to move a series of symbols to new locations, as well as to change a symbol's size in order to produce a Flash movie or static graphic.

If you needed to create info graphics for a Web site or geological study, you could use Generator to move and resize the seismic activity over an area based on data from instruments or based on historical data. You could also use other Generator commands to color-code activity in a specific area. Once you've separated your data from the design, you won't need to revisit the Flash files every time there's a thump in the night.

Using the Transform command is much like using the Transform panel (Window > Panels > Transform)—but you don't need to be inside the Flash authoring environment.

In our example we're going to rotate an oval 50 degrees, scale it to twice its size, and then move it to a new location on the stage.

Let's start a new Flash movie:

1. *Set the frame rate to 12 fps, Modify > Movie.*

2. *Set the stage dimensions to 500 x 300 and the background color to white.*

3. *Set up some layers (starting at the bottom and going up):*

GenCommand, FlashModify, Actions

4. *Choose Insert > New Symbol, then choose Movie Clip. Name our symbol "oval."*

5. *From the toolbox, select the Oval tool and create an oval on the stage. Although the oval can be any color you desire, for our example we're going to use blue with a black outline.*

6. *Select the oval clip on the stage and pull up the Info panel (Window >*
    Panels > Info). Change the width to 50 and the height to 100.

7. *Go back to our main timeline and pull up the library. Drag the oval*
    movie clip from the library (Window > Library) onto the stage. You do
    not need to specify an instance name.

8. *Using the Arrow tool, select the symbol instance oval and pull up the*
    Generator panel (Windows > Panels > Generator).

9. *Select the instance and in the Generator panel choose Transform from*
    the pop-up menu.

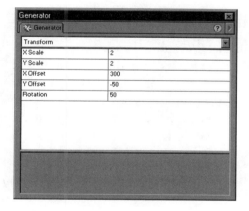

As you've probably guessed, we can specify a literal value or a variable for
any parameter using the {variableName} syntax. For this example, we're
going to type them in; however, feel free to define variables and specify the
values as a native data source (as we did in the other examples).

Let's set both X-Scale and Y-Scale—which specify the factors to scale the
instance horizontally and vertically, respectively—to 2. In the data source,
valid values are 0.0 to 10.0; 1.0 produces no change. With these settings,
our oval should scale to twice its original size.

The X-Offset and Y-Offset settings reposition the instance by the specified number of pixels when the movie is generated; the instance is moved relative to its registration point. Let's set the X-Offset to 300 and the Y-Offset to -50. With these settings our instance should move 300 pixels to the right and 50 pixels up from its original position.

In the Rotation field, type **50**. This will rotate the oval 50 degrees to the right. Negative numbers (-) rotate the instance to the left; positive numbers (+) rotate the instance to the right.

10. *Save your work before testing. Also, make sure the Generator checkbox is selected in the Publish settings.*

11. *Test the movie by selecting Control > Test Movie.*

If the oval doesn't grow to twice its original size, rotate 50 degrees, and then move over and up on the stage, you may want to look at the CD-ROM in the Chapter 5 folder (transform.fla) to make sure you followed the instructions correctly.

Try other values to get a feel for the ranges and the results.

Transforming with ActionScript

The Transform panel (Window > Panels > Transform)—like many of the other design-time edit panels (including the Sound and Effect panels)—modifies movie-clip instances in the authoring environment. As you've probably noticed, using the Transform command is similar to setting properties or using the Movie Clip object method to change the size, scale, rotation, and location of your movie clips.

Because most client-side interaction (such as games and navigation) must happen in real time, you'll want to use ActionScript to modify your movie clips.

In the next example we'll use ActionScript to duplicate our Transform command results.

1. *Drag another instance of the oval to the stage to the FlashModify layer. In the Instance panel (Window > Panels > Instance), name the instance "foval."*

2. *Place the instance somewhere near the bottom of the stage so that we can compare the Transform command and the ActionScripted movie clip on the stage when we test the movie.*

3. *In the first frame of the Action layer, set the x value to 300 by using the Movie Clip Object method:*

```
foval._x = "300";
```

4. *Next, set the y value of our instance to 50:*

```
foval._y = "50";
```

5. *Set the xscale to 200 to double its size:*

```
foval._xscale = "200";
```

6. *Set the yscale to 200 to double its size:*

```
foval._yscale = "200";
```

7. *Finally, set the rotation to 50. As with the Transform command, positive values are clockwise, and negative values are counterclockwise:*

```
foval._rotation = "50";
```

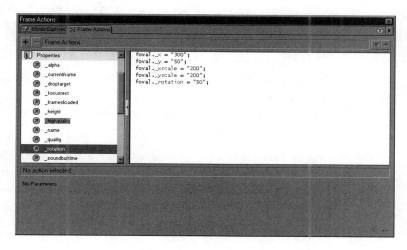

8. *Save your work before testing.*

9. *Test the movie by selecting Control > Test Movie.*

If your oval does not double in size, rotate 50 degrees, and move over and up on the stage, you may want to look on the CD-ROM in the Chapter 5 folder (transform.fla) to make sure you followed the instructions correctly.

Try other values to get a feel for ranges and results. Remember that any Flash variables you set can be Generator variables. For a fun experiment, try using Generator to set the Flash variables that determine the properties of a movie clip.

Symbol nesting and Generator commands

If you need to use more than one symbol command, such as Transform and Set Alpha, place the original symbol instance inside another movie clip or graphic symbol. By using this popular Flash authoring technique, you can apply a symbol command to the original instance inside the new symbol and add another command to the instance of the new symbol on the Stage.

On the Chapter 5 CD, see the nesting.fla for an example of symbol nesting if you're unfamiliar with the concept.

REPLACE

Using the Replace command, you can dynamically replace movie clips or graphic symbol instances with instances from the template's library (or from another template's library) when a template is processed. If, for example, you wanted to create an online catalog to be published every two weeks to a company's Web site, you could create placeholder symbols within Flash pointing to an external data source (for example, a text file). By placing the symbol names in an external-media file, you avoid having to modify the Flash file.

If you're creating multiple versions of a site to accommodate a number of different languages, the Replace command can automate the process by simply modifying a text file or database. The Replace command also comes in handy for personalized sites that allow users to display specific content such as news and sports.

Projects using the Enterprise edition's caching will also benefit from the Replace command since it allows a library's worth of content to be cached using external-media files for symbol replacement. Not only does this speed up file requests, it also lightens the server's load: By keeping the assets outside the main Flash file, you're minimizing file size, which means the user doesn't need to download an entire library for just one symbol.

In our exercise, we'll replace a symbol on the stage with a symbol from the local symbol library; then we'll create and replace the symbol with an external-media file or another symbol library.

Let's start a new movie:

1. *Set the frame rate to 12 fps, Modify > Movie.*

2. *Set the stage dimensions to 500 x 300 and the background color to white.*

3. *Set up some layers (starting from the bottom and going up):*

GenCommand, FlashModify, Actions

4. *Choose Insert > New Symbol; then choose Movie Clip. Name our symbol emptybox.*

5. *From the toolbox, select the Rectangle tool and create a square on the stage. Although you can make the square any color, for our example we're going to use a transparent box with a black outline.*

6. *Go back to our main timeline and pull up the library. Drag the empty-box movie clip from the library (Window > Library) onto the stage. You don't need to specify an instance name.*

You must use symbol libraries that are contained in either the template or an external-media file—you cannot use shared libraries. Use the External Media option with Generator when you need to use symbols housed outside of the template. See "Using External Media Files with the Replace Command" later in this example for more information.

7. *Let's create another symbol. Choose Insert > New Symbol, then choose Movie Clip, name the symbol smallcircle.*

8. *From the toolbox, select the Oval tool and create a circle on the stage. Although you can make the circle any color, for our example we're going to use a transparent box with a black outline.*

9. *Go back to our main timeline and select the empty box movie-clip instance.*

10. *Using the Arrow tool, select the symbol instance emptybox and pull up the Generator panel (Windows > Panels > Generator).*

11. *Select the instance and in the Generator panel choose Replace from the pop-up menu.*

12. *In the Replace Symbol field, choose True.*

This step specifies whether to replace the current symbol with the symbol specified in Symbol Name; values are True or False. In a production environment, you would likely use a variable here so that you could pass the value True or False to Generator based on a condition or value in your data source.

13. *In the Symbol Name field, type our symbol's name, smallcircle.*

This field specifies the symbol name that will replace the current instance. In a live production environment, we would also use the variable syntax {variableName} for each of the fields and pass those values in.

When specifying a symbol from the library for use with the Replace command, refer to the symbol by the name assigned to it in the library. If the symbol is contained within a folder in the library, reference it by folder name and symbol.

For example:

- If a symbol named my_symbol is in the root of the library, refer to it simply as my_symbol.

- If a symbol named my_symbol is within a folder named my_objects, refer to the symbol as my_objects/my_symbol.

- If a symbol named my_symbol is stored within the blue_symbols sub-folder inside the my_objects folder, refer to it as my_objects/blue_symbols/my_symbol.

14. *Save your work before testing. Also, make sure the Generator check-box is selected in the Publish settings.*

15. *Test the movie by selecting Control > Test Movie.*

If you still see the emptybox symbol when you test, you may want to look on the CD-ROM in the Chapter 5 folder (replace.fla) to make sure you followed the instructions correctly.

Replacing with ActionScript?

There really isn't a direct way of replacing symbols in ActionScript like you can do using Generator's Replace command. One way of replacing a symbol in ActionScript requires an empty movie clip and use of the attachMovie method:

```
anyMovieClip.attachMovie(idName, newname, depth);
```

The attachMovie method has the following arguments:

- idName. The name of the movie from the library to attach. This is the name entered in the Identifier field in the Symbol Linkage Properties dialog box.

- newname. A unique instance name for the movie clip being attached.

- depth. An integer specifying the depth level where the movie is placed.

This method creates a new instance of a movie clip in the library and attaches it to the movie clip specified by anyMovieClip. You can only remove movies attached via attachMovie by setting the movie clip's visibility to False or by using the removeMovieClip or unloadMovie method.

As you might imagine, the complexity of managing shared libraries combined with the custom ActionScript required and the fact that entire linked libraries need to be downloaded make this method of symbol replacement unsuitable for many projects. In addition, this method only works with Flash 5 and later, which means lower-end clients and devices won't be able to view your content, and you won't be able to produce JPGs, GIFs, PNGs, or MOVs.

In the chapter 5 folder on the CD-ROM (as_replace.fla), we've included an example of this method, which duplicates the functionality of the Replace command.

Using external-media files with the Replace command

Whenever possible, you'll want to keep external libraries of content. For example, you don't need to include actual symbols (that is, those containing content) in your base template. Instead, you can house the real symbols in a separate file so that if you need to update graphics used by multiple templates, you only have to change them in one place. Otherwise you would have to edit each template individually. An external-media file is basically an external library that Generator can access and search for symbols you specify when the template is processed. In contrast, when using shared libraries with Flash 5 and above, the entire shared library must be downloaded before it can be used.

Let's create our own external-media file, which we'll use with our last example.

Start a new movie:

1. *Set the frame rate to 12 fps, Modify > Movie.*

2. *Set the stage dimensions to 500 x 300 and the background color to white.*

3. *Choose Insert > New Symbol, then choose Movie Clip. Name our symbol triangle and then create a triangle.*

4. *Create four more symbols and four more movie clips: circle, oval, rectangle, and square.*

5. *Your library should look like this:*

6. **Save your work and call this fla shapes.fla.**

7. **In the Publish settings (File > Publish Settings), select only the Generator Template checkbox and publish the template.**

8. **Place the shapes.swt file in the same directory as the file we created for the Replace example.**

9. **Open the Replace example and go to the Publish settings (File > Publish Settings). Make sure the Generator Template checkbox is selected and click the Generator tab.**

10. **In the External Media option, click the Folder icon.**

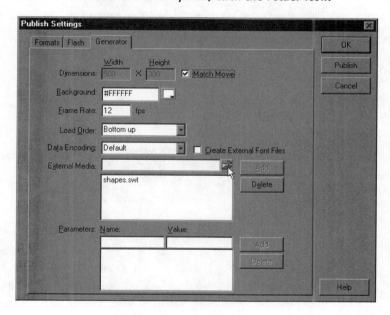

The shapes.swt file should be listed. If you don't see it, make sure the shapes.swt file is in the same directory as the Replace fla we created. Select the shapes.swt file.

Don't click Add yet!

You may notice that Flash puts the entire path in the field. We want to make the shapes.swt file relative to our file so that when we move it from server to server or from desktop to server, we don't need to open up the Flash file. Get rid of all the text in the field except shapes.swt and then click Add to close the Publish settings.

You cannot specify a Generator variable for the external-media file. For now, you need to keep track of the external-media file name when you want to update it.

11. *Click and select the emptybox instance on the stage. Pull up the Generator panel (Window > Panels > Generator) and type in* **triangle.** *We can type the name of any symbol that resides in either the template's library or the external-media file.*

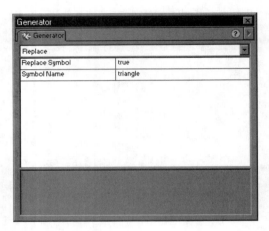

Remember: A symbol's location within the library matters. If your symbol resides in a folder, you must include the folder name when you reference it.

12. *Save your work, then test! A triangle should appear where the emptybox instance was on the stage.*

Use variable names instead of typing them into the Symbol name fields. Also, you can add more than one external-media file in the Publish settings. Experiment by adding multiple external-media files and using a native data source to choose symbols from those files.

REPLICATE

The Replicate command lets you display movie clips, graphic symbols, and buttons sequentially. The command displays a new symbol for each row of data in a data source. If, for example, you wanted to return the stock price of five stocks, you could use the Replicate command to show a different stock and stock price for each return from the five returns in the data source—and you don't even need to know in advance how many items the data source includes. The Replicate command will produce one symbol per data-source row until it runs out of rows. Since most databases work well with this method, the Replicate command can be used for all kinds of things—from creating sports scores to personalized news headlines and animated GIFs for PDAs. You can even use the command to return auction bids.

When you apply the Replicate command to a symbol instance, the original symbol determines the uses for values and objects in subsequent movie clips by providing variables to be filled in with values from each row of the Replicate command's data source.

The Replicate command uses its own data source, which you'll need to define unless you instead use a variable that's passed in when the template is processed. The data source must have at least one column and one row, but it does not require any mandatory column names. Instead, all columns in a row are used to specify variables for the replicated movie clip.

Let's say you were returning messages of the day for the company intranet: Your data source might look like this:

```
Date, department, message
10.14.00, Human resources, Make sure to turn in your 401k!
10.12.00, Accounting, All Expense reports need to be in by
10.16.00
10.14.00, IT, Backup starts at 5pm today-log off before 5pm.
```

In the first row we declare the column names that correspond to variable names within our movie clip.

In the following example we'll create a Flash movie that displays today's news about a company in a small window. We'll also create a version in animated GIF format for systems that can't display Flash (such as some PDAs).

Let's start a new Flash movie:

1. *Set the frame rate to 12 fps, Modify > Movie.*

2. *Set the stage dimensions to 300 x 300 and the background color to white.*

3. *Set up some layers (starting from the bottom and going up):*

Background, ClipLayer, Actions

4. *Choose Insert > New Symbol and choose Movie Clip. Name it textclip.*

5. *Create the following block of text inside the textclip movie clip on the first layer, and name the first layer texy.*

6. *Make sure that you make the text block as large as the area you wish the text to fill. Also, use a fixed-width block so that the words wrap automatically when different amounts of text come in.*

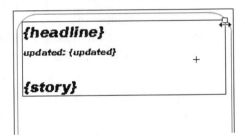

7. *In Frame 50 add a frame (Insert > Frame) so that the text spans across 50 frames of the timeline.*

If we wanted to make the delay between news stories longer or shorter, this is where we would add or remove frames.

8. *Go back to the main timeline and drag the text clip instance out of the library and onto the cliplayer on the stage.*

9. *Lock the cliplayer and create a background shape under the cliplayer on the background layer—this shape will be where the content comes in.*

10. *Select the testclip instance and pull up the Generator panel (Window > Panels > Generator). In the Generator panel, choose Replicate from the pop-up menu.*

11. *Select Data Source and specify the data source in the Parameters text box. For our example we're going to create a text file in a few moments so type in* **data.txt.**

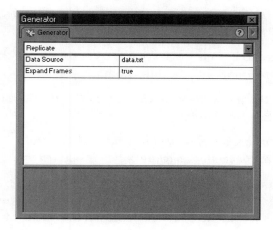

12. *Set Expand Frames to True.*

If you're creating templates in Flash 3 or later, set the option to False. If you're creating Flash 2–compatible templates, set the option to True. Also, if you set Expand Frames to False, our news widget will play in Flash and loop forever but the animated GIF will only play the first frame. Since we want to create an animated GIF, make sure you select True for the Expand Frame property.

13. *Save your work.*

14. *In an external text editor such as Notepad or Simpletext, type the following data source:*

```
headline, updated, story
company xyz gains!, 10.1.00, this is the first story of the day
there are many like them but this one is the first story of the
day.
company abc reports earnings, 10.9.00, this is the second story
of the day there are many like them but this one is the second
story of the day.
dow up record high, 10.7.0, this is the third story of the day
there are many like them but this one is the third story of the
day.
```

15. *Let's take a closer look at the data source.*

The column are named "headline," "updated," and "story"—monikers that correspond to the variable names we specified in Flash. We have three rows of data, which means that Generator will create three sets of content that will display based on our data source.

If we wanted to include special characters or commas in the data source, we'd need to follow the guidelines from Chapter 4.

16. *Save this file in the same directory as the file you're working on. Call this text file data.txt.*

17. *Let's go back to Flash and test our work (Control > Test Movie). Make sure the Generator Template option is selected in the Publish settings.*

Story 1 should appear, followed by Story 2, then Story 3, and they should loop continuously. If you're having trouble with this, open up the replicate.fla example in the Chapter 5 folder on the CD-ROM and compare your file with the example we provided.

18. *To create an animated GIF version, go to Publish settings (File > Publish Settings) and select the "animate GIF" checkbox. Click the tab to bring up the GIF properties.*

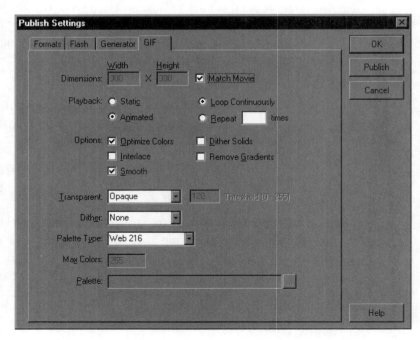

19. *In the playback area, select Animated and Loop Continuously.*

20. *Click Publish and go to the folder where you're publishing your work.*

Drag the GIF image into a browser to view the results, or open it with your favorite GIF tool such as Fireworks if you want to view the guts of the GIF.

Experiment using a longer or shorter span in the text-clip movie to make the animation go faster or slower. Adjusting the frame rate affects the animation speed as well. Make sure to test on many machines because the frame rate may vary from machine to machine.

Also, trying adding the variable name {mylabel} as a frame label and pass the value in via the text file. You can also use Generator variables as Flash variables in ActionScripts that can be replicated.

In the Chapter 5 folder on the CD-ROM, check the adv_replicate.fla to learn about other uses of the Replicate command.

Replicating and ActionScript

As with the Replace command, there's no easy or direct way to reproduce the functionality of the Replicate command with ActionScript. Although there are many ways to emulate the Replicate command, they all involve complicated and custom ActionScript or SmartClips. Generator creates new frames and physical Flash files—a capability Flash Player can't duplicate. ActionScript cannot generate Flash. What's more, Flash and ActionScript by themselves are not capable of creating complementary sets of graphics, such as animated GIFs. If your project requires multiple deliveries in many formats, there's no substitute for Generator.

POINTS TO REMEMBER

- You can use Generator commands to modify instances from setting alpha, tint, brightness, and color to transforming, replacing, and replicating content.

- In some cases, you can use ActionScript to duplicate Generator commands. Although ActionScript may be better suited for modifying alpha, tint, brightness, and color, it cannot be data-driven easily and will often require Flash 5 and above.

- Though powerful, ActionScript does not work as well for automating production and streamlining workflow because of its complexity as well as the testing it requires. Depending on the task, Generator commands can offer a quick and manageable solution.

- By using Generator commands to modify instances and create content, developers can produce content for delivery in other formats besides Flash, including JPG, GIF, PNG, and MOV.

- Because you can use Generator commands in conjunction with Generator variables, you can control many aspects and features of a Flash movie externally via any number of data sources.

- Think of Generator commands as server-side ActionScript to be modifying instances for alpha, brightness, tint, color, and replace.

- By employing symbol nesting, you can apply multiple Generator commands to one instance on the stage.

- External-media files provide a great way of managing libraries of content without modifying existing Flash movies.

CHAPTER 6

MEET THE GENERATOR OBJECTS

JUST AS GENERATOR OBJECTS ARE AT THE HEART OF THAT APPLICATION, this chapter is at the heart of this book. As placeholders for Generator-processed content, objects allow you to create complex data-driven elements such as charts, tables, and lists—items that would be difficult and time-consuming to create using standard Flash authoring techniques.

In this chapter, we'll examine the objects that come installed with Generator, show you how you can use them to create dynamic data-driven Flash elements, and go over a few tips and tricks. We'll also examine some custom objects that you can download from the Web to add functionality to Generator.

WHAT IS A GENERATOR OBJECT?

Although Generator objects are defined as placeholders for dynamic Generator-created content, this doesn't really begin to cover what they can do. The best way to answer the question, "What is a Generator object?" is by looking at the functionality objects provide. You can use objects to create charts, tickers, and lists. You can even use them to dynamically insert media into Flash movies.

The following is a quick overview of some of the object types included with Generator:

Charts: One of Generator's strengths is its ability to dynamically create data-driven charts. Generator comes with a variety of chart types, including bar, pie, line, stock, and scatter charts.

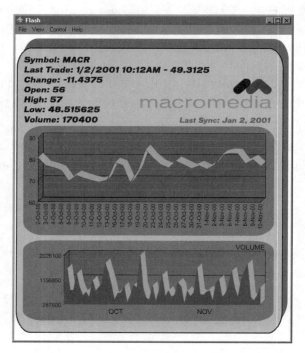

Insert Media: Generator can insert many types of graphics and media files into a Flash movie, including JPEG, PNG, GIF, Flash symbols, and other Flash movies or Generator templates.

Sounds: Generator can also be used to dynamically insert sounds into your Flash movie. It can insert both external (MP3) sound files and internal sounds that already exist in the movie's library.

Lists/Tickers: Lists and tickers often provide the clearest way to quickly display easy-to-understand information sets. They can show multiple records of data with either a fixed format or in a continuous loop that scrolls in all directions.

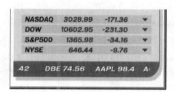

NASDAQ	3028.99	-171.36	▼
DOW	10602.95	-231.30	▼
S&P500	1365.98	-34.16	▼
NYSE	646.44	-9.76	▼

.42   DBE 74.56   AAPL 98.4   A

Plot: The Plot object allows you to dynamically insert and position multiple symbols into a Flash movie based on values defined in a data source.

Tables: Tables are powerful tools for displaying rows of related information. Generator allows you to dynamically create HTML or spreadsheet-like tables and insert them into your Flash movie.

Travel Advisory

	Location	Comment	
	Reykjavik Iceland	volcanic eruptions	7.02.99
	Atlanta USA	thunderstorms	6.28.99
	San Francisco USA	fog delays	6.26.99
	Paris France	road construction	6.14.99
	Oxaca Mexico	earthquake aftershocks	6.11.99
	Kyoto Japan	road construction	6.08.99

Custom objects: From creating complex menus to importing XML on the fly, there are dozens of Generator objects you can install and use right now to add new functionality to the program. Although these objects do not come installed with Generator, you can download them from the Web and add them to your existing Generator objects. In addition, you can use the Generator SDK to create and use your own Generator objects.

Are objects SmartClips?

You're probably thinking that Generator objects sound a lot like Flash 5 SmartClips: Both make it easy to create and insert dynamic, customizable, complex elements into your Flash movie. So are Generator objects just SmartClips? Not really, but it can be helpful to think of them as server-side SmartClips.

The main difference between SmartClips and Generator objects lies in where and when they're executed: SmartClips are executed on the client side in the Flash player (which means they require the Flash 5 Player and rely on the user's computer for processing). Generator objects, in contrast, are processed on the server side by the Generator server before the Flash movie is sent to the user (which means dynamic content can be generated without relying on the user's computer or Flash Player).

Using Generator objects

Now that you know what Generator objects are, how do you use them?

Locating the objects

GENERATOR OBJECTS
PANEL.

When you open Flash with the Generator extensions, one of the first things you'll notice is a new panel of objects. This is the Generator Objects panel, which you can access from Windows > Generator Objects. It contains all of the Generator objects that come installed with Generator. Any custom objects that you download and install will also appear in this panel.

Configuring the objects

In addition to the Generator Objects panel, you can also access the Generator Properties panel. This is where you specify properties to customize the functionality and output of Generator objects. You access this panel by double-clicking a Generator object on the stage, or selecting the object on the stage and then selecting Windows > Panels > Generator.

Generator object workflow

Workflow is pretty much the same for all object types. The steps below are typical of the workflow for using an object.

1. **Open the Generator Objects panel (Window > Generator Objects).**

2. **Click and drag an object from the panel to the stage.**

If the object inserts something into the movie (for example, a chart), it will do so in the timeline/movie clip in which in which it is placed. In most cases the position of the object will determine where the generated content (such as a chart) will be inserted in the movie.

3. **Open the Properties window for the object by double-clicking the object on the stage, or selecting the object and then selecting Window > Panels > Generator.**

4. **Set the properties for the object.**

5. **Test the movie.**

Dynamically specifying Generator properties

Because you can place a Generator variable just about anywhere that you can type, you can dynamically define the value of that variable when the template is processed.

Take, for example, the Generator object's Properties window: Instead of typing in a value for a property, you can place a Generator variable for the property and then pass in the value of that variable when the template is processed. Using this powerful technique, you can dynamically customize just about every aspect of your Flash movie and Generator template.

Specifying paths from Generator

Many objects include properties with paths to external data-source or media files (such as images or MP3s). These paths to external resources can be relative or absolute. However, keep in mind that if the path is relative, it is relative to the Generator template (.swt) in which the object exists.

The use of relative and absolute paths works a little differently when you employ middleware as a data source (see Chapter 8 for more on using Generator with middleware). The path to the middleware must be an absolute URL. Otherwise Generator treats the middleware just like a text file, and code within the middleware will not be processed. This applies to using Generator in both online and offline mode.

Getting information from Generator

When working with Generator objects, a number of errors can occur, such as data-source errors or incorrect paths to external media. Any errors or messages from the Flash movie or Generator objects will be displayed in the Output window (Window > Output).

It's a good idea to set the debugging level to Verbose by opening the Output window and selecting Options > Debug Level > Verbose. This ensures that any messages sent by Generator will be displayed in the Output window.

Customizing the Generator Objects panel

You can customize the Generator Objects panel by creating submenus that contain sets of objects—useful if you download a lot of custom objects, or if you want to organize existing objects by functionality.

To create a submenu in the Generator Objects panel:

1. *Close Flash.*

2. *Open up the Macromedia\Flash 5\generator\templates directory.*

3. *Create a folder called Custom Objects.*

4. *Copy any one of the .def files in the Template folder into the folder you just created.*

5. *Open Flash and then open the Generator Objects window (Window > Generator Objects).*

6. *At the top of the window, you should see a drop-down box with "common" selected. Click this box.*

7. *It will display the folder you just created; select Custom Objects.*

8. *The panel will change and show the object that you placed in the folder.*

9. *When you're finished, you can go back and delete the Custom Objects folder.*

INSERTING GRAPHICS WITH GENERATOR

The Insert GIF File, Insert JPG File, Insert PNG File, Insert Symbol, and Insert Flash Movie Generator objects allow you to dynamically insert various types of media in your Flash movie.

Inserting bitmapped files (.gif, .jpg, and .png) is one of the more CPU-intensive Generator tasks. Whenever possible, you should try to optimize image size (both file size and dimensions) or import the movie into Flash's library before Generator uses it. Inserting a GIF, JPG, or PNG file already embedded to a Flash movie will always be faster than inserting an image directly into a Generator template.

Insert GIF, Insert JPG, and Insert PNG properties

The Insert GIF File, Insert JPG File, and Insert PNG File objects have the following properties in the Generator Properties window:

File Name: This specifies the file path, relative or absolute URL (HTTP and FTP), database connection URL, or Java-class URL from which Generator will obtain the image data.

Scale to Fit: This specifies whether or not the image will be scaled to fit the object's placeholder. If this property is set to True, the image will be stretched to fit the object's placeholder (without necessarily maintaining the image's original aspect ratio). If the property is set to False, the image will retain its original size and aspect ratio.

Export As: This determines how the image will be compressed. Valid options are JPEG, which is a lossy compression scheme that works well with complex images such as pictures, and Lossless, which is a lossless compression scheme that works well with images which include large blocks of color.

JPEG Quality: If the Export As property is set to JPEG, this specifies the level of the compression. Values can range from 0 to 100. A lower value results in lower image quality and smaller file sizes. As the value increases, so do image quality and file size. A value of 100 allows JPEG files to be inserted into the movie without first decompressing and then recompressing the image data. This significantly improves the performance of the Insert JPEG object.

Cache: This specifies whether or not the image is cached. Valid values include True and False. This property is overridden by the cache settings in the Administration Servlet as well as by any cache parameters specified in the URL for the template. Setting this property to True will activate caching for the object if it is served from a Web server that has caching enabled on the Enterprise edition of Generator. If the files are served from a Web server that does not have the Enterprise edition of Generator installed, this property is ignored.

Frames: This setting—which only applies to the Insert GIF File object— specifies which frames to retrieve from an animated GIF file. You can specify All, Single, or an integer representing the frame number to retrieve. Single retrieves the first frame of the animated GIF, while All inserts the entire animated GIF.

Instance Name: This identifies the instance name of the object so that it can be targeted with ActionScript.

The following example demonstrates how to use the Insert GIF File object to dynamically insert a GIF file into a Flash movie. These steps and settings are repeated for the Insert PNG File and Insert JPEG File objects.

1. *Start a new Flash movie (File > New).*

2. *Drag the Insert GIF File object from the Generator Object panel into your movie.*

3. *Open the object's Properties window by double-clicking the Insert GIF object. Set the properties so that they match those in the following figure.*

4. *In the File Name property enter* **myimage.gif***. Now is a good time to save the Flash file to a location on your hard drive.*

5. *Copy the "myimage.gif" image from the Chapter 6 Insert Image folder on the companion CD into the same directory where the Flash file you're working on is saved.*

You can use any GIF image as long as the name and path specified in the File Name property match that of the image. The File Name property can be a relative or absolute file name or URL. If it's a relative path, it's relative to the location of the Generator template.

6. *Test the movie (Control > Test Movie) and view your results.*

If your image doesn't show up, make sure to check the path name and that the file is in the proper location. The Generator Output window will also tell you if there are any problems. If you still can't get it to work, look at the example in the Chapter 6 folder on the CD-ROM.

Finally, be aware that performance slows when you select a single frame other than Frame 1 from an animated GIF file.

Dynamically loading images into Flash at run time

If you need to dynamically insert images into your Flash movie at run time, you can create a simple template that only contains an Insert GIF File object (or JPEG or PNG). Instead of an image name, the File Name property would contain a Generator variable, whose value would be defined when the template is processed. You could then call the template with the ActionScript loadMovie command to dynamically load images into Flash, passing the image to be loaded through the URL.

For example, if the image variable were named {imageName}, the ActionScript code would look something like the following:

```
loadMovie("template.swt?imageName=myimage.gif", 0);
```

or more useful:

```
var image = "myimage.gif";
loadMovie("template.swt?imageName=" + image, 0);
```

Scaling inserted graphics proportionally

Setting the Scale to Fit parameter to True can distort and skew your image if its aspect ratio is not the same as that of the Generator object. This is because Scale to Fit will stretch the image to fit the Generator object exactly.

If you know that the size of the images being dynamically inserted into the Flash movie will always be the same, you can simply scale the Generator object to match the size of the image.

However, if you don't know how big the inserted image or symbol will be, you must use the Insert GIF/JPG/PNG/Symbol object with the Table object to ensure that the image's aspect ratio is maintained. (The Table object is discussed later in this chapter.)

1. *Create a new graphic or movie-clip symbol and name it "image".*

2. *Inside the symbol, place an Insert GIF/JPEG/PNG/Symbol object. Set the Scale to Fit parameter to False, then set the other parameters as desired. Do not resize the object's placeholder.*

3. *Close the symbol. Insert a Table object into the timeline in which you want to display the image. Resize the object placeholder to the size at which you want the image to be displayed.*

4. *Set the Table object's parameters to match those in the figure shown at right:*

Setting the Sizing parameter to Auto causes the Table object to automatically scale the image proportionally to fit within the size of the one table cell.

5. *Test your movie (Control > Test Movie). The image should now be scaled to the size you chose with its original aspect ratio maintained.*

This technique works best when the image being inserted is larger than the bounding box area; smaller images may appear pixelated.

The Insert GIF object and client CPU usage

Using the Insert GIF object can increase the CPU load of the movie in the Flash player because Generator places the image in its own movie clip before inserting it in the Flash movie. The Flash Player may continue to play the movie clip, redrawing the image, which leads to the increased CPU usage.

You can fix this by targeting the movie clip containing the image and telling it to stop playing:

1. *In the Generator properties windows for the Insert Gif object, set the Instance Name property (such as "MyGif").*

2. *Add the following ActionScript on the timeline containing the Insert GIF object:*

For Flash 5 Player:

```
MyGif.stop();
```

For Flash 4 Player:

```
tellTarget ("MyGif")
{
    stop ( );
}
```

Dynamically inserting images when you don't know image type

As we pointed out earlier in the chapter, Generator has a separate image object for each of the image types it supports:

```
Insert Gif
Insert Jpeg
Insert Png
```

If you need to dynamically insert images using Generator but don't know the image type beforehand, you can do one of two things:

- Create a movie clip with a layer for each image type that might be inserted. On each layer, place one Insert GIF/JPEG/PNG object.

Make sure that the object placeholders are the same size, have the same properties, and X, Y coordinates. For the image name, place the same Generator variable in each object. When Generator processes the template, it will attempt to insert the image into each object, but only the correct object will work. Other than throwing some errors into the logs, this will work fine.

- Use the Custom Insert Image object. This object determines the type of image being inserted and then passes it on to the correct Generator image object.

The Insert Image Custom Generator object is discussed in more detail in the Custom Generator Objects section later in the chapter.

Inserting symbols

The Insert Symbol object allows you to dynamically insert Flash symbols from your library into your Flash movie. You can also insert symbols from external symbol libraries. (Use the External Media setting in the Generator Publishing Settings tab to import libraries.)

The Insert Symbol object is similar to the ActionScript attachMovie() command, except that only the symbols being inserted in the movie are sent to Flash Player.

When authoring movies for Flash 2 and using the Insert Symbol object, make sure that the main timeline and any clips being inserted have the same number of frames.

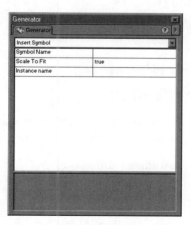

Symbol Name: This specifies which symbol from the Flash library to insert. If symbols are in folders, use a fully qualified name (for example, folder/folder/symbol name).

Scale to Fit: This specifies whether the symbol should be scaled to fit the boundaries of the gray box on the stage. If this property is set to True, the symbol will be stretched to fit the object's placeholder (without necessarily maintaining the image's original aspect ratio). If the property is set to False, the image will retain its original size and aspect ratio. (See the section above for information on how to scale the inserted symbol while maintaining its aspect ratio.)

Instance Name: This identifies the instance name of the object so that it can be targeted with ActionScript.

The Insert Symbol object works very much like the Insert GIF/JPG/PNG objects:

1. *Drag the Insert Symbol file to the stage.*

2. *Add a new movie-clip symbol to the library (Insert > Symbol) and call it MySymbol.*

3. *In the Generator Properties window for the Insert Symbol object, set the Symbol Name property to the name of the symbol we just created, MySymbol.*

4. *Test the movie (Control > Test Movie).*

You should see the symbol you created in the same space as the Insert Symbol object. If you don't see the symbol, make sure you entered its name correctly. If you continue to have problems with it, view the example on the included CD-ROM in the Chapter 6 folder, insert_symbol example.

Referencing movie clips stored in folders within the library

As we've just discussed, the Insert Symbol Generator object allows you to dynamically load symbols from your library and place them in your movie.

It's good practice to create folders within your library to organize your symbols; however, this can make it tricky to reference the symbols from Generator.

To reference symbols contained within folders, you must reference the complete path to the symbol.

For example, if you had the following library structure:

you would specify the following for the Symbol Name property of the Insert Symbol object:

```
folder1/mySymbol1
```

This will load the symbol contained within the folder.

Inserting a Flash movie file

The Insert Flash Movie object allows you to employ Generator to dynamically insert an entire Flash movie within your Flash movie. It works in much the same way as the Insert GIF/JPG/PNG objects.

The Insert Flash Movie object is similar to the ActionScript LoadMovie command—except, of course, that the movie is included on the server side, and not when the Flash movie is playing in the Flash Player.

The Insert Flash Movie object has the following properties:

File Name: This specifies the file name, relative or absolute URL (HTTP and FTP), database connection URL, or Java-class URL of the location of the Flash movie that Generator will load.

Cache: This specifies whether or not the file is cached. Valid values include True and False. This property is overridden by the Cache settings in the Administration Servlet and by any cache parameters specified in the URL for the template. Setting this property to True will activate caching for the object if it is served from a Web server that has caching enabled on the Enterprise edition of Generator. If the files are served from a Web server that does not have the Enterprise edition of Generator installed, this property is ignored.

Scale to Fit: This specifies whether the inserted Flash movie will be scaled to fit the boundaries of the gray box on the stage. If this property is set to True, the inserted movie will be stretched to fit the object's placeholder (without necessarily maintaining the image's original aspect ratio). If the property is set to False, the Flash movie retains its original size and aspect ratio. (See the section "Inserting GIF/JPG/PNG Properties" earlier in this chapter for information on how to scale the inserted Flash movie while maintaining its aspect ratio.)

Expand Frames: If set to True, this expands the timeline containing the movie file so that the entire inserted movie can play. Otherwise, the Flash movie is inserted into a movie clip. Generally, this property should be set to False.

Instance Name: This identifies the instance name of the object so that it can be targeted with ActionScript.

To insert a Flash movie, you must already have created a .swf. For the example below, you can use the example Flash movie in the InsertMovie folder on the CD-ROM.

1. *Drag the Insert Flash Movie object onto the stage.*

2. *Copy the .swf from the CD-ROM into the same directory as the Flash movie you're working on.*

3. *Set the properties to match those in the following figure:*

4. *Test the movie.*

You should see your movie (loaded SWF) in the same area that the Insert Flash Movie object was placed.

> If you're using Generator Developer Edition, you cannot use the Insert Flash Movie object to insert the output of another Generator template. The Developer edition can only process one template at a time; requesting a template from another template will cause the server to freeze.

THE ART OF THE CHART

Some of the most powerful and popular Generator objects are those that allow you to dynamically add charts to your Flash movie. These objects include the Basic Charts object, the Stock Chart object, and the Pie Chart Object:

- The Basic Charts object allows you to create bar, line, area, scatter, stacked bar, stacked line, stacked area, and stacked scatter charts.

- The Stock Chart object allows you to create high-low-close, open-high-low-close, and candlestick charts.

- The Pie Chart object allows you to create pie charts.

Building charts with the Basic Charts object

In this section, we'll use the Basic Charts object to create a dynamic line chart.

The following are the properties for the Basic Charts object. (Remember: Not all properties are used with each chart type you can create with the Basic Charts object.)

Data Source: This specifies the data source from which the chart will be built. The data can be retrieved from any source that Generator can use, including URLs, files, and databases.

Chart Type: This specifies the type of chart to create. Valid chart types are Bar, Line, Area, Scatter, Stacked Bar, Stacked Line, Stacked Area, and Stacked Scatter.

Symbol: This specifies the name of the symbol in the library to use for plotting points in scatter charts. This is only used if the Chart Type property is set to Scatter or Stacked Scatter.

Max Data Entries: This specifies the maximum number of values displayed in the chart (both the maximum permitted and the minimum number for which space is allotted). For example, if Max Data Entries is set to 10, Generator will create a chart with space for 10 entries. If there are more than 10 values in the data source, only the first 10 will be charted. If there are less than 10 values in the data source, all of the values will be charted and space will be reserved for the rest of the chart. If the property is set to Default, all values will be displayed. This property applies to all chart types except scatter and stacked scatter.

Gap: This specifies the amount of space between bars in a bar chart. Each unit is equal to one-twentieth of a pixel. This property only applies to bar and stacked bar charts.

Depth: This specifies the amount of depth to render chart elements (that is, how three-dimensional the chart element will look). Each unit equals one-twentieth of a pixel. The Depth property applies to all chart types except scatter.

Labels: This specifies whether labels will appear along the left side of the chart. Valid values include On and Off.

Label Format: This specifies the font that will be used to display the labels on the left and bottom of the chart. Valid values include Arial, Time, and Courier. This setting is ignored if an external symbol file is specified in the Symbol File property (see the "Customizing Value and Label Formatting Using the External Symbol File Property" section below).

Horizontal Label Orientation: This specifies whether the labels on the bottom of the chart will be displayed vertically or horizontally. Valid values include Horizontal and Vertical. The labels on the bottom of the chart are defined by the HLABEL column in the data source.

Horizontal Label Scale: This specifies the size of the label on the bottom of the chart. The label can be scaled to fit the chart element (Scale to Fit) or displayed at the symbol size (Fixed). Half and Double display the symbol at half or double its original size. You can also enter a numerical scale factor to apply to the symbol. For example, entering 0.50 scales the label to one-half the symbol size.

Value Display: This specifies where and when the chart values will be displayed on the chart. Valid values include Always, Never, and Rollover. If Rollover is specified, the value will be displayed when the user mouses over the chart element. This property only applies to bar, stacked bar, scatter, and stacked scatter charts.

Value Scale: This indicates whether or not the text that displays the value should scale to fit within the chart element's area or be displayed at a fixed size. Valid values include Scale to Fit, Fixed, Half, and Double. These properties work the same as in the Horizontal Label Scale property. This property only applies to bar, stacked bar, scatter, and stacked scatter charts.

Value Format: This specifies the font to be used to display the value within the chart. Valid values include Arial, Times, and Courier. This property only applies to bar, stacked bar, scatter, and stacked scatter charts.

Value Placement: This specifies where chart values should be displayed within the chart. Valid values include On Bar, Over Bar, Over Chart, and Under Chart. This property only applies to bar, stacked bar, scatter, and stacked scatter charts.

Symbol File: This specifies the path to a Generator template that will be used to format the labels and values in the chart. This property allows you to obtain more advanced formatting control by linking to an external Generator template (SWT file).

If you're creating a scatter chart and are using position labels, you must specify a symbol file. Labels are available to all chart types; values are available to bar, stacked bar, and scatter charts only.

See below for more information later in this chapter on using the Symbol File property.

Grid Lines: This specifies whether or not grid lines are displayed behind the chart. Valid values are On and Off.

Grid Scales: This specifies how the number of grid lines will be determined. The first valid value is Auto, which builds the grid lines based on the data in the chart. The other valid value is Manual, which allows you to specify how the grid lines are specified using the Major Grid Lines and Minor Grid Lines properties (see "Creating and Formatting a Line Chart Using the Basic Charts Object" below).

Major Grid Lines: If the Grid Scales property is set to Manual, this specifies the number of major grid lines that will be drawn in the chart.

Minor Grid Lines: If the Grid Scales property is set to Manual, this specifies the number of minor grid lines that will be drawn in the chart.

Min Y-Pos Type: This setting determines where on the Y axis the chart's lowest value will be plotted. Valid values include Absolute and Relative. If the property is set to Absolute, the minimum value of the chart will be determined by the value in the Min Y-Pos property. If the property is set to Relative, the minimum value of the chart will be the percentage specified in the Min Y-Pos property above the lowest value in the data source.

In most cases you can just ignore this setting and use the default value of Absolute.

Min Y-Pos: If the Min Y-Pos Type property is set to Absolute, this specifies the lowest Y value that will be used in the chart. If the Min Y-Pos Type property is set to Relative, this specifies the percent above the lowest value in the data source where the lowest value will be displayed.

In most cases, you can use the default value of 0.

Max Y-Pos Type: This setting determines where on the Y axis the chart's highest value will be plotted. Valid values include Absolute and Relative. If the property is set to Absolute, the maximum value of the chart will be determined by the value in the Max Y-Pos property. If the property is set to Relative, the maximum value of the chart will be the percentage specified in the Max Y-Pos property below the highest value in the data source.

In most cases you can just ignore this setting and use the default value of Absolute.

Max Y-Pos: If the Max Y-Pos Type property is set to Absolute, this specifies the highest Y value that will be used in the chart. If the Max Y-Pos Type property is set to Relative, this specifies the percent below the highest value in the data source where the highest value will be displayed.

In most cases, you can use the default value of 0.

Origin: This specifies the position of values that equal 0 along the left side of the chart. In most cases you can ignore this setting and use the default of 0.

Border: This specifies whether or not to draw a border around the Chart object's bounding box. Valid values include True and False. The color of the border is determined by the color specified in the Color property.

Border Thickness: If the Border property is set to True, this setting specifies the thickness of the border in *twips* (one-twentieth of a pixel). This also specifies the width of major grid lines.

Line Thickness: This specifies the thickness of chart lines (such as in a line chart), measured in twips.

Color: This specifies the color of various items in the chart, including the border and gridlines. If a color is not specified in the data source for chart elements, this property also sets the colors for those Chart objects. Valid values include Web-safe color names (blue), Web hexadecimal values (#000000), and regular hexadecimal values (0x000000).

Instance Name: This identifies the instance name of the object so that it can be targeted with ActionScript.

Customizing value and label formatting using the External Symbol File property

As mentioned earlier, the External Symbol File property allows you to specify the path to a Generator template that will be used to format the labels and values in the chart. This gives you greater control over label and value formatting.

Using an external symbol file allows you to specify the font type, size, and color of the values as well as to dynamically insert text and other Generator objects that you want to associate with the label or value.

To do this, you must create another Generator template that will act as a formatting template for our value display. The chart will get its formatting settings for its values from this template.

To create an external symbol file:

1. *Create a new Flash movie.*

2. *Set the file to publish as a Generator template (.swt) in the Publish Settings window.*

3. *Create a new movie-clip symbol (Ctrl-F8) and call it chartValue1 for value formatting, and chartLabel1 for label formatting. (The name must be exactly like this).*

4. *Open the symbol to edit and place a Generator variable called {value} near the center point.*

The font type, color, and size that you choose for the {value} variable will be used to display the value in your chart. If you were setting label formatting, you would insert a {label} variable into the chartLabel1 symbol.

Any variables in your data source are also available for use in the external symbol file.

5. *Save and publish the file. The resulting Generator template (.swt) is the file that Generator will use as the external symbol file.*

You can insert more than just text in your chart using this method. You could, for example, place an Insert Symbol object into the formatting SWT and then dynamically insert a symbol to be displayed with the value and label. Note, however, that the variables are not evaluated until they're in the movie that's loading the external symbol file. Thus, any resources dynamically loaded (such as symbols) must be present or available in the chart's movie, not the formatting template.

Creating the data source for the Basic Charts object

All of the charts created with the Basic Charts object use a Generator column data source. However, each chart type uses different column headings. The following lists the chart types you can create with the Basic Charts object as well as the columns you can use in their data source.

Bar: Each row of the data source represents one bar in the bar chart.

> **value:** This required value specifies the value for the current chart section.
>
> **color:** This specifies the color for the current chart section. If no value is specified, the bar color will be determined by the Color property of the object.
>
> **hlabel:** If the Labels property is set to On, this column specifies which labels will be displayed under each chart section.
>
> **URL:** Defines a URL that the user will be redirected to when they click the pie piece for the current row. Cannot be used if "goto" or "gotolabel" is defined.
>
> **goto:** Defines the frame number in the current Flash movie that the movie will go to when the user clicks the bar for the current row. Cannot be used if a URL or "gotolabel" is defined.
>
> **gotoLabel:** Defines a frame label in the current Flash movie that the movie will go to when the user clicks the bar for the current row. Cannot be used if a URL or "goto" is defined.
>
> **window:** If the URL has a value, this property defines the browser frame/window that the URL will be opened in when the user clicks the bar. The following are valid values:
>
> - _top: Opens the URL in the current browser window and loads the URL in the top frame.
> - _self: Opens the URL in the current browser window and loads it in the current frame. This is the default value.
> - _blank: Opens the URL in a new browser window.

Stacked Bar: The Stacked Bar Chart data source is a Generator column data source, with each row representing one level/section of each bar. All of the rows for a value column make up a single bar.

> **color:** This defines the color of the current level of the bar sections. For example, if the color of the first row of data were set to Red, all of the first sections of each stacked bar piece would be red.

value1, value2, … value *n*: Each value column represents one stacked bar section.

Line: Each row of the data source represents one point on the line chart.

value: This specifies the value for the current chart section, and is a required value.

color: This specifies the color for the line chart. Only the color defined in the first row of data is used. If no color is defined, the color will be determined by the Color property of the object.

hlabel: If the Labels property is set to On, this column specifies the labels that will be displayed under each chart point.

Stacked Line: Each row of the data source represents one line in the chart, with subsequent lines building on the values of the lines below them in the data source.

color: This specifies the value for the line represented by the current row of data.

value1, value2, … value *n*: These fields specify the values used to construct the line represented by each row of data.

Area: Each row of the data source represents one point on the area chart.

value: This required value specifies the value for the current chart section.

color: This specifies the color for the Line chart. Only the color defined in the first row of data is used. If no color is defined, the color will be determined by the object's Color property.

hlabel: If the Labels property is set to On, this column specifies the labels that will be displayed under each chart point.

Stacked Area: Each row of the data source represents one line in the chart, with subsequent lines building on the values of the lines below them in the data source. This is similar to the stacked line chart except that the body of the line is filled in with a solid color.

color: This specifies the value for the line represented by the current row of data.

value1, value2, … value *n*: These fields specify the values used to construct the line represented by each row of data.

Scatter: The scatter chart allows you to plot points on a chart based on a column data source.

X: This specifies the X coordinate to plot the item that the current row represents.

Y: This specifies the Y coordinate to plot the item that the current row represents.

symbol: This specifies the symbol used to plot the item that the current row represents. If no symbol is specified, Generator will insert a default symbol (a dot).

color: If no symbol is specified, this determines the color of the default symbol used to plot the item represented by the current row.

hlabel: This specifies the horizontal label for the item that the current row represents.

Scatter Line: The scatter line chart allows you to plot points on a chart based on a column data source. This is similar to the scatter chart except that the points plotted are connected by a line in the order that they appear in the data source.

X: This specifies the X coordinate to plot the item that the current row represents.

Y: This specifies the Y coordinate to plot the item that the current row represents.

symbol: This specifies the symbol used to plot the item that the current row represents. If no symbol is specified, Generator will insert a default symbol (a dot).

color: If no symbol is specified, this determines the color of the default symbol that will be used to plot the item represented by the current row.

hlabel: This specifies the horizontal label for the item that the current row represents.

Creating and formatting a line chart using the Basic Charts object

In this section we'll create a data-driven stock chart that displays the name of the market and the market values of the day. We'll also use it to create a GIF for PDA, cell phone, and device deployment.

1. *Create a new Flash movie (File > New).*

2. *Set the stage dimensions to 400 x 280 and the background color to Black.*

3. *Create five layers and name them, from the bottom up, "chartbg," "chart frame," "market text," "date text," and "chart."*

4. *In the "chartbg" layer, create a blue (#508CC8) rectangle. In the Options area use the Rectangle Corner Radius settings to set the corner radius to 40.*

It doesn't matter what color or shape we use for our example; however, if you want your results to resemble ours, you'll need to follow this example closely.

5. *Using the Info panel (Window > Panels > Info), set the height and width of the shape to the following: Width: 380, Height: 248, X: 10, Y: 29.*

6. *In the market text layer, use the Text tool to create a Generator variable named {market}.*

Make sure that you stretch the text block as large as the area you wish the text to fill. Any time that you have different amounts of text coming in you should use a fixed-width block so that the text will wrap automatically.

7. *On the Chart layer drag the Basic Charts object onto the stage. Set its properties to match those in the following figure:*

Generator		
Generator		
Basic Charts		
Data Source	chartdata.txt	
Chart Type	Line	
Symbol		
Max Data Entries	default	
Gap	0	
Depth	300	
Labels	on	
Label Format		
Horizontal Label Orientation	vertical	
Horizontal Label Scale	fixed	
Value Display		
Value Scale		
Value Format		
Value Placement		
Symbol File	labels.swt	
Grid Lines	on	
Grid Scales	Auto	
Major Gridlines	5	
Minor Gridlines	3	
Min Y-Pos Type	Relative Percent	
Min Y-Pos		
Max Y-Pos Type	Relative Percent	
Max Y-Pos		
Origin		
Border	false	
Border Thickness	1	
Line Thickness	20	
Color	0x000000	
Instance name	OurChart	

For a more detailed description of each data source parameter for all the Generator charts, consult the appendixes at the back of this book.

8. **Enter chartdata.txt** *in the Data Source field; this is the text file that we're going to create to feed Generator the data.*

If we were creating a line or scatter chart, we could specify multiple data sources by entering a semicolon-delimited list of data sources.

You can also place Generator variables into all of the property fields and define them dynamically when the template is processed.

9. *Save your work. Name the file mychart.fla and place it in a new folder; this is where we'll keep the files used in this movie.*

Creating the data source

Now we'll create the data source that we'll base the chart on.

1. *Using any text editor, create a new file and enter the following column names:*

value, color, hlabel

value is the value of the stock for that particular row of data, or interval.

color determines the color of our Line chart. Only the color in the first line will be used. You can specify any Web-safe color name, Web hexadecimal, or regular hexadecimal value.

hlabel specifies the labels that will be displayed on the bottom of the chart if the Labels property is set to On. We'll use this to display the market's start and close times.

2. *Enter the following data into your data source (or use the copy from the CD-ROM):*

3240.54,green,Open
3144.81,,
3168.05,,
3199.30,,10:00am
3199.07,,
3186.85,,
3167.15,,
3173.22,,
3150.87,,
3127.17,,11:00am
3129.78,,
3105.26,,

```
3134.47,,
3144.51,,
3172.86,,
3161.83,,12:00pm
3197.24,,
3193.17,,
3227.67,,
3252.79,,
3225.35,,
3218.37,,1:00pm
3228.12,,
3218.34,,
3212.12,,
3225.66,,
3238.47,,
3249.55,,2:00pm
3254.19,,
3234.40,,
3239.08,,
3218.43,,
3216.73,,
3226.47,,3:00pm
3186.30,,
3180.80,,
3181.60,,
3200.87,,
3190.40,,
3168.38,,4:00pm
3168.17,,
3168.51,,
3168.49,,Close
```

3. *Save this file into the same directory as the .fla and name it chartdata.txt.*

Notice that the "hlabel" column only contains a value every five rows. This prevents the labels from running together when you're using large amounts of data to build your chart.

4. *Switch back to Flash and open the Generator Publish Properties tab. In the Parameters section, enter* market *for the name and* NASDAQ

for the value. This sets the Generator variable {market} equal to "NASDAQ." When you've entered the data, click the Add button and close the Publish Settings window.

These parameters are only used for testing the template; they won't be included with the final Generator template.

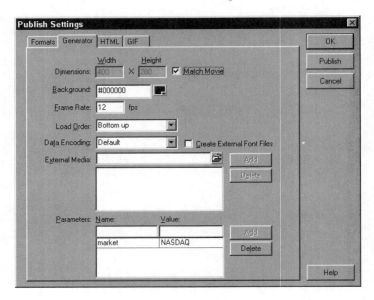

5.   **Test the movie (Control > Test Movie).**

Now back to our movie: You may notice that the labels have defaulted to Arial. This is because we have not yet created a symbol file. We also need to add some graphics behind the chart to make it more engaging.

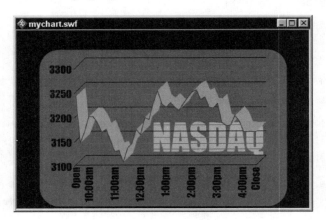

We didn't specify a border in the chart settings because we wanted to create one ourselves. However, we cannot see the exact amount of space that the chart will take up when working in Flash. This can make it difficult to create a background that lines up with the chart.

Framing that chart

Next, we'll create an image of the generated chart, which we'll use as a guideline in the Flash authoring environment to help us create and position our own background image and border.

1. *Revisit the Publish settings and check the PNG Publish setting. Publish the movie, then close the window.*

2. *Add a new layer to the movie and call it* chart guide. *Make this a Guide layer by right-clicking the layer name and selecting Guide. Click the first frame in the Chart Guide layer and import the PNG we just published (File > Import, choose mychart.png).*

We can now see the chart and the amount of space it will use.

3. *Using the Line and Paint tools (or whichever tools you're comfortable with), create a frame on the Chart Frame layer.*

Refer to the following figure to match it to the example or feel free to create your own. Keep testing your movie to get it exactly the way you want.

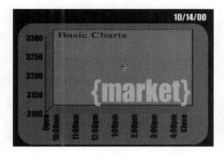

4. *Save your work before we create an external symbol file to customize the format of our chart labels.*

Creating the symbol file

Finally, we need to create the symbol file specified in the chart's Symbol File property. Doing so will give us greater control over label and value formatting in the chart.

1. *Create a new Flash movie. Make sure to set it to publish as a Generator template in the Publish Settings window.*

2. *We need to insert two movie clips that contain the fonts for the charts' labels. Create a new graphic or movie-clip symbol (Insert > New Symbol) and name it chartLabel1. The name must be exactly the same.*

3. *Open the new symbol and create a text block with a variable named {label}. Use the font and size you wish to use for the labels of the chart.*

For our example, we're going to use Impact with a font height of 16. If you don't have that font, feel free to use another. It doesn't matter where you place the text within the symbol; however, the text is easier to locate if it's positioned in the center of the symbol.

This symbol will be used to format the chart's labels.

4. *Create a new symbol and call it chartValue1 (again, the name must be exact). Then repeat Step 2.*

This symbol will be used to format the values of the chart.

5. *Save the file in the same directory as the mychart.fla file and name it labels.fla.*

This is the name of the Symbol File property that we specified in our chart.

6. *Publish the movie by selecting File > Publish. This will create the SWT file and save it into the same directory as the .fla.*

7. *Switch back to the mychart.fla file and test the movie (Control > Test Movie).*

Voila! You should now see a fairly nice-looking stock chart. Note that the chart labels and values are now the same as those specified in the symbol file.

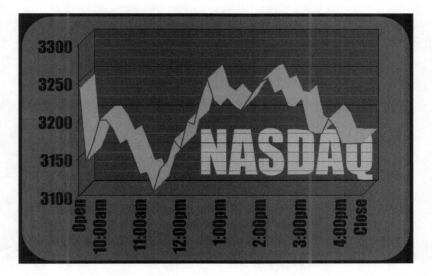

8. *If you're happy with the appearance of the chart and background, you can delete the Guide layer within the chart.*

GIF it up

The last thing we need to do is edit our movie so that we can dynamically create GIF files from it. This will allow us to use the chart with cell phones, PDAs, and other devices that can only display GIFs (not Flash movies).

1. *Open the Publish Settings window (File > Publish Settings). Check the Select GIF Image (.gif) tab and uncheck PNG (since we no longer need to create a guide). Click the GIF tab and select Static in the Playback area.*

The GIF tab is where you will set all of the GIF settings for the Generator-created GIF.

Note: If this were an animated Flash chart or if our movie had multiple frames, we could place labels inside the Flash movie that Generator could use to grab the image or image series.

To specify a single frame for a static GIF, place a frame label called #static on the frame of the Flash movie timeline to be included in the static GIF.

To specify a range of frames to be included in an animated GIF, place a frame label called #first on the first frame of the range of frames in the timeline to be included in the animated GIF and place a frame label called #last on the last frame of that frame range.

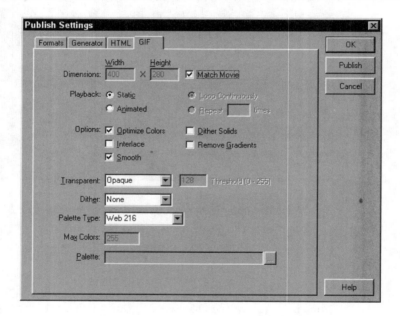

2. **Publish the movie (File > Publish) and look in the folder that contains the .fla.**

You should see a GIF file in that folder. The .gif contains an image of the chart. If you're unhappy with image quality, you can tweak the settings in the GIF tab under the Publish Settings window (File > Publish Settings).

You have now created a complete, Generator-driven line chart. You can create other chart types (such as bar and area) with the Basic Charts object using the steps and techniques we employed to create the line chart above.

If, for instance, you wanted to convert the line chart to a bar chart, you would only have to make two changes:

1. *Change the Chart Type property to Bar.*

2. *Edit the data source and add a color value for each row under the Color column.*

This will determine the color of the bar piece for that row of data.

Creating clustered bar charts with Generator

(Thanks to Robb Corrigan for developing the following technique.)

The trick to creating clustered bar charts is in how you format the data. A typical data source for a bar chart might look like the following:

```
COLOR, HLABEL, VALUE
#0000FF, Company A Net Sales (1998), 1.00
#FFFF00,Company A Net Sales (1999),1.69
#FF0000,Company A Net Sales (2000),1.64
```

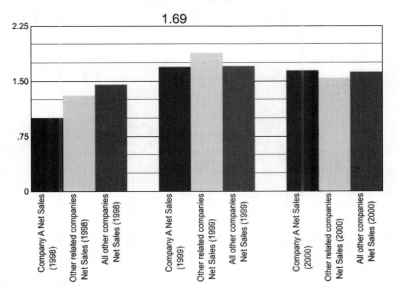

For a *clustered* bar chart, you would format your data as follows:

```
COLOR, HLABEL, VALUE
#0000FF,Company A Net Sales (1998),1.00
#FFFF00,Other related companies Net Sales (1998),1.30
#FF0000,All other companies Net Sales (1998),1.45
#FFFFFF,,0
#0000FF,Company A Net Sales (1999),1.69
#FFFF00,Other related companies Net Sales (1999),1.88
#FF0000,All other companies Net Sales (1999),1.70
#FFFFFF,,0
#0000FF,Company A Net Sales (2000),1.64
#FFFF00,Other related companies Net Sales (2000),1.54
#FF0000,All other companies Net Sales (2000),1.62
#FFFFFF,,0
```

Notice that the groups are now separated by a blank column (#FFFFFF,,0). This allows you to represent additional measures within the same chart.

Inserting stock charts

The Stock Chart object allows you to dynamically create high-low-close, open-high-low-close, and candlestick stock charts. Because these work similarly to basic charts, we won't build demos of these.

Simple Candle Stick Chart created with the Stock Chart object.

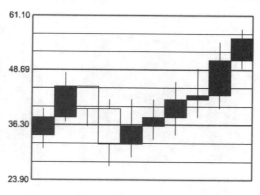

Stock charts have the following properties in the Generator panel:

Data Source: This specifies the data source from which the chart will be built. Data can be retrieved from any source that Generator can work with, including URLs, files, and databases. See below for more information on data sources.

Chart Type: This specifies the type of stock chart to create. Valid values include High-Low-Close, Open-High-Low-Close, and CandleSticks.

Max Data Entries: This specifies the maximum number of values displayed in the chart (both the maximum permitted and the minimum number for which space is allotted). For example, if Max Data Entries is set to 10, Generator will create a chart with space for 10 entries. If there are more than 10 values in the data source, only the first 10 will be charted. If there are fewer than 10 values in the data source, all of the values will be charted and space will be reserved for the rest of the chart. If the property is set to Default, all values will be displayed. This property applies to all chart types except Scatter and Stacked Scatter.

Start Offset: This specifies how far to the right or left of the chart data will begin to be plotted. The default is 0, which means that data will be plotted from the far left side of the chart.

Gap: This specifies the amount of space between sections in the chart. Each unit is equal to one-twentieth of a pixel.

Open Column: This specifies the column name in the data source to use as the open data. This is useful if you need to use a data source that does not have the default column names.

Close Column: This specifies the column name in the data source to use as the close data. This is useful if you need to use a data source that does not have the default column names.

High Column: This specifies the column name in the data source to use as the high data. This is useful if you need to use a data source that does not have the default column names.

Low Column: This specifies the column name in the data source to use as the low data. This is useful if you need to use a data source that does not have the default column names.

Labels: This specifies whether or not labels will appear along the left side of the chart. Valid values include On and Off.

Label Format: This specifies the font that will be used to display the labels on the left and bottom of the chart. Valid values include Arial, Time, and Courier. This setting is ignored if an external symbol file is specified in the Symbol File property.

Horizontal Label Orientation: This specifies whether the labels on the bottom of the chart will be displayed vertically or horizontally. Valid values include Horizontal and Vertical. The labels on the bottom of the chart are defined by the HLABEL column in the data source (see "Stock Chart Data Source" below).

Horizontal Label Scale: This specifies the size of the label. The label can be scaled to fit the chart element (Scale to Fit) or displayed at the symbol size (Fixed). Half and Double display the symbol at half or double its original size, respectively. You can also enter a numerical scale factor to apply to the symbol. For example, entering **0.50** scales the label to one-half the symbol size.

Value Display: This specifies where and when the chart values will be displayed on the chart. Valid values include Always, Never, and Rollover. If Rollover is specified, the value will be displayed when the user moves over the chart element.

Value Format: This specifies the font used to display the value within the chart. Valid values include Arial, Times, and Courier.

Value Scale: This indicates whether or not the text that displays the value should scale to fit within the chart element's area or be displayed at a fixed size. Valid values include Scale to Fit, Fixed, Half, and Double. These properties work the same as in the Horizontal Label Scale property.

Value to Display: This specifies which column value will be displayed.

Value Placement: This specifies where chart values should be displayed within the chart. Valid values include On Bar, Over Bar, Over Chart, and Under Chart.

External Symbol File: This specifies the path to a Generator template that will be used to format the chart's labels and values. This gives you more formatting control by linking to an external Generator template (SWT file). See the basic chart example above for more information on creating and using external symbol files.

Grid Lines: This specifies whether or not grid lines are displayed behind the chart.

Grid Scales: This specifies how the number of grid lines will be determined. The first valid value is Auto, which builds the grid lines based on the data in the chart. The other valid value is Manual, which allows you to set how the grid lines are specified using the Major Grid Lines and Minor Grid Lines properties (see next entry).

Major Grid Lines: If the Grid Scales property is set to Manual, this specifies the number of major grid lines that will be drawn in the chart.

Minor Grid Lines: If the Grid Scales property is set to Manual, this specifies the number of minor grid lines that will be drawn in the chart.

Min Y-Pos Type: This setting determines where on the Y axis the chart's lowest value will be plotted. Valid values include Absolute and Relative. If the property is set to Absolute, the minimum value of the chart will be determined by the value in the Min Y-Pos property. If the property is set to Relative, the minimum value of the chart will be the percentage specified in the Min Y-Pos property above the lowest value in the data source.

In most cases you can just ignore this setting and use the default value of Absolute.

Min Y-Pos: If the Min Y-Pos Type property is set to Absolute, this specifies the lowest Y value that will be used in the chart. If the Min Y-Pos Type property is set to Relative, this specifies the percent above the lowest value in the data source where the lowest value will be displayed.

In most cases, you can use the default value of 0.

Max Y-Pos Type: This setting determines where on the Y axis the chart's highest value will be plotted. Valid values include Absolute and Relative. If the property is set to Absolute, the maximum value of the chart will be determined by the value in the Max Y-Pos property. If the property is set to Relative, the maximum value of the chart will be the percentage specified in the Max Y-Pos property below the highest value in the data source.

In most cases you can just ignore this setting and use the default value of Absolute.

Max Y-Pos: If the Max Y-Pos Type property is set to Absolute, this specifies the highest Y value that will be used in the chart. If the Max Y-Pos Type property is set to Relative, this specifies the percent below the highest value in the data source where the highest value will be displayed.

In most cases, you can use the default value of 0.

Border: This specifies whether or not to draw a border around the object's bounding box. Valid values include True and False. The color of the border is determined by the color specified in the Color property.

Border Thickness: If the Border property is set to True, this setting specifies the thickness of the border in twips (one-twentieth of a pixel). This also specifies the width of major grid lines.

Line Thickness: This specifies the thickness of chart lines, measured in twips.

Color: This specifies the color of various items in the chart, including border and grid lines. If a color is not specified in the data source for chart elements, this property also sets the colors for those chart objects. Valid values include Web-safe color names (blue), Web hexadecimal values (#000000), and regular hexadecimal values (0x000000).

Instance Name: This identifies the instance name of the object so that it can be targeted with ActionScript.

Stock chart data source

The data source for stock charts is a simple column data source. Each row of data represents one set of related information. The data source shows the default column names, though you can change some of these via the object's Properties settings.

open: This is the value of the opening price. You can change this column's name via the object's Open Column property.

close: This is the value of the closing price. You can change this column's name via the object's Close Column property.

high: This is the value of the high price. You can change this column's name via the object's High Column property.

low: This is the value of the low price. You can change this column's name via the object's Low Column property.

color: This specifies the color for the current chart section. If no value is specified, the color will be determined by the object's Color property.

hlabel: If the Labels property is set to On, this column specifies the labels that will be displayed under each chart section.

URL: Defines a URL that the user will be redirected to when he or she clicks the chart section for the current row. Cannot be used if "goto" or "gotolabel" is defined.

goto: Defines a frame number in the current Flash movie that the movie will go to when the user clicks the chart section for the current row. Cannot be used if URL or "gotolabel" is defined.

gotoLabel: Defines a frame label in the current Flash movie that the movie will go to when the user clicks the chart section for the current row. Cannot be used if URL or "goto" is defined.

window: If the URL has a value, this defines the browser frame/window that the URL will be opened in when the user clicks the chart section. Valid values are as follows:

- _top: Opens the URL in the current browser window and loads the URL in the top frame.
- _self: Opens the URL in the current browser window and loads the URL in the current frame. This is the default value.
- _blank: Opens the URL in a new browser window.

Pie charts

The Generator Pie Chart object allows you to dynamically create and insert pie charts in your Flash movies.

Creating a data source

Before we can create a pie chart, we must first create a data source that specifies the values for the chart's pie sections.

The data source—which is specified in the Data Source section of the Generator Properties panel—must be a valid Generator column from any data source that Generator can access and retrieve data from. For our example, we'll use a simple text file as the object's data source.

The pie chart data source is in the Column data layout (which replicates a database column/row structure). The following is a basic pie chart data source:

```
value, color
5, blue
7, red
6, yellow
```

The first row defines variable names, and subsequent rows define variable values (one row for each pie section). The value and color variables are required and must be defined in every pie chart data source. The pie chart that uses this data source will have three colored pie pieces: blue, red, and yellow, with values of 5, 7, and 6.

In addition to the value and color variables, a number of other valid variables can be passed to the Pie Chart object through the data source. These include URL, "goto," "gotolabel," and "window."

The following is a listing of valid columns in the pie chart's data source:

value: This number represents a pie piece's value. The size and area of each pie piece is determined by this value. Values will be rounded down to the nearest whole number.

color: Defines the color of the pie section for the current set of data.

URL: Defines a URL that the user will be redirected to when he or she clicks the pie piece for the current row. Cannot be used if "goto" or "gotolabel" is defined.

goto: Defines a frame number in the current Flash movie that the movie will go to when the user clicks the pie piece for the current row. Cannot be used if URL or "gotolabel" is defined.

gotoLabel: Defines a frame label in the current Flash movie that the movie will go to when the user clicks on the pie piece for the current row. Cannot be used if URL or "goto" is defined.

window: If the URL has a value, this defines the browser frame/window that the URL will be opened in when the user clicks the pie section. Valid values include the following:

- _top: Opens the URL in the current browser window and loads it in the top frame.
- _self: Opens the URL in the current browser window and loads it in the current frame. This is the default value.
- _blank: Opens the URL in a new browser window.

In addition to the above values, you can define your own column variables and values, which you can then use to format the pie chart's value presentation (See "Advanced Formatting" in the next section).

Now that we've looked at the data source, let's create one for our pie chart:

Create a data source with the same variables and values as the data source above. You can use any text editor (such as Windows Notepad), or you can use the data source from the CD-ROM. Name the file data_1.txt and place it in the same directory that you intend to save your pie chart.

Inserting the Pie Chart object

1. *Create a new Flash movie and name it pie_chart_1.fla. Make sure that File > Publish Settings > Generator Template (.swt) is set.*

2. *Open the Generator Object panel (Window > Generator Objects) and drag the Pie Chart object into your movie.*

3. *Now you need to tell the Pie Chart object where the data source we created is located: With the Pie Chart object selected, enter **data_1.txt** for the Data Source row in the Generator Properties tab.*

4. *Once you've entered the data source, preview the movie by selecting Control > Test Movie.*

You should see a pie chart with three pieces (blue, red, and yellow). The value for each section should appear within its pie piece.

PIE CHART WITH DEFAULT SETTINGS.

If you cannot see your pie chart, try the following:

- Make sure that the path to your data source is in the same directory as your pie chart's .fla.

- Make sure you set the pie chart movie to be published as a Generator template.

- Check your data source: Each item of data must be separated by a comma, and each row must end with a line return.

Now that we've created a basic pie chart, we can use its data source to make more advanced charts. By adding a few variables and values, we can make the pie sections clickable and capable of redirecting the user to another Web page.

5. *Create a new data source that looks like the data source below. (You can use the data source from the CD-ROM.)*

```
value, color, URL, window
5, blue, "http://www.macromedia.com", "_blank"
7, red, "http://www.flash.com", "_top"
6, yellow, "http://www.shockwave.com", "_self"
```

6. *Save your data source and name it data_2.txt.*

7. *Update the Data Source property in the Properties window to point to the new data source.*

8. *Preview the pie chart in your browser (F12).*

You can now click each pie section and be redirected to its associated URL in the data source. The "goto" and "gotolabel" variables work the same way, except that they redirect to different frames within the Flash movie. Note that the URL sometimes opens in a new window and sometimes opens in the current window. This is determined by the "window" variable that we added to the data source.

Pie Chart Properties tab

Now that we've created a data source and some basic pie charts, let's begin to look at how we can further customize our pie chart by adjusting the object's properties.

The Pie Chart object has the following properties:

Data Source: This specifies the path to the pie chart's data source. It can be a relative or absolute path to a file or URL, a database connection URL, a Java-class connection URL, or a Generator variable that will translate into a data source in the proper format.

Depth: This specifies the amount of depth to render the chart (that is, how three-dimensional the chart will appear). Each unit equals one-twentieth of a pixel.

Value Display: This specifies when chart values will be displayed on the chart. Valid values include Always, Never, and Rollover. If you specify Rollover, the value will be displayed when the user mouses over the chart element.

Value Format: This specifies the font used to display the value within the chart. Valid values include Arial, Times, and Courier.

Value Placement: This specifies where in the chart the value will be placed. Valid values include Inside (the value will be displayed within its pie section), Outside (the value will be displayed outside of its pie section), and Auto (the value's placement will be determined based on the size of the value and pie section).

Value Scale: This specifies the size of the value. The value can be scaled to fit the chart element (Scale to Fit) or displayed at the symbol size (Fixed). Half and Double display the symbol at half or double its original size, respectively. You can also enter a numerical scale factor to apply to the symbol. For example, if you were to enter **0.50**, the label would be scaled to one-half the symbol's size. A negative scale value will flip the value labels (so that they're upside-down and backwards).

External Symbol File: By specifying the path to an external symbol file, this property gives you greater control in formatting value labels because it links to an external Generator template (.swt) that provides formatting information. This property is described in more detail in the "Advanced Formatting" section below.

Border: This specifies whether or not to draw a border around the object bounding box of the chart. Valid values include True and False. The color of the border is determined by the color specified in the Color property.

Border Thickness: If the Border property is set to True, this setting specifies the thickness of the border in twips (one-twentieth of a pixel).

Color: This specifies the color of the chart's border. Valid values include Web-safe color names (blue), Web hexadecimal values (#000000), and regular hexadecimal values (0x000000).

Instance Name: This identifies the instance name of the object so that it can be targeted with ActionScript.

We're now ready to further customize our movie by adjusting the chart's property settings.

9. *Match the pie chart's Property settings to those in the following figure.*

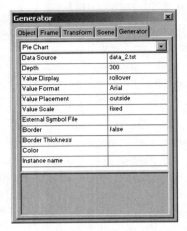

10. *Now test your movie (Control > Test Movie).*

By adjusting the chart's properties, we've created a more compelling and interactive three-dimensional pie chart.

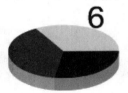

Play around with different settings and see how they affect the chart's appearance and functionality.

You'll probably notice that the properties don't give you much formatting control over the way each pie section's value is displayed (you can only specify one of three font types). To further customize our chart, we'll need to employ some more advanced techniques.

Advanced formatting

You can obtain more advanced formatting control by linking to an external Generator template (SWT file) through the External Symbol File property, which you'll find in the pie chart's Properties tab. This allows you to specify font type, size, and color of the values; it also allows you to dynamically insert text and other Generator objects to be associated with each pie section.

To do this, we need to create another Generator template that will act as a formatting template for our value display. The pie chart will get the formatting settings for its values from this template.

1. *Create a new Flash file and enable Generator Template (.swt) in the Publish Settings window.*

2. *Create a new movie-clip symbol and name it chartValue1 (the name must appear exactly like this). You may also name the movie clip chartLabel1, though there's no difference in how it functions.*

3. *Open the symbol you wish to edit and place a Generator variable called {value} near the center point.*

The font type, color, and size that you choose for the {value} variable will be used to display the value in your pie chart.

4. *Save your file in the directory that contains your pie chart and name it value_1.fla.*

5. *Once you've saved the .fla, publish the movie. This will create a file named value_1.swt, which we'll import into the pie chart movie.*

6. *Open your pie chart movie, and in the Generator Properties window find the External Symbol File setting. For its value, enter the name of the formatting template you just created (value_1.swt).*

7. *Preview your movie and move your mouse over the pie sections. Note that the values are now formatted just like the {value} variable in the value_1.swt file.*

You can use this technique for more than just formatting the value. You can also dynamically insert additional text, images, or other Generator objects into your value presentation. Let's add a label to each pie chart section.

8. *Open up the data source, add a column variable called "label," and save it as data_3.txt.*

Your data source should look something like the following data source. You may also use the data source on the CD-ROM.

```
Value, color, URL, window, label
5, blue, "http://www.macromedia.com", "_blank", "Macromedia"
7, red, "http://www.flash.com", "_top", "Flash.com"
6, yellow, "http://www.shockwave.com", "_self", "Shockwave.com"
```

9. *Open value_1.fla, then open the chartValue1 movie clip. Add a Generator variable called {label}.*

The font type, size, and color you choose to create the {label} variable will determine how the label is formatted on the pie chart.

10. *Save the file as value_2.fla, publish it, and then switch back to the pie chart movie.*

11. *Update your pie chart movie to point to the new data source (data_3.txt) and the new value template (value_2.swt).*

12. *Preview the movie and move your mouse over the pie sections. Your pie chart should now display both a value and a label for each section.*

3D PIE CHART WITH
CUSTOM VALUE/LABEL
FORMATTING.

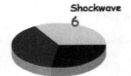

You can use this method to insert more than just text in your pie charts. You can employ it to place an Insert Symbol object into the value_1.swt file and then dynamically insert a symbol to be displayed with the value and label. Note, however, that the variables are not evaluated until they're in the pie chart movie. Thus, any dynamically loaded resources (such as a symbol) must be present or available in the pie chart movie, not the value_1.swt template.

3D PIE CHART WITH
ADVANCED VALUE
FORMATTING.

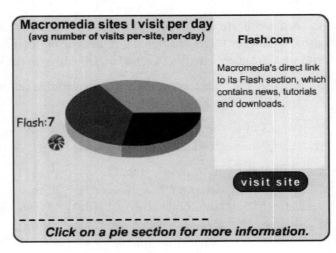

The preceding figure pulls together everything we've discussed here into one pie chart, using "gotolabel" in the data source and advanced formatting to dynamically insert a graphic symbol along with a label and value for each pie chart.

You can view the source for this movie on the CD-ROM in the Chapter 6 folder.

INSERTING SOUNDS

You can add sounds to Generator templates using the Insert Sound and Insert MP3 Generator objects.

The Insert Sound object dynamically inserts sounds that are contained in the Flash library (similar to how Insert Symbol works with graphic symbols).

The Insert MP3 object dynamically inserts external MP3 files into your Flash movies.

If you have the Enterprise edition of Generator and have enabled and configured the Generator caching feature using the instructions in Chapter 10, you can specify caching for MP3 files using the Cache property in the Generator panel. You cannot use caching with the Insert Sound object.

The Insert Sound object has the following properties in the Generator panel:

Sound Symbol: This specifies the name of the sound symbol in the Flash library that will be dynamically placed into the Flash movie by Generator. Use a fully qualified path name if the sound symbol is contained within a folder.

Loop Count: This specifies the number of times the sound will loop (play).

Instance Name: This identifies the instance name of the object so that it can be targeted with ActionScript.

The Insert MP3 object includes the following properties in the Generator panel:

File Name: This specifies the name of the MP3 file to be inserted into the Flash movie. The name can point to any source that returns the actual MP3 file, including a URL or file name.

Cache: This specifies whether or not a file is cached. Valid values include True and False. This property is overridden by the cache settings in the Administration Servlet and by any cache parameters specified in the URL for the template. Setting this property to True will activate caching for the object if it is served from a Web server that has caching enabled on the Enterprise edition of Generator. If the files are served from a Web server that does not have the Enterprise edition installed, this property is ignored.

Stream: This determines whether or not the Flash movie containing the MP3 file will stream when loading into the Flash player. Valid values include True and False.

If Stream is set to True, the movie's main timeline will be expanded to contain the entire MP3 file. The sound will begin to play as soon as it starts to load into the Flash player. However, because it automatically expands the main timeline, you should only set the object to stream if the Insert MP3 object is the only item in the movie. You can then use a LoadMovie ActionScript command from another movie to load the streaming Flash movie, and still have graphics displayed to the user.

If Stream is set to False, the MP3 will be placed in a movie clip within the movie. The MP3 will not begin to play until the entire movie clip containing the MP3 has loaded. As a rule, you should set the Stream property to False if you're inserting small files. If you don't, your users may experience long download times.

Delay: This specifies the time, in seconds, before the sound begins to play.

Add Stop Action: If the Stream property is set to True, this specifies whether or not a stop action will be placed at the end of the generated movie.

If the Stream property is set to True, a stop action will be placed at the end of the movie and the MP3 file will only play once.

If Stream is set to False, no stop action will be inserted, and the SWF and MP3 will continuously loop.

If your Insert MP3 object does not have this property then make sure that you have installed the latest Generator patch available from: http://www.macromedia.com/generator/

Instance Name: This identifies the instance name of the object so that it can be targeted with ActionScript. This is particularly useful if you're creating buttons to play and pause an MP3.

When using the Insert MP3 object, your movie's frame rate will be set to 12 frames per second regardless of the rate set in the Movie Properties box.

TABLE, LIST, AND TICKER OBJECTS

One of Generator's most powerful features is its ability to easily connect to data sources (such as databases) and display large amounts of data in useable formats. The Table, List and Ticker objects can all organize and display large amounts of data in a user-friendly format.

Table object

The Generator Table object allows you to insert HTML-like tables into your Flash movie.

The Table object has the following properties:

Data Source: This specifies the column data source from which the table will be built. It can be retrieved from any source from which Generator can retrieve data, including URLs, files, and databases. See "Table Object Data Source" below for more information on the data source.

Rows: This specifies the number of rows in the table.

Columns: This specifies the number of columns in the table. This setting, along with the Rows property, determines how the data-source rows are grouped.

Horizontal Alignment: This specifies how the content of each column will be aligned horizontally within the table cell. Valid values include Center, Left, and Right.

Vertical Alignment: This specifies how the content of each column will be aligned vertically within the table cell. Valid values include Center, Top, and Bottom.

Sizing: This specifies how the symbols within each cell will be scaled. Valid values include Auto (automatically scales content based on cell size), Fixed (does not scale content), and Half and Double (which scale the content by half and double the original size, respectively).

Default Symbol: If the data source doesn't specify a "clip" column, this determines the movie clip that will be used to build each cell.

Row Labels: This specifies a comma-delimited string of labels to be used as row labels. For example, if you had a table with four rows, and wanted to label each one, you could set the property to row1, row2, row3, row4.

Column Labels: This specifies a comma-delimited string of labels to be used as column labels. For example, if you wanted to label each column in a four-column table, you could set this property to col1, col2, col3, col4.

Label Format: This specifies the font to be used to display the values for the row and column labels. Valid values include Arial, Times, and Courier.

Label Sizing: This specifies the size of the label. The label can be scaled to fit the chart element (Scale to Fit) or displayed at the symbol size (Fixed). Half and Double display the symbol at half and double its original size, respectively. You can also enter a numerical scale factor to apply to the symbol. For example, if you entered **0.50,** the label would be scaled to one-half the symbol size.

Symbol File: This specifies a path to an external symbol file, giving you more control over how you format value labels by linking to an external Generator template (.swt) that provides formatting information. See the line chart and pie chart examples above for more information on this property.

Border: This specifies whether a border is drawn around each cell of the table. Valid values include True and False. Border color is determined by the color specified in the Border Color property.

Border Color: If the Border property is set to True, this specifies the border color for the table. Valid values include Web-safe color names (blue), Web hexadecimal values (#000000), and regular hexadecimal values (0x000000).

Border Thickness: If the Border property is set to True, this setting specifies the thickness of the border in twips (one-twentieth of a pixel).

Instance Name: This identifies the instance name of the object so that it can be targeted with ActionScript.

Table object data source

The Table object uses a Generator column data source, which has one required column, "clip." The "clip" column determines which symbol will be used to create the cell for the current row of information. This column can be omitted if the default Symbol property of the object is used to define the symbol used to build each cell.

You can also define your own column variables and values, which will be made available to use in the Table object as each cell is constructed. This allows you to dynamically insert text, images, and other media into each cell.

Generator uses the values in the Columns property of the object to determine how to group rows of data sources in table rows.

Take a look at the following data source, which contains eight rows of data:

```
Clip, var1, var2
GeoClip,0,0
LocateClip, "Reykjavik", "Iceland"
EventClip, "volcanic eruptions",0
DateClip, "7.02.99",0
WeatherClip,0,0
LocateClip, "Atlanta", "USA"
EventClip, "thunderstorms",0
DateClip, "6.28.99",0
```

If the Columns property is set to 2, the table will contain two columns with four rows of data. If the Columns property is set to 4, the table will contain four columns with two rows of data.

Creating lists and tickers

Generator provides several objects that make it easy to display sets of data in lists and tickers. The following sections covers lists, scrolling lists, tickers, and multipage lists.

Lists, scrolling lists, and tickers

The Scrolling List and Ticker objects are similar and have the same properties.

- The List object creates a nonscrolling list of items.

- The Scrolling List object creates a list of items that can be scrolled. To make the list scroll, you must specify an instance name for the list and provide buttons with ActionScript to control the scrolling.

- The Ticker object creates a list that scrolls in a continuous loop— useful for creating stock tickers.

Lists, scrolling lists, and tickers have the following properties in the Object panel:

Data Source: This specifies the data source for the object. The data source is a Generator column data source with one required column named "clip," which specifies the movie clip used to construct the current item in the object. See the "Scrolling List, List, and Ticker Data Source" section below for more information on the data source.

Orientation: This specifies whether the items inserted by the object are stacked next to each other (Horizontal) or on top of each other (Vertical).

Mask to Box: This specifies whether the list or ticker will be masked to fit the object's bounding box. Setting this property to True will add a mask to the list or ticker. Items outside the object's bounding box will not be visible. If the property is set to False, all items will be visible, regardless of their location on the stage.

Scale to Fit: This specifies whether the content of the list will be scaled to fit within the bounding box. Valid values include "True" and "False". This property only applies to the List Object.

This property can be used in conjunction with the Set Color Command in order to dynamically create legends for charts.

If your List Object does not have this property make sure that you have downloaded and installed the latest Generator patch from: http://www.macromedia.com/generator/

Step Size: This specifies the scrolling speed of the list or ticker and is measured in the number of pixels that the list or ticker should scroll in a single frame. The motion will appear smoothest to the human eye at 1 pixel per frame. This property applies to Scrolling List and Ticker objects only.

Spacing: This specifies how list or ticker items will be spaced. Valid values are Fixed and Auto. Fixed creates a list in which each item will take the amount of space specified in the Item Space option. Auto creates a list or ticker in which each item will use just as much space as it needs.

Item Space: If the Spacing property is set to Fixed, this specifies the number of pixels between each item in the list or ticker.

Horizontal Alignment: This specifies how each element will be aligned horizontally within the list or ticker.

Vertical Alignment: This specifies how each element will be aligned vertically within the list or ticker.

Instance Name: This identifies the instance name of the object so that it can be targeted with ActionScript.

Scrolling List, List, and Ticker data source

Here is a description of the data source for these objects:

clip: This defines the symbol that will be used to create the current element of the list or ticker. Any variables defined within the data source will also be available for use in the symbol defined in this field.

instanceName: This allows you to specify an instance name for the movie clip created for the current row of information. This is separate from the Instance Name property for the object, which gives an instance name for the movie clip that contains all of the individual movie clips of the list or ticker.

In addition to the above values, you can define your own column variables and values. These will be made available for use in the List/Ticker object as each item is generated.

The List/Ticker objects work by creating a movie clip that contains the list items. The movies clips specified in the "clip" column of the data source are then created, inserted in that movie clip, and positioned. Knowing how Generator creates the object comes in handy if you need to write ActionScript that acts on the movie clips created by the List/Ticker objects.

For instance, it's very simple to create buttons that control list scrolling:

1. *Create a new Flash movie (File > New).*

2. *Create a new movie-clip symbol and name it "clip."*

3. *Add two variables to your newly created movie clip and name them {stock} and {price}. You can use any color for the variables.*

4.   *Open the Generator Objects window and drag the Ticker object into your movie.*

5.   *Set the properties of this object to match those in the figure below:*

6.   *Make sure that the Data Source property is set to tickerData.txt and that the Instance Name property is set to "ticker."*

7.   *We now need to create the data source for the object. Create a new text file and name it tickerData.txt.*

8.   *Open the text file and enter the following data:*

```
clip, stock, price
clip, MACR, 56
clip, AMZN, 32
clip, LU, 15
clip, P, 22
```

This will create a ticker containing four items.

9.   *Save the text file and switch back to Flash.*

10. *Test your movie. You should see a simple ticker with the data from the data source.*

Adding buttons to control tickers

1.   *Using the above example, create two buttons, which will be used as Play and Pause buttons.*

2.   *Place each button on the stage.*

3. *To control the Ticker, we need to use the Instance Name property (set in the object's properties) to target the movie clip with ActionScript. Assuming the Instance Name property is set to "ticker," add the following code to the Pause button:*

```
on(release)
{
    ticker.stop();
}
```

4. *Add the following ActionScript to the Play button:*

```
on(release)
{
    ticker.play();
}
```

5. *Test the movie. You should be able to stop and start the ticker with the buttons we just created.*

This technique also works with the Scrolling List object. In addition, you can use ActionScript to reverse the Ticker and Scrolling List objects and make them go back to their beginnings. To do this, simply create a loop in ActionScript that continually tells the Ticker or Scrolling List object to keep going to the previous frame, as in the following:

```
ticker.prevFram();
```

Remember that the Ticker and List objects are just movie clips with their own timelines. By using ActionScript to target those timelines, you can do some pretty advanced and powerful things.

Multipage lists

The Multipage List object creates a series of pages to display large lists of data in smaller, more manageable chunks. Users are able to navigate through the data sets with navigation buttons that are automatically added to the object's output.

The Multipage List object has the following properties in the Generator panel:

Data Source: This specifies the path to the data source used to create your multipage list. See the data source section below for more information on data-source format.

Items per Page: This specifies the number of items that will be displayed on each page. It also determines the number of pages that will be created. For example, if you have 30 items and need to list 3 items per page, 10 pages will be created (30 divided by 3 equals 10).

Previous Symbol: This specifies the symbol used to create the Previous button to navigate pages. If this field is blank, a default button will be created and inserted.

Home Symbol: This specifies the symbol used to create the Home button that takes the user to the first page of the list when pressed. If this field is blank, a default button will be created and inserted

Next Symbol: This specifies the symbol used to create the Next button to navigate pages. If this field is blank, a default button will be created and inserted.

Text Symbol: This specifies the name of the symbol used to create each item of information. The symbol—which is similar to the "clip" column in List objects—should contain variables that match those defined in the data source.

Symbol Spacing: This specifies the amount of space between elements in the list. Units are specified in twips (one-twentieth of a pixel).

Line Spacing: This specifies space between list items (not lines of text). Each unit represents one-twentieth of a pixel. Valid values include all integers; the default setting is 50.

External Symbol File: This specifies the path to an external Generator template (SWT) file that contains resources to be used in the object. When processing the template, Generator first searches the external symbol file (if specified) for any symbols referenced in the data source. If the symbols are not found, Generator uses the symbols specified in the current SWT file or the default symbols for those parameters.

Instance Name: This identifies the instance name of the object so that it can be targeted with ActionScript.

When the object is created, the following ActionScript variables are placed within the Multipage List object. These can be accessed in conjunction with the Instance Name property to target the variables.

- numPages: the number of pages in the list.
- numItems: the number of items in the list.
- currentPage: the (1 based) page number currently displayed.

Multipage List object data source

The data source for the Multipage List object is a Generator column data source with each row representing one item of the list. The data source can have the following columns:

Text: This required column has no clear purpose. In most cases, you'll just add it to the data source and leave its value blank.

instanceName: This column allows you to specify an instance name for the movie clip created for the current row of information. This is separate from the object's Instance Name property, which assigns an instance name to the movie clip containing all of the list's individual movie clips.

In addition to the above values, you may also define your own column variables and values. These will be made available for use in the Multipage List object as each item is generated.

Creating a Multipage List object

To create a simple Multipage List object:

1. *Open Flash and create a new file.*

2. *Open the Generator Objects window and drag the Multipage List object into the movie.*

3. *Set the properties to match those in the following figure:*

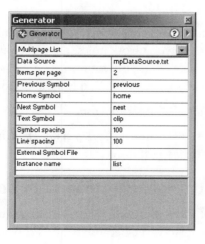

4. *Make sure the Data Source property points to mpDataSource.txt.*

5. *Create three new graphic symbols called Next, Previous, and Home. These will be used to create the Next, Previous, and Home buttons for the list.*

6. *Open the symbols you just created and add some graphics. Although it's not important what you add, the button's function should be obvious.*

7. *Create another graphic symbol and call it Clip. Enter four Generator variables named {team1}, {team2}, {score1}, and {score2}. The layout should appear similar to the following figure:*

```
{team1}                        {score1}
{team2}                        {score2}
```

8. *Now we need to create the data source for the list: Create a new text file, name it mpDataSource.txt, and open it with a text editor.*

9. *Enter the following data:*

```
team1, team2, score1, score2, text
Seattle, Washington, 102, 94
Los Angeles, Cleveland, 98, 97
New York, Miami, 77, 81
Atlanta, Portland, 94, 85
Houston, Chicago, 97, 79
Boston, Sacramento, 92, 108
```

Note that we included a "text" column that doesn't include any values. This is because the object won't work unless a "text" column is included. You do not, however, need to use the column. As long as you make sure to create it, you don't need to worry about adding values for it.

10. *Save the file and switch back to Flash.*

11. *Test the movie. You should now have a simple multipage list that you can navigate with the buttons you created.*

Positioning buttons in Multipage List objects

The Multipage List object is useful for displaying large amounts of data in a user-friendly manner. However, because the object does not allow you to position the navigation buttons, your design and interface options are severely limited.

To address this problem, in this section we describe how to position the navigation buttons anywhere you want and to make those buttons smarter by adding ActionScript code that tells them their position in the list.

The Multipage List object works like the other List and Ticker objects, essentially creating a bunch of movie clips and keyframes, each with different content. To move among items, you simply move around the List object's timeline.

This example makes use of the Multipage List object we created earlier. If you did not build that example, you can view the .fla's source in the Chapter 6 folder on the accompanying CD-ROM.

1. *Open the Multipage List object we created earlier.*

2. *Make sure to give the Multipage List object an instance name: In the object's Properties window, enter* list *in the Instance Name column.*

3. *To get rid of the buttons automatically inserted by the object, open the symbol library and edit the Next graphic symbol. Delete all of the graphics in the symbol, but do not delete the symbol itself. Do the same thing for the Previous and Home buttons.*

If you do this, Generator will no longer automatically insert buttons into the list (actually, it will, but the symbols will be empty).

Now all we have to do is to create our own buttons and add some ActionScript to make them work.

4. *Create three buttons (nextButton, previousButton, homeButton) and place them on the main timeline (or in the same movie clip as the Multipage List object).*

5. *Add the following code to each button:*

```
Next :
on(release)
{
    if(list._currentFrame == list._totalFrames - 1)
    {
        list.gotoAndStop(1);
    }
    else
    {
        list.nextFrame();
```

```
    }
}

Prev :
on(release)
{
    if(list._currentFrame == 1)
    {
        list.gotoAndStop(list._totalFrames);
    }
    else
    {
        list.prevFrame();
    }
}

Home :
on(release)
{
        list.gotoAndStop(1);
}
```

6. Test your movie (Control > Test Movie).

You can now navigate your list with custom-positioned buttons.

Basically, the code in the Next button checks to see if it is on the last frame of the List object. If it is, it goes to the first frame; if it's not, it goes to the next frame. The Previous button does the same but in reverse.

Now not only can you position your buttons, but they wrap when you get to the end or beginning of the list.

Targeting a List/Ticker item with ActionScript.

When Generator creates the List and Ticker objects, it's really just creating nested movie clips and applying tweens or ActionScript to those symbols.

Using the Instance Name property in conjunction with the instanceName field in the data sources for the objects, you can target individual items of the lists and tickers, and control them with ActionScript.

For example, if the Instance Name property for a List object were list, and the values for the instanceName column in the data source were named `item_1`, `item_2`, and so on, you could target each item with the following code:

```
list.item_1
```

If, for example, you wanted to make the first item invisible, you would write the following:

```
list.item_1.alpha = 0;
```

This is a simple example; however, you can use this technique to do some very advanced things.

USING THE RADIO BUTTON OBJECT

The Radio Button object allows you to dynamically create and place HTML-like radio buttons in your Flash movie. In addition, Flash variables placed in the movie can indicate the currently selected button. By using this in conjunction with ActionScript, you can access and use the radio buttons' data.

The Radio Button object has the following properties in the Generator panel:

Data Source: This specifies the data source that will be used to create the radio buttons. The column-formatted data source has one required column: "text." See the "Radio Button Data Source" section below for more information on the data source.

On Symbol: This specifies which symbol will be used to create the on/selected state of the radio button. If no symbol is specified, Generator will use a default graphic for the button's on/selected state.

Off Symbol: This specifies which symbol will be used to create the off/unselected state of the radio button. If no symbol is specified, Generator will use a default graphic for the button's off/unselected state.

Text Symbol: This specifies the symbol used to create and format the text for each radio button. The symbol must contain a Generator variable named {text}, which will be used to create the label for the button. This is a required property.

Line spacing: This specifies the space between each radio button, measured in twips (one-twentieth of a pixel).

Selected by Default: This specifies the radio button that will be the default-selected button. The property takes a number that represents the index of the row of the data source whose button will be selected as the default. For example, if you wanted the button created from the second row of the data source to be the default button, you would set the field as 2. If the field is left empty or contains an invalid value, the first button will be set as the default.

Selected Button Variable: This specifies the name of the Flash variable used to store the currently selected button. This variable can be used in conjunction with the Instance Name field below to target the variable.

Instance Name: This identifies the instance name of the object so that it can be targeted with ActionScript.

Radio Button object data source

The data source for the Radio Button object is a column data source with the following required field.

Text: This specifies the text/label for the current button being inserted. The value of this field will be inserted into the symbol specified in the Text Symbol property to create the label for the Radio Button represented by the row. This is a required value.

You can also define your own column variables and values. These will be made available for use in the symbol specified in the Text Symbol property for the object when it's inserted into the movie.

Using the Selected Button variable property

All you need to do to figure out which button is currently selected is write some simple ActionScript: Simply target the variable using the instance name and variable name specified in the Radio Button object's properties. For example, if the Selected Button variable were set to the default of radioVar, and the Instance Name property were set to the default of radioButton, you could find out the index of the selected button by using the following ActionScript:

```
var selectedIndex = radioButton.radioVar;
```

This code will give you the position index of the currently selected button and store it in the selectedIndex variable.

Although this is fairly simple, it can be tedious to try to keep track of which button equals which index. The following technique demonstrates how you can pass a string value through the button instead of a number.

1. **Add the following code to the symbol specified in the object's Text Symbol property:**

```
name = "button{index}";
value = "{text}";
```

This code accomplishes two things: The first line gives the movie clip an instance name so that we can reliably target it with ActionScript code, and the second line sets an ActionScript variable that stores the value of the radio button. The value is set by Generator and passed in through the {text} variable of the data source.

2. **Next, add a column named "index" to the data source. For each row of the data source, add the index of the current row for the index value. For example:**

```
text, index
Rockfish, 1
Tuna, 2
Shark, 3
Sturgeon, 4
```

3. **To get the value of the selected button, use the following ActionScript:**

```
selected = radioButton.radioVar;
selectedValue = radioButton["button" + selected]["value"];
```

This stores the value of the currently selected button in the selectedValue variable.

You can now use the variable just as you would any other Flash variable.

THE PLOT OBJECT

The Plot object allows you to dynamically place and position symbols within your Flash movie. It's similar to the duplicateMovieClip and attachMovieClip ActionScript commands, except, of course, that the Plot object is processed on the server side.

The Plot object has the following properties in the Generator panel:

Data Source: This specifies the path to the column data source that will be used by the object. See the "Plot Data Source" section below for more information on the data source.

Min X-Pos: This specifies the minimum X coordinate position of any of the symbols inserted with the Plot object.

Max X-Pos: This specifies the maximum X coordinate position of any of the symbols inserted with the Plot object.

Min Y-Pos: This specifies the minimum Y coordinate position of any of the symbols inserted with the Plot object.

Max Y-Pos: This specifies the maximum Y coordinate position of any of the symbols inserted with the Plot object.

X Column: This specifies the column name in the data source whose value will determine the X position of the symbol being inserted. The default value is X.

Y Column: This specifies the column name in the data source whose value will determine the Y position of the symbol being inserted. The default value is Y.

X-Scale Column: This specifies the column name in the data source whose value will determine the X scale of the symbol being inserted. The default value is X-Scale.

Y-Scale Column: This specifies the column name in the data source whose value will determine the Y scale of the symbol being inserted. The default value is Y-Scale.

Rotate Column: This specifies the column name in the data source whose value will determine the Rotation of the symbol being inserted. The default value is Rotate.

Symbol Name Column: This specifies the column name in the data source whose value specifies the symbol name for the symbol to be inserted by the object. The default value is Symbol Name.

Instance Column: This specifies the column name in the data source whose value will specify the instance name for the symbol being inserted. The default value is instanceName.

Border: This determines whether a border will be drawn around the bounding box of the Plot object. Valid values include True and False. The border's color is determined by the color specified in the Border Color property.

Border Color: If the Border property is set to True, this specifies the color of the border. The default color is black. Valid values include Web-safe color names (blue), Web hexadecimal values (#000000), and regular hexadecimal values (0x000000).

Border Thickness: If the Border property is set to True, this setting specifies the thickness of the border in twips (one-twentieth of a pixel).

Instance Name: This identifies the instance name of the object so that it can be targeted with ActionScript. All of the symbols inserted by the Plot object will be placed within one larger movie clip whose instance name will be specified by this property.

The data source for the Plot object is a Generator column data source. Each row of the data source represents a symbol that will be placed in the Flash movie. This allows you to insert and position multiple symbols into a Flash movie with a single Plot object.

Plot data source

The Plot object's data source has the following column headings:

Symbol Name: This specifies the name of the symbol to be inserted in the Flash movie. You can change the name of this column by using the object's Symbol Name Column in the object's property.

X: This specifies the X coordinate where the symbol will be inserted, relative to the Plot object's position on the stage. For instance, if the Plot object were at X coordinate 20 on the stage and this value was 20, the symbol would be placed at X coordinate 40 (20 + 20 = 40). You can change the column name by using the X Column in the object's properties.

Y: This specifies the Y coordinate where the symbol will be inserted. The coordinate is relative to the Plot object's position on the stage. For instance, if the Plot object were at Y coordinate 20 on the stage and this value was 20, the symbol would be placed at Y coordinate 40 (20 + 20 = 40). You can change the column name by using the Y Column in the object's properties.

X-Scale: This specifies the X scale of the symbol being inserted. You can change the column name by using the X Scale Column in the object's properties.

Y-Scale: This specifies the Y scale of the symbol being inserted. You can change the column name by using the Y Scale Column in the object's properties.

Rotate: This specifies the rotation of the symbol being inserted. You can change the column name by using the Rotate Column in the object's properties.

instanceName: This specifies the instance name for the symbol being inserted. You can change the column name by using the Instance Column in the object's properties.

You can also define your own column variables and values. These will be made available for use in the symbols being inserted into the movie by the Plot object.

When authoring movies to publish as Flash 2 that use the Plot command, make sure that the main timeline and any clips being plotted have the same number of frames.

Positioning symbols relative to the timeline

When symbols are inserted into a Flash movie by the Plot object, their X, Y coordinates are relative to the position of the Plot object, not to the movie's timeline in which the symbol is being inserted.

To specify the symbols' X, Y coordinates relative to the timeline, you simply place the Plot object at coordinates 0,0. This will position any object-inserted symbols relative to both the Plot object and the timeline.

Using database data with objects that have required column names

All of the List and Ticker objects, along with a few other objects such as the Radio Button object, have required column names in their data source. This can make it difficult to retrieve data directly from databases since your table column names may be different from those required by the object you're using.

One solution would be to change your table's column names to match those required by Generator—not a good option because it ties your data too closely to Generator.

Another option would be to have Generator retrieve the data from middleware, which would in turn connect to the database and return a data source with the correct column names. (See chapter 8 for more information on using Generator with middleware.) However, this is overkill if all you're doing is changing column names.

A third—and better—option would be to us the SQL statement AS in your SQL query to specify the column names in the result set returned to Generator.

For example, let's say you have a table called Weather with the following columns:

```
graphic, forecast, high, low
```

In you wanted to convert the "graphic" column to "clip," your SQL statement would look something like the following:

```
SELECT graphic AS clip, forecast, high, low FROM Weather
```

This would return a result set with the following columns:

```
clip, forecast, high, low
```

You can use the AS modifier more than once per statement, and you can employ it on just about anything that returns a value, such as the following:

```
SELECT count(*) AS numDays FROM Weather.
```

CUSTOM OBJECTS

Generator has its own SDK that anyone can use to create his or her own custom Generator objects. In addition, a number of useful objects have been created and released on the Macromedia Flash Exchange. (See Chapter 14 for more on the SDK.)

This following examines some of the more useful objects and explains how to use them.

All of the objects discussed in this chapter can be downloaded from the Macromedia Flash Exchange at the following URL:
http://www.macromedia.com/exchange/flash

Select Box object

The Select Box object creates HTML-like Select boxes and is similar in function to the Flash 5 Menu SmartClip—except, of course, that Generator creates the boxes on the server side (as opposed to the client side like Flash 5).

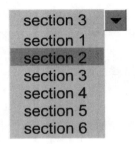

The Select Box object has the following properties in the Generator Properties panel:

Data Source: This is the Generator Column data source that will be used by the object to create the Select box. It can be derived from any valid data source that Generator can connect to, including files, URLs, or database connections. See the "Select Box Data Source" section below for more information on the data source.

Section: Up: This is the name of the symbol in the Flash library that will be used to create the default section of each section piece. It must contain a Generator variable named {title} that will be used to display the value of the section.

Section: Over: This is the name of the symbol in the Flash library that will be used to create the hover/mouse-over portion of each section piece. This will be viewed when the user moves the mouse over the section piece. It must contain a Generator variable named {title} that will be used to display the value of the section.

Button: up: This is the name of a symbol in the Flash library that will be used to create the default view of the button that opens and closes the Select box.

Button: down: This is the name of a symbol in the Flash library that will be used to create the mouse-down view of the button that opens and closes the Select box. The name will be displayed when the user presses the button.

Instance Name: This specifies the instance name of the Select box and can be used in conjunction with the Selected Variable property to determine which section of the Select box has been selected. The default value is selectBox.

Menu Direction: This specifies the direction that the Select box will open. Valid values are Up or Down, with Down the default value.

Button Placement: This specifies whether the button that opens and closes the select box will be on the right or left of the section pieces. Valid values are Right and Left, with Right the default value.

Select Piece Y Offset: This setting specifies, in pixels, the amount that a lower section piece will overlap the section piece above it. This can be used to create borders around your entire Select box.

Selected Variable: This specifies the name of the Flash variable in which the current Select box's selection is stored. The variable is placed within the same movie clip as the Select box, which means it can be accessed by using the Instance Name property. The default value is Selected.

Select box data source

The Select Box object's data source contains the following fields:

title: This determines the text that will be displayed for each section piece and is analogous to the text between the <option></option> tags in an HTML Select box.

value: This determines the value of the section piece. This value will be stored in the Selected variable when the section is selected. If no value is specified for a section in the data source, the title will be used as the value. This is analogous to the Value attribute of the option tag of an HTML Select box.

selected: This specifies whether or not the current section is the default section selected. Valid values include True and False. If more than one section in the data source has True in the selected column, the last section with a value of True will be set as the default section.

Building a Select box

1. *Download and install the Select Box object from the Macromedia Flash Exchange. Make sure to restart Flash after you've installed the object.*

2. *Create a new Flash movie.*

3. *Create two graphic symbols in the Flash library and give them the following names: sectionUp and buttonDown.*

4. *Open the sectionUp symbol and create a graphic for the Up state for the section. Draw a white box with a black border. Inside the box (on a separate layer) add a Generator variable called {title} (make sure the color is not white). Make sure the graphics are set at x, y coordinate 0, 0 measuring from the top left corner.*

5. *Duplicate the sectionUp symbol and name the new copy sectionOver. Open the new symbol and change the background color to light gray.*

6. *Open the buttonUp symbol and draw a dark gray box with a black border. Make sure the graphics are set at x, y coordinate 0, 0 measuring from the top left corner.*

7. *Duplicate the buttonUp symbol and name the new copy buttonDown. Open the symbol to edit and change the background color to light gray.*

8. *Open the Generator Objects panel (Window > Generator Objects) and drag the Select Box object onto the stage.*

9. *Set the Objects settings so that the Properties window looks like the following figure:*

10. *On the main timeline, create a new layer and place a dynamic text field. For the text field's variable property, enter **selectBox.selected**.*

We'll use this field to display the value of the currently selected section.

11. **With a text editor, create a file called selectDataSource.txt and save it in the same directory as your .fla.**

12. **Open the text file and enter the following information:**

```
title, value, selected
1, "section 1",
2, "section 2", true
3,
```

13. **Save the text file and test your movie. You should see a fully functioning Select box.**

If you receive any error messages or don't see the text box, make sure you've installed the Select Box object, and check each step for errors. Remember: You must always restart Flash after you've installed a custom object.

You can now use your Select box. Note that when you select a section, its value is displayed in the dynamic text field.

Also notice that each section contains its own border. You can make all sections share one border by adjusting the "Select Piece Y Offset" variable. Set the property to 1 (the exact setting will depend on the width of the border in the section pieces). Retest your movie and notice that your sections now share a border.

Tree/Hierarchical Menu object

The Tree Menu object—which creates advanced hierarchical menus—is useful for creating Flash-based navigation menus.

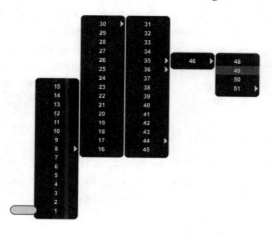

Here are the properties for that object:

Data Source: This specifies the path to the object's data source. The data source is a column data source and can be retrieved from any source from which Generator can retrieve data, including URLs, files, and databases. See the "Tree/Hierarchical Menu Data Source" section below for more information on the data source.

Header Symbol: This specifies the symbol in the symbol library that will be used for the header for each section of the menu. This field is not required; if left blank, no header will be added.

Footer Symbol: This specifies the symbol in the symbol library that will be used for the footer for each section of the menu. This field is not required; if left blank, no footer will be added.

Instance Name: This specifies the instance name for the generated menu and is used to open and close the menu as well as to detect the menu's state.

Section Padding: This determines the menu's sensitivity, specifying the amount of padding (in pixels) that will be added around each section. The menu will not close until the mouse moves off of this padding.

Left Padding: This determines the amount of padding on the far left side of the menu. This determines how far to the left of the menu the user will be able to close the menu.

Right Padding: This determines the amount of padding on the far right side of the menu. This determines how far to the right of the menu the user will be able to close the menu.

Close: This specifies how much of the menu will close when the user moves off one of its sections. Valid values include All and First Level. If this property is set to All, the entire menu will close when the user moves the mouse off of it. If it's set to First Level, all but the first level of the menu will close when the user moves the mouse outside of the menu. The default value is All.

Tree/Hierarchical Menu data source

The data source for the Tree Menu object is one of the more complex Generator object data sources. In this column data source, each row represents a menu piece, and the columns are as follows:

upClip: This is the symbol used to build the up/default stage of the menu piece. The symbol must contain a variable named {title} that will be used to display the title of the menu section. This column is required.

overClip: This is the symbol used to build the mouse-over stage of the menu piece (activated when the user moves his or her mouse over the menu piece). The symbol must contain a variable named {title} that will be used to display the title of the menu section. This column is required.

num: This is a unique index for each pie section. This number must be unique among each row, and it must not skip any numbers. Thus, Row 1 should be 1, Row 2 should be 2, and so on. If a number is skipped, only the rows below the skipped number will be built.

parent: This number determines the parent menu piece of the current row. Menu pieces with the same parent make up menu sections. Menu pieces on the first/main section of the menu have a parent of zero (0).

direction: This determines whether the section for the current menu piece will open up or down. All sections with a common parent should have the same "direction" setting. Valid values are Up and Down.

title: This determines the text that will be displayed in the menu piece.

URL: Defines the URL that the user will be redirected to when he or she clicks the menu section for the current row. Cannot be used if "goto" or "gotolabel" is defined.

goto: Defines a frame number in the current Flash movie that the movie will go to when the user clicks the menu section for the current row. Cannot be used if URL or "gotolabel" is defined.

gotoLabel: Defines a frame label in the current Flash movie that the movie will go to when the user clicks the menu section for the current row. Cannot be used if URL or "goto" is defined.

window: If URL has a value, this defines the browser frame/window that the URL will be opened in when the user clicks the pie section. Valid values include the following:

- _top: Opens the URL in the current browser window and loads the URL in the top frame.
- _self: Opens the URL in the current browser window and loads the URL in the current frame. This is the default value.
- _blank: Opens the URL in a new browser window.

If the "url," "goto," and "gotolabel" columns are all specified, they will be processed in the following order: "url," "goto," "gotoLabel." As soon as one of the columns is found, its action is added to the button, and the next menu piece is processed.

To open and close the menu, create a button with the following ActionScript:

```
on (rollOver)
{
    menu.gotoAndStop(2);
}
```

This assumes the Instance Name property of the menu was set to Menu.

You should make sure that the button that activates the menu overlaps the Tree Menu object. This will ensure that when the user moves the mouse off the button, the menu won't close.

Lets make a simple tree menu using the object:

1. *Download and install the Select Box object from the Macromedia Flash Exchange. Make sure to restart Flash after you've installed the object.*

2. *Create a new Flash movie.*

3. *Create two movie clips named Up and Over.*

4. *Open the Up symbol and draw a dark-blue box with a yellow border. Also add a Generator variable called {title}. Make sure that the movie clip's contents are at coordinates 0,0 when measuring from the top left corner of the graphics.*

5. *Open the Over symbol, then repeat Step 4 but make the background color of the box light blue.*

6. *With a text editor, create a file called treeData.txt and save it in the same directory as your.fla.*

7. *Open the text file and enter the following information:*

```
upClip, overClip, num, parent, direction, title
up, over,  1, 0, up, 1
up, over,  2, 0, up, 2
up, over,  3, 0, up, 3
up, over,  4, 0, up, 4
up, over,  5, 1, up, 5
```

```
up, over,   6, 1, up, 6
up, over,   7, 1, up, 7
up, over,   8, 1, up, 8
up, over,   9, 1, up, 9
up, over,   10, 3, up, 10
up, over,   11, 3, up, 11
up, over,   12, 3, up, 12
up, over,   13, 3, up, 13
up, over,   14, 10, up, 14
up, over,   15, 10, up, 15
up, over,   16, 10, up, 16
up, over,   17, 12, down, 17
up, over,   18, 12, down, 18
up, over,   19, 12, down, 19
up, over,   20, 12, down, 20
up, over,   21, 12, down, 21
```

8.   *Drag the Tree Menu object onto the first frame of the movie and place it in the bottom left of the stage.*

9.   *For the data source, enter* **treeData.txt**. *Make sure that Header Symbol, Footer Symbol are blank and Close is set to "All".*

10.   *Set the Instance Name property to "menu."*

11.   *Create a new layer above the current frame.*

12.   *Place a button in the new layer and add the following code:*

```
on (rollOver)
{
    menu.gotoAndStop(2);
}
```

13.   *Make sure that the button is placed over the placeholder for the Tree Menu object.*

14.   *Test the movie.*

You should just see the button. Move your mouse over the button, and the menu should open. You can now navigate the button. Note that clicking the pieces won't cause anything to happen because we didn't specify a URL, "goto," or "gotoLabel" in the data source.

The menu we just created will work in a Flash 3 or higher movie (though you'll have to change the code in the button that opens the movie to use Tell Target). If you place the menu in a Flash 4 or higher movie, a variable is placed in the Tree Menu movie clip that specifies whether the main menu section is open or closed. If the Instance Name property of the object is set to Menu, you can access the variable with the following code:

```
menu.menuState
```

If you choose Debug > List Variables when testing your movie, your output will resemble the following:

```
Variable __level0.menu.menuState = "closed"
```

Of course, if the menu is open, the variable will equal "open."

Although our menu works well, it can be difficult to tell which menu pieces open new sections. You can get around this problem by creating additional Up and Over clips, using arrows (or some other symbol) to indicate that the piece opens a new section. Then, in the data source, you would simply add the new symbols to the upClip and overClip section for the pieces that open new sections.

Insert Date/Time

These two simple but useful objects make the server's date and/or time available for use in your Generator template. They do this by placing the date and/or time in a Generator variable. You can then use the variable anywhere in your movie that you would use other Generator variables.

Here are the properties for the Insert Date/Time objects:

Date/Time Format: This property determines the format in which the date/time will be displayed. Valid values are Short, Medium, Long, Full, and Raw. The exact output for each format will depend on your operating system and locality. The Raw format outputs the time in milliseconds (from midnight GMT, January 1, 1970).

Variable Name: This specifies the name of the Generator variables where the object's date/time will be stored.

It's good practice to place the object in a frame before its variable is used because Generator doesn't always process the template in the same order (that is, it doesn't always process the object before the variable that uses output from that object).

If you use more than one Date and/or Time object in your movie, make sure to give each one a separate Variable Name property. If you don't, the value of one object may overwrite the value of the other object.

Using the object is very simple:

1. *Download and install the Insert Date/Time objects from the Macromedia Flash Exchange. Make sure to restart Flash after you've installed the object.*

2. *Create a new Flash movie.*

3. *Create two keyframes on the main timeline.*

4. *In the first frame, place the Insert Date or Insert Time object into the movie.*

5. *Add a Stop action to the second frame.*

6. *Add a Generator variable to the second frame. The variable name should be the same as the Variable Name property for the object. If you didn't change the setting, this should be either serverDate or serverTime.*

7. *Test the movie.*

You should now see the date or time displayed in your Flash movie. This is a handy way to let your users know the last time Generator created the Flash movie. It's also helpful for maintaining version control when developing your projects.

The following code demonstrates how to use the Insert Date/Time object to construct a Flash 5 ActionScript Date object. The code determines whether it's day or night where the server is located.

```
myDate = new Date("{serverTime}");
var serverHour = myDate.getHours();

if(serverHour < 6 || serverHour < 19)
{
    trace("it is day at the server");
}
else
{
    trace("it is night at the server");
}
```

The output format for the Time object is set to Raw, and the variable name is set to serverTime.

Insert Text

It may seem odd that there's a custom Generator object that dynamically inserts text into a Flash movie. After all, can't you already do this with Generator? Well, yes and no. Although you can dynamically insert text into Flash movies using Generator, it's difficult to dynamically set that text's properties (for example, font type, size, and color). The Insert Text object allows you to do this, as well as dynamically set a number of other properties.

Here are the properties for the Insert Text object:

Text: This is the text that will be inserted into the Flash movie.

Color: This specifies the color of the text. This can be any Web-safe color name (blue), Web hexadecimal value (#000000), or regular hexadecimal value (0x000000).

Size: This specifies the font size of the text

Type: This specifies the font used to display the inserted text.

Font File: This is the path to the Generator external font file that displays the font. Note that at the time this book was written, you had to use an external font file when employing the object on Mac, Linux, and Solaris systems.

Bold: This specifies whether or not the inserted text will be displayed in bold. Valid value are True and False.

Italic: This specifies whether or not the inserted text will be displayed in italic. Valid value are True and False.

Alignment: This specifies the alignment of the inserted text. Valid values are Left, Right, Center, and Justified.

Letter Spacing: This specifies the space between letters, measured in half-pixels.

Line Spacing: This specifies the space between lines of text, measured in points.

Transparency: This specifies the alpha/transparency level of the inserted text. Valid values include any number between 1 and 100. The default value is 100.

Using the object is simple:

1. *Download and install the Insert Text object from the Macromedia Flash Exchange. Make sure to restart Flash after you've installed the object.*

2. *Create a new Flash movie.*

3. *Place the Insert Text object into your movie.*

4. *Resize the object on the stage to match the width of the text field in which the text will be inserted. This will determine the point at which the text begins to wrap to the next line.*

5. *Enter some text into the Text property of the object.*

6. *Test the movie. You should see the text you specified inserted in the movie.*

7. *Try out different settings for the object and retest the movie.*

Remember: You can place Generator variables for the values of Generator objects and then dynamically pass in the value of those variables when the template is processed.

For more information on the Insert Text object, see Chapter 14, which shows how to build the Insert Text custom object.

XML Column Data Source object

The XML Column Data Source object (XML object) allows you to use certain forms of XML as a Generator data source. This is especially useful when you consider the amount of free and commercial XML content available on the Internet. Good sources for XML content include the RTF data format as well as the following Web sites:

- Slashdot.org

- moreover.com (more than 300 free XML news feeds)

- Wired.com

- ScreamingMedia.com

This object works much like the Insert Date/Time object. It simply takes some XML and creates a Generator column data source, and then stores it in a Generator variable. You can then use that variable anywhere in your Generator movie, including as the data source for other Generator objects.

The XML must contain tags in the following format, and it must be contained in a valid XML document:

```
<tag>
    <item_1>Data_A</item_1>
    <item_2>Data_B</item_2>
    <item_3>Data_C</item_3>
</tag>
<tag>
    <item_1>Data_D</item_1>
    <item_2></item_2>
    <item_3>Data_E</item_3>
</tag>
<tag>
    <item_1>Data_F</item_1>
    <item_2>Data_G</item_2>
    <item_3>Data_H</item_3>
</tag>
```

Assuming you set the Element Name property to "tag" (see the "Properties" section below), the object would parse the XML and make the following data source available to other Generator objects:

```
Item_1, item_2, item_3
Data_A, Data_B, Data_C
Data_D,, DatavE
Data_F, Data_G, Data_H
```

The second tag above, item_2, contains no data. This is to ensure that the object holds the item's space in the data source so that the data is mapped correctly to each column heading.

Here are the properties for the object:

XML Path: This specifies the path to the XML that the object will convert into a Generator column data source. This can contain a path to a file or URL. It can also contain a Generator variable that includes the XML; however, the variable must be preceded by a pound sign (#). The object cannot retrieve data from "fgjdbc," and "fgftp" data sources.

Variable Name: This is the name of the variable that contains the column data source created by the object.

Element Name: This is the element/tag name of the tag that contains the data to be used by the object. The tags contained within the Element Name tag will be converted into column headers in the new data source, and the tag's values will be used as the values for the data source. In the example above, the Element Name property is set to "tag."

Max Number of Items: This specifies the maximum number of data row that the object-created data source can contain.

Clip Name: This setting allows you to specify that an additional clip name be added to the data source. The value for the column is specified in the Clip Value property. This is useful if you're using the object with objects that require a "clip" column.

Clip Value: This is the value that will be placed on each row for the column added in the Clip Name property.

Image Tag: The name of the tag that specifies an image's name. It will be used with the Image Path property to create a path to the image.

Image Path: This is the base path to the images specifies in the Image Tag property. This will be used to create a path to the image.

To see how the object works, view the Slashdot file on the CD-ROM. Here, we use the XML object to get data from Slashdot.org and create a Flash movie that displays news headlines.

Note, that the XML object exists in a frame before the variable that uses it: The XML Object is in Frame 1, and the Replicate command that uses the data from the XML object is in Frame 2. This ensures that the objects are processed in the correct order.

If you're using more than one XML object in your movie, make sure to give each one a separate Variable Name property. If you don't, the value of one object may overwrite the value of the other object.

Advanced Data Source object

This useful object allows you to use any comma-separated value (CSV) formatted file as a Generator data source. It also adds the following functionality:

- The ability to sort the data source

- The ability to filter the data source

- The ability to limit the number of rows in the data source

- The ability to add an additional column and value to the data source

- The ability to add an "index" column that specifies the current row's index to the data source

- The ability to add or replace the column headers (useful if your CSV file contains only data and no headers)

As you can see, this object adds to Generator the type of logic that previously required middleware.

This object functions in much the same way as the XML object and the Insert Date/Time objects. A CSV file or Generator data source is specified, and the object creates a new Generator column data source and stores it in a Generator variable. You can then use the variable anywhere in the template that you would use any other Generator variable, including as the data source for other objects.

Here are the properties for this object:

Data Source: This specifies the path to the object's data source for the object. The data can come from any comma-separated file (including Generator templates) and be retrieved from any source that Generator's able to retrieve data from, including URLs, files, and databases.

Variable Name: The name of the variable that contains the column data source created by the object.

Set Headings: This allows you to rename column headings. It takes a comma-separated list of column names and, if defined, will add or replace the column headings with the data source passed in. For instance, if this field were to contain col1, col2, col3, col4, the data-source header fields in the new data source would be col1, col2, col3, and col4. You would then access each row's value with these new header names.

Set Heading Action: This specifies whether the column headings specified in the Set Headings property will replace or add to the data-source headings of the data source, or will add to the headings of the data source (effectively moving each row down by one). Valid values are Replace and Add. The default value is Add.

Limit Column: This specifies a column name that you want to filter the data source by. The type of filter that will be applied is specified in the

Action property, and the values that the column will be filtered against are specified in the Limit Value property.

Action: This specifies how the column specified in the Limit Column property will be filtered against the data specified in the Limit Value column. Valid values are Contains, Contains ignore case, Equals, Equals ignore case, Begins with, Begins with ignore case, Ends with, and Ends with ignore case. The default value is Equals.

Limit Value: This specifies the value that the values in the column specified in the Limit Column property are tested against, with the rule specified in the Action column.

For example, if the Limit column were set to Col1 and the Action column were set to Equals, and the Limit value were set to Foo, the resulting data source would only contain rows where the value in Col1 equaled Foo.

Sort Column: This specifies the column that the data source will be sorted by. The default (see the Sort By property) will sort according to the locality of the operating system it's being run on. Thus, if you're running on a French operating system, the object will sort according to French language rules.

Sort By: This specifies how to sort the data source by the column specified in the Sort By property. Valid values include Alphabetical, Alphabetical Desc (reverse alphabetical order), Reverse (which reverses the order of the data source), and Custom (which allows you to specify your own sorting rules in the Custom Sort Rules property).

Custom Sort Rules: If the Sort By column is set to Custom, this specifies the custom sorting rules for the column.

Here are three simple sets of rules:

English Alphabetical
< a,A < b,B < c,C < d,D < e,E < f,F < g,G < h,H < i,I < j,J < k,K < l,L < m,M < n,N < o,O < p,P < q,Q < r,R < s,S < t,T < u,U < v,V < w,W < x,X < y,Y < z,Z

English Alphabetical Desc
< Z,z < Y,y < X,x < W,w < V,v < U,u < T,t < S,s < R,r < Q,q < P,p < O,o < N,n < M,m < L,l < K,k < J,j < I,i < H,h < G,g < F,f < E,e < D,d < C,c < B,b < A,a

Norwegian
< a,A< b,B< c,C< d,D< e,E< f,F< g,G< h,H< i,I< j,J < k,K< l,L< m,M< n,N< o,O< p,P< q,Q< r,R< s,S< t,T < u,U< v,V< w,W< x,X< y,Y< z,Z < å=a?,Å=A? ;aa,AA< æ,Æ< ø,Ø

For a more in-depth discussion of the sorting rules syntax see:

```
http://java.sun.com/products/jdk/1.2/docs/api/java/text/
RuleBasedCollator.html
```

Max Number of Items: This specifies the maximum number of rows of data contained within the data source created by the object.

Clip Name: This setting allows you to specify the name of an additional clip to be added to the data source. The value for the column is specified in the Clip Value property. This is useful if you're using the object with objects that require a "clip" column.

Clip Value: This specifies the value that will be placed on each row for the column added in the Clip Name property.

Index Label: If this is specified, a column with the name set in the property will be added to the data source. The value of the column will be the current index of each row of data. Thus, Row 1 will be 1, Row 2 will be 2, and so on.

The object can be useful if all you want to do is manipulate, sort, and filter your existing Generator data sources. Adding to its utility is the fact that it lets you use non-Generator data sources as Generator data sources.

1. *Download and install the Advanced Data Source object from the Macromedia Flash Exchange. Make sure to restart Flash after you've installed the object.*

2. *Create a new Flash movie with two keyframes.*

3. *Place the Advanced Data Source object into the first frame.*

4. *For the data source, enter the following:*

```
http://chart.yahoo.com/table.csv?s=amzn&a=10&b=1&c=2000&d=1&
e=2&f=2001&g=d&q=q&y=0&z=macr&x=.csv
```

This URL will return a comma-separated file of stock data for the symbol and date range specified in the URL. This URL will return the stock price of Amazon.com (AMZN) for each day from October 10, 2000, to February 2, 2001. You can enter the URL in your Web browser to see what the raw data looks like.

If you look at the data in the browser, you'll notice that it has column headings but the names are different than those we need for our line chart. Thus, we have to use the object to replace the headings:

1. **Set the Set Column Heading property to , , , , value,.**

2. **Set the Set Column Action property to Replace.**

3. **Although we don't need to change the Variable Name setting, it's important to note that its value is dataSource.**

4. **Switch to the second frame and add a stop action.**

5. **In Frame 2, add a Basic Chart Generator object to the movie. Scale it to the size you want the chart to be.**

6. **For the data source, enter #{dataSource}. This is the variable that will be created by the Advanced Data Source object. The pound sign (#0) tells the Chart object that the data source contains the actual data source, not just a path to the data.**

7. **Set the Chart Type property to Line.**

8. **Test your movie.**

You should see a simple line chart created from the data source created by the Advanced Data Source object.

SIMPLE LINE CHART
CREATED WITH DATA
FROM ADVANCED DATA
SOURCE OBJECT.

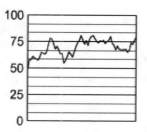

One thing to pay particular attention to is how we chained two objects together. The Advanced Data Source created data that the Basic Charts object used. If you wanted to do something similar with an XML data source, you could have the XML Data Source object create a data source that is then passed to the Advanced Data Source object, which manipulates and finally passes the data to the Chart object. The Chart object then creates the actual line chart. Be sure to place the objects in their own frame in the order that you want them to be processed.

If you're using more than one Advanced Data Source object in your movie, make sure to give each one a separate Variable Name property. If you don't, the value of one object may overwrite the value of the other object.

Insert Flash Variables object

The Insert Flash Variables object converts a Generator column data source into Flash 4 ActionScript pseudo-arrays. ActionScript can then use these Flash arrays/variables within the Flash movie.

For example, the object would convert the following Generator Column data source:

```
forecast, high, low
sunny, 77, 73
partly cloudy, 73, 52
into the following Flash variables:
forecast_0 = "sunny"
forecast_1 = "partly cloudy"
high_0 = "77"
high_1 = "73"
low_0 = "53"
low_1 = "52"
length = 2;
```

There is only one property for this object:

Data Source: This is a Generator column data source that the object will use to create Flash variables. The data can come from any valid source that Generator can connect to, including files, URLs, or database connections.

To use the object:

1. *Download and install the Insert Flash Variables object from the Macromedia Flash Exchange. Make sure to restart Flash after you've installed the object.*

2. *Create a new Flash movie.*

3. *With a text editor, create a file called flashVariablesData.txt and save it in the same directory as your .fla.*

4. *Open the text file and enter the following information:*

```
forecast, high, low
sunny, 77, 73
partly cloudy, 73, 52
```

5. *Save the text file.*

6. Drag the Insert Flash Variables object into your movie.

7. Set the data source property for the object to flashVariables.txt.

8. Test your movie.

You shouldn't see anything other than a white background. Now select Debug > List Variables to get a list of all Flash variables currently in the movie. Something similar to the following should appear in your Output window:

```
Level #0:
    Variable __level0.$version = "WIN 5,0,30,0"
    Variable __level0.forecast_0 = "sunny"
    Variable __level0.high0 = "77"
    Variable __level0.low0 = "73"
    Variable __level0.forecast1 = "partly cloudy"
    Variable __level0.high1 = "73"
    Variable __level0.low1 = "52"
    Variable __level0.length = "2"
```

Note that the object inserted a variable called Length, which contains the number of items in the data source. This makes it easier and more efficient to loop through all of the variables.

You can now use these variables just as you would a record set. Simply use the array access operator to loop through the variables. (If you're publishing your movie as a Flash 4 movie, then you need to use the eval() command to loop through the variables.)

```
for(i = 0; i < length; ++i)
{
    trace("----- Row " + i + " -----");
    trace("forecast : " + __root["forecast" + i]);
    trace("high     : " + __root["high" + i]);
    trace("low      : " + __root["low" + i]);
    trace("");
}
stop();
```

You will have to place the code that accesses the variables in a frame after the frame that contains the Insert Flash Variables object. This ensures that the objects and code are processed in the correct order.

The Insert Image object

This is a Generator object that allows you to dynamically insert an image into a Generator template. It can insert GIF, JPG, and PNG image files as well as replace InsertGifFile, InsertJpgFile, and InsertPngFile generator objects.

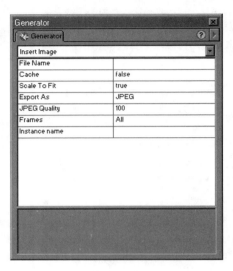

Because the object uses the image's file extension to determine its type, the image must end in .gif, .jpg, .jpeg, or .png.

The properties for the object are the same as those for the Insert GIF/JPEG/PNG objects. See the section "Inserting graphics with Generator" earlier in this chapter for a more thorough discussion of the properties.

Installing custom objects on the server

The Extension Manager will only install objects on the Windows and Mac platforms—fine if you just want to use the objects within the Flash authoring environment. However, once you're ready to move your templates to the server, you need to make sure that the custom objects are installed there. This involves manually moving the object files from your authoring machine to the server. Directions for installing each object are included in the documentation that comes installed with each object.

POINTS TO REMEMBER

- Generator objects are at the heart of Generator and dynamically insert content such as charts, tickers, and lists into Flash movies.

- Generator objects can be thought of as server-side SmartClips.

- In addition to the objects that come installed with Generator, you can download objects from the Macromedia Flash Exchange.

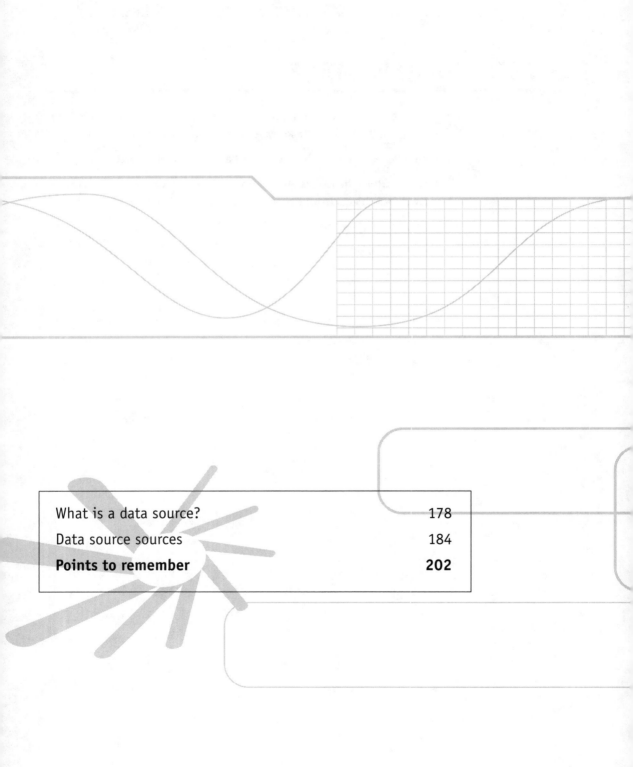

CHAPTER 7

GENERATOR DATA SOURCES

IF YOU HAVE READ THROUGH THE BOOK CHAPTER BY CHAPTER, YOU HAVE already had some exposure to data sources from Chapter 6. As you have probably figured out by now, data sources are at the core of Generator; they are almost as important as the Generator objects. Why is that? We keep talking about creating dynamic data-driven content; well, the dynamic and data-driven parts come from the data sources.

This chapter will explain what exactly a Generator data source is, show the different formats that it can take, and finally will discuss all of the different sources from which Generator can retrieve data. Understanding data sources is one of the most important skills in working with Generator. Once you have a good grasp on how Generator handles data sources, you can begin to do some very advanced things.

WHAT IS A DATA SOURCE?

So what exactly is a Generator data source? Basically, it is a source of data formatted in a way that Generator understands. In most cases, this means comma-delimited text, but a data source can also be a database table. In addition, with Java data sources you can use other types of data, such as XML, as Generator data.

Generator understands two data source formats. They are the Name/Value pair format, and the Column format. Let's look at each format in a little more depth.

Name/Value data source format

The Name/Value format is used to pass multiple Name/Value pairs into Generator. Here is a simple Name/Value formatted data source:

```
name, value
day, "March 28"
year, "2001"
```

The first row is required in every Name/Value data source and tells Generator that this is a Name/Value data source. Each subsequent row is a Name/Value pair. The first column is the *name* of the variable, and the second column on the same row is the *value* of the variable. Although you cannot see them here, each row ends with a line return. Line returns are very important, because they are used by Generator to determine when it reaches the end of the row.

The data source above creates two Generator variables:

```
day = March 28
year = 2001
```

Let's use the data source above in a simple template.

1. *Create a new Flash movie and call it nameValue.fla.*

2. *In the same folder where you saved the movie, create a text file called nameData.txt.*

3. *Copy the example data source from the text above into the text file and save it.*

The Generator
Environment
Variables button.

4. Open the nameValue.fla file and click the Generator Environment Variables button (it is the one at the top right of the screen that looks like a globe with two arrows).

You use the Generator Environment Variables window to load data into Generator which is accessible to the movie clip / time line it is loaded into, and all the movie clips contained within that time line.

The Column Name/Value
data layout button and
Name/Value data layout
button in the Generator
Environment Variables
window.

5. You will notice two buttons in the window that look like documents. Hold your mouse cursor over each one to see its name. These buttons tell Generator the type of data source format that you will be loading. Because we are going to load a Name/Value data source, click the Name/Value data layout button.

6. Now, in the text field of the window, enter the path to the data source that you just created (nameData.txt).

Note that this field accepts more than just a text file data source. It can take a data source from any source from which Generator can retrieve data. These sources will be covered in more detail later in the chapter.

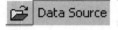

The Data Source File
Browser button in the
Generator Environment
Variables window.

You can also click the Data Source File Browser button to locate the data source. But since we know that our data source is in the same directory as our template, we don't need to do this.

7. Click the OK button.

8. In your movie, select the Text Tool and place two Generator variables into your movie. One named "{day}" and one named "{year}". Your movie should look something like this:

Template with variables
on main timeline.

9. *Finally, we have to tell Flash to publish the movie as a Generator template. Go to File > Publish Settings and make sure that the Generator Template (.swt) checkbox is checked.*

10. *Click OK and test your movie. You should see the values of the variables defined in your Name/Value data source.*

So what just happened? Well, you defined a couple of Name/Value pairs in a data source, loaded that data source into Generator, and then used the names as Generator variables in order to display their values in the movie.

Of course, you could use these variables anywhere that you can place Generator variables, such as the values for object properties for an object in the Generator panel.

Basically, the Name/Value data source format is used to pass Name/Value pairs to Generator.

Column data source format

The Column data source format is used to pass multiple rows of related information to Generator. It's very similar to a database table or result set in that the first row contains the column names, and each subsequent row contains related data separated into columns. A comma separates column headings and values, and each row of data ends with a line return.

Here is an example of a Column data source:

```
day, high, low, forecast
"Monday", "82", "72", "Sunny"
"Tuesday", "81", 75, "Cloudy"
"Wednesday", "77", "68", "Rain"
```

This is a Column data source that gives weather data about each day of the week (or in our case, the first three days of the week). The first row defines the column headings. Each heading is separated by a comma. You can also think of these as defining the variable names.

The rest of the rows define the values for the column that they are in. You can think of these as defining the variable values.

For example, in row 1:

```
day = Monday
high = 82
```

```
low = 72
forecast = Sunny
```

In row 2:

```
day = Tuesday
high = 81
low = 75
forecast = Cloudy
```

And so on.

But how can a variable have more than one value? It can't, but the objects that use the Column data source format, such as the Pie Chart object, know that each row is separate from the others.

Formatting data within the data source

The fields in the Name/Value and Column data sources are separated by commas, and each row ends in a line return. But what if we need to place a comma inside our data? Won't that confuse Generator? Yes and no. If you just place a comma within your data it will confuse Generator. However, if you escape the comma and tell Generator that the comma is part of the data, Generator will work just how you want it to.

Escaping commas

Escaping commas is very simple. Notice that in the data sources we created above, we wrapped the values in double quotes. Double quotes tell Generator that all of the text in between them is actually part of the data. So if you want to add a comma to your text, just wrap all of the data in double quotes.

So the following data source

```
name, value
text, "Christian ate a banana, pear, and apple."
```

will create a Generator variable that prints out:

```
Christian ate a banana, pear, and apple.
```

If you didn't place the double quotes around the data, Generator would become confused and would only print out:

```
Christian ate a banana
```

This is because it would see the comma and think that it had reached the end of the data. That's why it is always a good idea to wrap your data in double quotes.

Escaping double quotes

Notice that when we wrapped the data in double quotes, Generator removed them from the data it printed out, which is what we wanted. But what if we wanted to print out the double quotes? All we have to do is to escape the double quotes by placing a backslash (\) in front of them.

For example:

```
name, value
text, "Har'el said, \"Monkeys also eat bananas, pears and apples.\""
```

This creates a Generator variable (named "text") that prints out:

```
Har'el said, "Monkeys also eat bananas, pears and apples."
```

If we didn't escape the double quotes, Generator would become confused, and would only print out:

```
Har'el said, Monkeys also eat bananas
```

Wait a minute. How did the "Monkeys also eat bananas" get in there? Shouldn't it only have printed "Harel said"?

Remember that Generator figures out where a set of data ends by finding commas, not by double quotes. So in this case, Generator found the first two double quotes and removed them. Then it continued to include data until it found the comma, which was no longer wrapped in double quotes (since we didn't escape the first two, Generator removed them). That is why there was more data included in the variable.

Escaping backslashes

So if you use backslashes to escape double quotes, how do you escape backslashes? Simple: you escape a backslash with another backslash.

For example:

```
name, value
text, "You escape the \\ character like this \\\\"
```

This will create a Generator variable named "text" that will print out:

```
You escape the \ character like this \\
```

Why does the second set of backslashes have four backslashes? That is because we are escaping two backslashes. Because there is one backslash escaping each backslash, there are a total of four.

Escaping curly brackets

You also need to escape curly brackets because Generator uses curly brackets to denote its variables. To escape curly brackets, you simply double each bracket.

For example:

```
name, value
text, "A Generator variable looks like this : {{variableName}}"
```

This will print:

```
A Generator variable looks like this : {variableName}
```

This also works if you only have one curly bracket:

```
name, value
Text, "This is an opening curly bracket : {{"
```

This will print:

```
This is an opening curly bracket : {
```

Adding line returns to data sources

As we already mentioned, Generator uses line returns to determine when it has reached the end of a row of data. But what if we want to have a line return within our data? All we have to do is escape the line return.

First though, we need to figure out how to place a line return within our data source. Generator uses a \n (backslash - n) to denote a line return. Whenever Generator sees this, it will read it as a line return (you can also use \n\r).

Escaping line returns is just like escaping commas. All you have to do is place it within double quotes.

For example:

```
name, value
text, "This is text \n with a line return."
```

This will create a variable named "text" that prints out:

```
This is text
 with a line return.
```

Notice that the left margins of the two lines of text are not the same. This is because after the \n there is a space. In order to get rid of the space, simply remove it like so:

```
name, value
text, "This is text\nwith a line return."
```

This will then print out:

```
This is text
with a line return.
```

Using \n as a line return can be very useful, especially when using a native data source and middleware to create your data sources. See the "Native Data Sources" section below for more information on native data sources, and see Chapter 8 for more information on using middleware with Generator.

DATA SOURCE SOURCES

Now that you know what a data source is, where can Generator get its data from?

One of Generator's biggest strengths is that it can load data from just about anywhere, including from URLs, FTP sites, databases, Java classes, and text files. In addition, you can also define data sources within Generator itself. Using Java classes, you add support for just about any type of data or data source to Generator.

The sections below discusses all the different sources Generator can get its data from.

Native data sources

You can define entire data sources within Generator itself. This is called a *native* data source, and it is very useful when developing or debugging your template.

A native data source is merely a data source created and defined within Generator. This creation and definition is usually done in one of two areas: in the Environment Variables window and in the data source parameter for certain Generator objects.

Native data sources are just like regular data sources except for two things:

1. They begin with a pound sign (#). This tells Generator that the data following the pound sign is the actual data source, and not a path to the data source.

2. Line returns are represented by "/n/r" when the native data source is defined within an object's data source property field.

This works for both Name\Value and Column data sources.

Defining a native data source in the Generator Environment Variables window

1.   *Open up the FLA that you created in the example above (nameValue.fla). Rename it nativeName.fla.*

2.   *Open the Generator Environment Variable window. Remove "nameData.txt" and in its place type the following:*

```
#name, value
day, "March 28"
year, "2001"
```

Notice that this is the same data source that was in the text file, except that there is a pound sign (#) at the very beginning of the data source. Again, this tells Generator that the window contains the actual data source, and not a path to the data source.

Generator Environment
Variables window with
native data source.

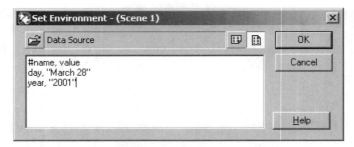

3.   *Close the window by clicking the OK button.*

4.   *Test your movie.*

You should see the day and year variable values printed out in the movie.
If you do not, make sure that the variables are on the main timeline.

Defining a native data source for Generator objects

The preceding technique will also work when defining data sources
for Generator objects. Let's create a simple pie chart that uses a native
data source.

1.   *Open Flash and create a new file. Name it "nativePie.fl."*

2.   *Open the Generator Objects window (Window > Generator Objects),
     and drag the Pie Chart object into your movie.*

3.   *Double-click on the object's placeholder and open the Properties panel
     for the object.*

4.   *For the data source property, enter the following:*

#value, color/n/r2, blue/n/r4, red/n/r6, green

5.   *Test the movie.*

You should see a pie chart with three slices colored blue, red, and green.

Let's look at the data source you entered. It starts off with a # (pound sign).
This tells Generator that the property contains the actual data source and
not a path to the data source. Next is "value, color /n/r". This is the column
headings for the data source. The /n/r is read by Generator as a line return
and thus the end of the row. You only use /n/r to denote a line return when
the native data source is defined within the object's data source property.

The rest of the data contains three rows of data that translate into:

```
2, blue
4, red
6, green
```

You can also enter the data source by clicking the data source button and entering it normally. Once you click OK, Generator will automatically translate it into a native data source for you.

At first glance, defining a data source in the Generator panel probably doesn't seem too useful. In fact, it is much more complicated than using a text file. However, you have to remember that instead of typing the actual data source in, you could place a Generator variable as the data source and then pass in the entire data source for the pie chart through the URL when the template is processed.

If you defined the following native data source in your Generator Environment Variable window

```
#name, value
pieData, "value, color\n2, blue\n4, red\n6, green"
```

you could then place the following as the data source for your pie chart:

```
#{pieData}
```

The pieData variable will be replaced by the data source and will be used to create the pie chart.

You could even use this technique to pass multiple data sources through a single data source. This would allow you to only have to make one call from Generator to load multiple data sources for multiple objects.

Text-based data sources

If you are reading through the book chapter by chapter, then you should already be familiar with text file–based data sources as we used them in Chapter 6. Generator can retrieve text file-based data sources from the file system, URL, and FTP site.

However, the most important thing to realize is that the data source does not have to actually *be* a file, but rather Generator only has to *think* it's a file. This allows you to use middleware to dynamically create the data source without having to write an actual text file to the file system. We cover this concept in much more depth in Chapter 8.

Loading a data source from the file system

The easiest way to load a text-based data source is via a file. This is the way that you usually load data when developing your templates, and it is the technique we have been using throughout the book to test our templates.

You can enter either a relative or absolute path to a file. If you enter a relative path, it is relative to where the Generator template is saved. As a general rule, you should always try to enter a relative path when developing as this makes it easier for other users to work on the same template without having to change the path.

You can specify a path to a data source in the data source property field of objects that require data sources, and also in the Generator Environment Variable window.

Here are some examples of data source paths, both relative and absolute:

Relative:

- data.txt: Text file is in the same directory as the template.
- data/data.txt: Text file is in a sub-directory called data that is a child of the directory that the template is in.
- ../data.txt: Text file is in a directory that is the parent of the directory that the template is in.

Absolute:

- C:\temp\data.txt: Text file is in the C:\temp directory.
- /temp/data.txt: (UNIX-based systems) Text file is in the temp directory, which is a child of the root directory.

Loading a data source from a URL

Loading a text-based data source from a URL is as simple as entering the URL to the data source.

For example:

```
http://www.domain.com/data/data.txt
```

If you need to specify the port number for the Web server, you add it to the end of the domain name like so:

```
http://www.domain.com:8080/data/data.txt
```

This URL connects to the Web server at `www.domain.com` listening on port 8080.

You can also point the URL to a middleware file that creates and returns a text-formatted Generator data source. The URL would look similar to

```
http://www.domain.com/data/data.asp
```

Of course, the file extension would depend on the type of middleware you were using. The example above is using ASP. This topic is covered in much more depth in Chapter 8.

Loading a data source from an FTP site

Finally, you can also load a data source from an FTP site. Although this technique is not used very often, it can be useful if you need an easy way to make your data source password-protected.

There are two ways to connect to a FTP server from Generator. The first uses a standard FTP URL and can be used if you do not need to pass a user name or password to log onto the server.

Here is an example of an FTP URL that Generator could use to load a text-based data source:

```
ftp://ftp.domain.com/pub/data/data.txt
```

The file exists on an FTP server called "ftp" at the "domain.com" domain. It exists in the "/pub/data/" directory and is named "data.txt".

If you need to pass a username and password to log into the FTP server, you have to use a slightly different format—the FGFTP format.

Here is an example:

```
fgftp://username|password@ftp.domain.com:23/data/data.txt
```

This tells Generator to connect to the FTP server at `ftp.domain.com` listening on port 21. Generator will pass the username and password to log into the server and will look in the "/pub/data/" directory for the data source named "data.txt". Notice that the user name and password are separated by a pipe (|) character.

If you leave the port section empty, Generator will use a default value of 21.

This will also work if you need to log onto a site anonymously. Here is an FGFTP URL that logs onto the site above, anonymously passing the user's email address.

```
fgftp://anonymous|generator@domain.com@ftp.domain.com:23/
data/data.txt
```

Retrieving a data source from a database

In addition to being able to load data from text files, Generator can also connect directly to most databases to retrieve its data.

When connecting to a database, Generator sends an SQL command (defined by the user) that returns a result set. Because the Generator Column data source format is just like a result set, Generator can easily use the result set as a Column data source.

Note: You can also retrieve a Name\Value data source by connecting to a database. Do this by having your SQL command only return one row of data. If it returns more than one row of data, the last row of data will be used. If the SQL query returns two columns named "name" and "value," then all of the data will be included in the data source (see the "Using data from a database with objects that have required column names" section below for more information).

Generator can connect to any database with an ODBC or JDBC database driver. By default, Generator requires a database with an ODBC driver, but with a little extra work, you can make Generator connect to a database with a JDBC driver.

Connecting to a database via ODBC

ODBC is a database driver supported by such databases as Microsoft Access, FileMaker Pro, and Microsoft SQL server. It requires that you configure a Data Source Name (DSN) in the operating system that points to the database. The database is then accessed through the DSN.

The connection string necessary to connect to a database is a little intimidating at first. But once you break it down into parts, it is pretty easy to understand.

Let's take apart the following database connection string used by Generator:

```
fgjdbc:///?driver=sun.jdbc.odbc.JdbcOdbcDriver&url=jdbc:odbc:
myDataSourceName&userid=username&password=password&query=
select%20*%20from%20weatherTable
```

This connection string connects to the database defined by the DataSource Name (DSN) named "myDataSourceName". It passes a username and password to the DSN and runs the following SQL query: "select * from weatherTable".

Let's look at each section in more detail:

fgjdbc:/// This tells Generator that the string is a database connection string.

?driver=sun.jdbc.odbc.JdbcOdbcDriver This tells Generator which JDBC driver to use to connect to the database. The driver name is case sensitive. Generator actually always uses a JDBC driver to connect to databases. By default, it uses the driver specified here, which is a JDBC-ODBC bridge and is rather slow. See below for information on how to connect to a database using a native JDBC driver.

&url=jdbc:odbc:myDataSourceName ODBC databases require that a DataSource Name (DSN) be set up on the system in order to connect to the database. This string specifies the name of the DSN that Generator should connect to. In this string, the DSN name is "myDataSourceName". You must first set up the DSN in your system's properties before this can be used. JDBC databases do not require a DSN.

&userid=username This specifies the username required to log into the database. If a username is not required, you can leave the field blank, but you must specify the userid field like this: **&userid=**.

&password=password This specifies the password required to log into the database. If a password is not required, you can leave the field blank, but you must specify the password field like this: **&password=**.

&query=select%20*%20from%20weatherTable This specifies the SQL query to be executed on the database. The actual SQL query is URL encode. For the most part, this means that you have to replace spaces with %20.

In most cases the query will be a select statement that returns a result set. However, it is possible to execute delete, insert, and update statements. But since Generator is expecting to receive a result set back (and in most cases these commands do not return result sets), it will log an error to the log file (which you can ignore).

You can also specify SQL commands that run stored procedures. Just create the query the same way you would if you were manually executing the stored procedure on the database.

Connecting to a database using JDBC

As we just discussed, Generator can connect directly to any ODBC database via the ODBC-JDBC bridge. In order for this to work you have to have a database with an ODBC driver, and you have to set up a DSN to point to the data source.

However, one of the disadvantages of this is that the ODBC-JDBC bridge is inherently slow because the connections must be converted from JDBC to ODBC. If you are using a database with native JDBC drivers, then you can gain some extra speed and flexibility by having Generator use those drivers to connect directly to the database.

We will use the JDBC drivers for the MySql database in order to demonstrate this. MySql is an open source mid-tier database that supports a large subset of the SQL standard. It also works very well with Java and other middleware languages (especially PHP). You can find more information on MySql and download a free working version from `http://www.mysql.org`.

Here is how you can connect directly to a MySql database from Generator.

1. *Download the MySql JDBC drivers. You can choose from a number of drivers from*

   `http://www.mysql.com/downloads/api-jdbc.html`

2. *Install the drivers so that Generator can locate them. This is done by unjarring/unzipping the drivers into the "Generator 2\classes" directory. Make sure that when you unjar or unzip the files, you maintain the directory structure of the jar file.*

3. *Restart Generator.*

4. *Within the Generator template, change your connection string to use the MySql JDBC drivers.*

Here is an example string:

`fgjdbc:///?driver=org.gjt.mm.mysql.Driver&url=jdbc:mysql:`
`%2f%2fwww.domain.com:3306%2fdbName&userid=username&password=`
`password&query=select%20columnName%20from%20Table`

Let's look at each part of the string:

fgjdbc:/// This tells Generator to read the rest of the string as a JDBC URL.

?driver=org.gjt.mm.mysql.Driver This is the name of the MySql JDBC driver. This will be different depending on the database you are connecting to and the JDBC driver that you are using.

&url=jdbc:mysql:%2f%2fwww.domain.com:3306%2fdbName This is the MySql JDBC connection string (make this point to whichever drivers you are using). The %2f are URL encoded forward slashes (/). www.domain.com is the address that the database server is located at, and 3306 is the port that the database is listening on for connections. Finally, "dbName" is the database name within the database server that Generator will connect to.

&userid=username This specifies the username required to log into the database. If a username is not required, you can leave the field blank, but you must specify the userid field like this: **&userid=**.

&password=password This specifies the password required to log into the database. If a password is not required, you can leave the field blank, but you must specify the password field like this: **&password=**.

query This is a URL-encoded SQL query that will be executed.

This technique works for any database with JDBC drivers such as Oracle, Sybase, MySql, and mSql.

Using data from a database with objects that have required column names

As we have just discussed, Generator can retrieve its data directly from any database that has an ODBC or JDBC driver.

However, some objects, such as the scrolling list object, require that the data source contain certain column names (such as "clip"). One solution to this would be to change your table's column names to match those required by Generator. But that is not a good option, because it ties your data too closely to Generator, making it difficult to use with other applications or programs.

Another option is to have Generator retrieve the data from some middle-ware that would in turn connect to the database and return a data source with the correct column names. However, that can be overkill if all you are doing is changing the column names. Furthermore, you may not have the resources necessary to develop or deploy the middleware.

The third option is to use the SQL "AS" statement in your SQL query to specify the column names in the result set returned to Generator.

Thus if you had a table in your database named "Weather" with the following columns

```
graphic, forecast, high, low
```

and you wanted to convert the "graphic" column to "clip," your SQL statement would look something like:

```
SELECT graphic AS clip, forecast, high, low FROM Weather
```

This would return a result set with the following columns:

```
clip, forecast, high, low
```

You can use the AS modifier more than once per statement, and use it on just about anything that returns a value such as

```
SELECT count(*) AS numDays FROM Weather.
```

Retrieving a data source from a Java class

Generator also allows you to write Java classes that can be used to provide data to Generator. Although this is probably the most complex and advanced way to get data into Generator, it is also the most flexible, because it allows you to use all Java's advantages and features to gather and format data for Generator.

Using a Java-based data source from within Generator

In order to call a Java data source from within Generator, you need to use the FGJAVA URL. You can call it from the data source property of Generator objects, and also from the Generator Environment Variable window. Here is an example URL:

```
fgjava://JavaClassName?param1=foo&params2=bar
```

Let's look at this URL section by section:

fgjava:// This tells Generator that it needs to retrieve the data source from a Java class.

JavaClassName This is the name of the Java class from which the data source will be retrieved.

?param1=foo&param2=bar These are Name/Value pairs that will be sent to the Java data source. The first Name/Value pair starts with a question mark, and then the rest of the Name/Value pairs are separated by & (ampersand). The values must be URL encoded. Not all Java data sources require Name/Value pairs.

Creating a Java-based data source

The following example shows how to create a simple Java data source. The data source creates a column data source using hard-coded weather data. Of course, in most cases you would retrieve the data from other sources, such as a database or XML file. But we want to be able to concentrate on the Java code related to Generator, so we will just hard-code the data in some arrays. This example requires at least a rudimentary knowledge of Java and how to compile Java classes.

Here is the code for a basic Java data source:

```java
import java.util.Hashtable;
import java.io.ByteArrayInputStream;
import java.io.InputStream;

public class WeatherSource
{
    public static InputStream getStream(Hashtable params)
    {
        int numDays = 7;

        String tempNum = (String)params.get("numDays");

        if(tempNum != null)
        {
            try
            {
                numDays = Integer.parseInt(tempNum);
```

```
        }
        catch(NumberFormatException nfe)
        {
        }
        if(numDays > 7 || numDays < 0)
        {
            numDays = 7;
        }
    }
    String[] days = {"Monday", "Tuesday", "Wednesday",
                    "Thursday", "Friday", "Saturday",
                    "Sunday"};
    String dailyHighs[] = {"85", "82", "87", "87", "80",
                    "81", "89"};
    String dailyLows[] = {"62", "63", "60", "59", "65",
                    "68", "62"};
    String dailyGraphics[] = {"Sunny", "Cloudy", "Rain",
                    "Sunny", "Cloudy", "Sunny",
                    "Cloudy"};

    String[] dailyForecast = new String[numDays];
    dailyForecast[0] = "Sunny and clear with temperatures
                    rising. Highs in the mid 80s.";
    dailyForecast[1] = "Sunny early then becoming cloudy.
                    Highs in the lower 80s.";
    dailyForecast[2] = "Rain with highs in the upper 80s.";
    dailyForecast[3] = "Cloudy early, becoming sunny by
                    midday. Highs in the upper 80s.";
    dailyForecast[4] = "Clouds moving in early with
                    temperatures in the lower 80s.";
    dailyForecast[5] = "Sunny and pleasant. Highs in
                    lower 80s.";
    dailyForecast[6] = "Cloudy and very muggy. Highs
                    near 90.";

    StringBuffer sb = new StringBuffer("day, forecast, high,
                                    low, graphic \n");

    for(int i = 0; i < numDays; i++)
```

```java
        {
            sb.append("\"" + days[i] + "\"" + ",");
            sb.append("\"" + formatForGenerator
                        (dailyForecast[i]) + "\"" + ",");
            sb.append("\"" + dailyHighs[i] + "\"" + ",");
            sb.append("\"" + dailyLows[i] + "\"" + ",");
            sb.append("\"" + dailyGraphics[i] + "\"");
            sb.append("\n");
        }

        InputStream is = new ByteArrayInputStream
                        (sb.toString().getBytes());

        return is;
    }

    public static String formatForGenerator(String string)
    {
        char[] charArray = string.toCharArray();
        StringBuffer tempBuffer = new StringBuffer();

        for(int i = 0; i < charArray.length; i++)
        {
            if(charArray[i] == '\"')
            {
                tempBuffer.append("\\\"");
            }
            else if(charArray[i] == '\\')
            {
                tempBuffer.append("\\\\");
            }
            else
            {
                tempBuffer.append(charArray[i]);
            }
        }
        return tempBuffer.toString();
    }
}
```

Note: The fully commented code is available on the included CD-ROM.

Now let's examine the code section by section to determine what it is doing.

```
import java.util.Hashtable;
import java.io.ByteArrayInputStream;
import java.io.InputStream;
```

The first section of the code is simply importing some classes that are necessary for this class. As this is a very simple example, we are only importing those classes that will always be used when creating a Java-based data source.

```
public class WeatherSource
```

This declares our class, which is named "WeatherSource."

```
public static InputStream getStream(Hashtable params)
```

We then create a function with the signature above. This is very important as every Generator Java data source must have this function with this signature. This is the function that Generator calls to process the Java data source.

The function returns an InputStream to Generator. This is how the code returns the data source it creates to Generator.

The Hashtable passed into the function by Generator contains Name/Value pairs passed in by the user via the FGJAVA URL when calling the Java class from within Generator.

```
int numDays = 7;
String tempNum = (String)params.get("numDays");
```

First we initialize an integer variable to 7. This will be used to store the number of days of weather information to place within our data source. The next line then retrieves the value for the number of days specified by the user via the FGJAVA URL. The URL would look something like this:

```
fgjava:///WeatherSource?numDays=5
```

Because the user may not have specified the Name/Value pair, we first store it in a temporary variable and then check its value.

```
if(tempNum != null)
{
    try
    {
        numDays = Integer.parseInt(tempNum);
    }
```

```
catch(NumberFormatException nfe)
{
}

if(numDays > 7 || numDays < 0)
{
    numDays = 7;
}
}
```

We check to see if the tempNum variable is null. If it is, it means that the user did not specify the Name/Value pair for the tempNum value, and so we just use the default value of 7 for the numDays variable.

If it is not null, then we attempt to convert the value passed in by the user to a number. If we can't, we use the default value of 7. If we can convert it to a number, we make sure that the number is between 0 and 8 (i.e. valid numbers include 1 - 7). If it is not, we use the default value of 7; otherwise we use the number passed in by the user.

That may seem like a lot of work just to get the value of one parameter passed in by the user. But you have to remember that Generator has no way of checking that the correct values are passed in, and thus you have to manually do all of the checking.

```
String[] days = {"Monday", "Tuesday", "Wednesday",
                "Thursday", "Friday", "Saturday",
                "Sunday"};
String dailyHighs[] = {"85", "82", "87", "87", "80",
                "81", "89"};
String dailyLows[] = {"62", "63", "60", "59", "65",
                "68", "62"};
String dailyGraphics[] = {"Sunny", "Cloudy", "Rain",
                "Sunny", "Cloudy", "Sunny",
                "Cloudy"};

String[] dailyForecast = new String[numDays];
dailyForecast[0] = "Sunny and clear with temperatures
                rising. Highs in the mid 80s.";
dailyForecast[1] = "Sunny early then becoming cloudy.
                Highs in the lower 80s.";
dailyForecast[2] = "Rain with highs in the upper 80s.";
```

```
dailyForecast[3] = "Cloudy early, becoming sunny by
                    midday. Highs in the upper 80s.";
dailyForecast[4] = "Clouds moving in early with
                    temperatures in the lower 80s.";
dailyForecast[5] = "Sunny and pleasant. Highs in
                    lower 80s.";
dailyForecast[6] = "Cloudy and very muggy. Highs
                    near 90.";
```

This section of code is pretty simple. All we are doing is creating some data in arrays to use to build our data source. Normally, this is where you would retrieve your data from a more dynamic source, such as a database or XML news feed. However, we want to be able to concentrate on the Generator-related code, so we will just use hard-coded variables.

Now that we finally have our data, we can begin to put our data source together. We do this by looping through the data and creating a Column-formatted data source that will be stored in a StringBuffer object.

```
StringBuffer sb = new StringBuffer("day, forecast, high, low,
                                    graphic \n");
```

First we create a StringBuffer object to store our data source. We initialize the object with the column headings (first row) of our data source. Remember that Generator looks for a line return to determine when it has reached the end of a row of data, so we have to add a line return to the end of the row. We do this in Java by inserting \n (backslash-n).

```
for(int i = 0; i < numDays; i++)
{
    sb.append("\"" + days[i] + "\"" + ",");
    sb.append("\"" + formatForGenerator
               (dailyForecast[i]) + "\"" + ",");
    sb.append("\"" + dailyHighs[i] + "\"" + ",");
    sb.append("\"" + dailyLows[i] + "\"" + ",");
    sb.append("\"" + dailyGraphics[i] + "\"");
    sb.append("\n");
}
```

We loop through the data for the number of days defined by the user and for each day create a row in our Column data source.

There are a couple of things to note. First, we are wrapping all of our data in double quotes. Because Java uses double quotes to denote the beginning and end of a string, we have to escape the quotes like so \" (backslash-double quote). Second, all of the data is separated by commas. And finally, at the end of the loop (and thus each row of data) we place a line return \n (backslash-n).

You have probably also noticed that we are using the formatForGenerator method. This method, whose code is included above, takes a string and formats it to be used by Generator. For a more detailed discussion of this method, see Chapter 8.

We now have a StringBuffer object that contains an entire Generator Column-formatted data source. All we have left to do is send that data source back to Generator. We do this by writing the data source to an InputStream that will be returned to Generator.

```
InputStream is = new ByteArrayInputStream
                 (sb.toString().getBytes());
```

First we get the bytes of the StringBuffer and pass them to a ByteArrayInputStream constructor which is a subclass of InputStream. We then return the InputStream (which now contains our data source) to Generator.

```
return is;
```

You can now compile the code. That is all there is to creating a Java-based data source.

Installing a Java-based data source

Installing a Java data source is very simple. You need to place the file(s) for the data source (which will end in .class) into the Generator 2\classes directory and then restart Generator.

Remember that if you create a template using a Java data source, you will have to install the Java data source files on the server before those templates will work on the server.

POINTS TO REMEMBER

- The Name/Value Generator data source format is used to bring Name/Value pairs into Generator.

- The Column Generator data source format is used to bring result set-like rows of related information into Generator.

- You must escape some characters such as double quotes, commas, line returns, and curly brackets in order to display them with Generator.

- Generator can retrieve data from multiple sources, including text files via file, URL, or FTP server, databases, and Java classes.

- Native data sources are data sources that are defined within the Generator template and are useful when developing and debugging.

- You can use middleware to dynamically create text-based data sources.

- You can manually install JDBC database drivers and have Generator use them to connect directly to a database.

- Using Java data sources you can add support for other forms of data such as XML.

CHAPTER 8

USING MIDDLEWARE WITH GENERATOR

MIDDLEWARE IS THE VIRTUAL GLUE THAT HOLDS OUR WEB APPLICATIONS together. When used properly, middleware will connect your Generator-driven application with a wide variety of databases and systems.

The word *middleware* refers to any programming language that can be used to manipulate and format data and then make that data available to Generator. Examples of middleware are JSP, ASP, PHP, and Cold Fusion, as well as client-side languages such as JavaScript, Flash 4 and 5, and ActionScript.

In this chapter we'll talk about and create examples from each of the most popular middleware languages. Although we won't try to teach you each language—that would require six more books!—we will go into depth about how each one relates to Generator.

WHY USE MIDDLEWARE WITH GENERATOR?

Macromedia created Generator for one purpose: To quickly and efficiently create dynamic Flash movies and media. While this means that Generator has been optimized to perform *that* task extremely quickly, it also means that the program doesn't contain much logic that would allow it to manipulate data. By integrating Generator with middleware, however, you can essentially create a logic layer for Generator while also making available the other advanced features of whatever middleware language you're using.

In some cases, middleware can retrieve data even faster than you could using Generator directly—say, if the middleware were to provide some form of data caching, or if it were integrated tightly with a particular data source (such as a database). What's more, by using middleware, you enable Generator to make use of data from more sources and in a wider range of formats. For example, you could use middleware to retrieve data from a network server, or to convert and use XML as a Generator data source.

The examples in this chapter and on the CD-ROM use Java servlets, JSP, PHP, ASP, Cold Fusion, and ActionScript. However, the concepts and techniques described here apply to any middleware language you can use with Generator.

When to use middleware

Although you'll need to determine precisely when and how to use middleware with Generator on a case-by-case basis, there are some simple guidelines that can help you make your decision.

You should use middleware with Generator when you need to:

- Filter or modify data from a data source. For example, some Generator objects require specific column headings. Instead of renaming table-column headings in your database to be compatible with Generator, you could simply filter the data through middleware, adding or modifying column headings so that Generator can use them.

- Pass user-input data directly to Generator. For instance, if you had a pie chart that displayed data collected from information users supplied to an HTML form (or Flash movie), you would need to use middleware to receive and format the data before sending it on for use by Generator.

- Extend Generator's functionality. For example, you could use middleware to access and transform XML into a Generator data source, to cache frequently used data for Generator, or to add expanded logging.

GENERATOR DATA SOURCES

As discussed earlier, Generator understands just two data formats: Name/Value format and the result-set-like Column format. Since getting your data into a format Generator can understand is 90 percent of your job when working with middleware, the sooner you understand how to do so, the sooner you'll be able to retrieve and manipulate that data.

The following table provides an example of each type of data source.

Column Data Source	Name / Value Data Source
Color, value, title	Name, value
"Blue", "5", "Yankees"	"Winner", "Yankees"
"Green", "9", "Mets"	"Loser", "Mets"
"Red", "7", "Cubs"	

Most of the examples in this chapter use Column format. As far as the code required within the middleware, using the Name/Value format is not much different than using the Column format: You just need to format the data differently.

The Column data source consists of a comma-delimited file with one or more rows. Each row is delimited by a line return, and the values of each section are divided by commas. The first row contains the column headings for the data source; subsequent rows contain the values for those headings. You may find it helpful to think of the Column data source as a database result set, with the first row containing the table's column names and subsequent rows containing rows of related data. Thus, in the Column data source above, *color* equals *blue* in Row 1, *green* in Row 2, and *red* in Row 3.

The data contained within the data source must be formatted so that it does not confuse Generator. This requires escaping any special character used by Generator.

Displaying special characters within Generator

Line Return (\n)	\n (when data is surrounded by double quotes)
Comma (,)	, (when data is surrounded by double quotes)
Backslash (\)	\\
Double Quote (")	\"

For example, let's say you want to insert the following sentence in a Flash movie using Generator:

Cathy said "those kitties are cute, but mischievous".

If you attempted to pass this sentence directly to Generator in a data source, Generator would see the first quote as the beginning of the data and would only insert the following:

those kitties are cute, but mischievous.

You need a way to tell Generator that the quotes are part of the data to be displayed, *not* a special character to be used by Generator. Here is what the sentence would look like formatted for Generator:

"Cathy said \"those kitties are cute, but mischievous \"."

As you can see, we made two changes: First we enclosed the entire string in quotes. This was necessary because our sentence contained another character used by Generator—a comma. By enclosing the data in quotes, we're telling Generator that the comma is part of the data—not a character delimiting the end of the section of data. By enclosing the data in double quotes, we also escape the line returns (\n), which means that the *literal* line returns can be placed within the data.

The second change we made was to escape the quotes we wanted to display by placing a backslash in front of them. By doing this, we tell Generator that the quotes are part of the data to be displayed—that is, they *do not* signify the end of a block of data.

You'll also need to escape backslashes (\) (this works the same as double quotes): If you want to display a backslash in your data, you simply place a backslash in front of it ("\\"). This tells Generator that the next backslash is a backslash to be displayed rather than an escape character.

As a general rule, you should enclose all values within double quotes in order to escape any commas and line returns within the data. This is particularly important if the data is being dynamically generated or retrieved.

The following is an example of a Column data source formatted for Generator:

```
Group, songTitle, filePath, comments
"The Smiths", "How Soon is Now", "c:\\mp3s\\hatful_of_hollow",
"This is the \"best\" song!"
"Radiohead", "Airbag", "c:\\mp3s\\OK_Computer", "This song,
which is on the OK Computer cd, starts off great"
```

All data is enclosed in double quotes, and literal double quotes and backslashes are escaped by placing a backslash in front of them.

INTEGRATING MIDDLEWARE WITH GENERATOR

The following describes the three primary ways to integrate middleware with Generator; all of the examples included in this chapter use some variation of one of these.

Middleware with URL strings

One of the primary ways you'll use middleware is to collect and format data sent to Generator via the URL/query string when calling the Generator template. Although this technique works well and is simple to implement, you can run into problems if you attempt to send a large amount of data from a browser through the query string. This technique also leads to larger downloads for users because the browser must download the data before it can pass it to Generator. One benefit of this technique is that it makes it easy for users to view the raw data.

Middleware with data sources

You can also use middleware to gather and format information, and then create a data source. In this case, the Generator template would point directly to the middleware, and the middleware would return data in a format Generator understands. In essence, Generator thinks it's getting its data from a text file when it's actually retrieving the info from middleware—a powerful technique since it provides the power and flexibility of middleware while still allowing you to isolate the logic required to process that data. Plus, you avoid the problems inherent in passing data through the URL. The main downside of this technique is that you have to make a separate call to the middleware for each data source required.

Middleware in front of Generator

Finally, you can use middleware to add functionality to Generator. In such a scenario, your middleware (usually a Java servlet) would sit in front of Generator. This way, when a template is requested, the custom servlet would be called instead of Generator. The servlet can then modify the request or add data before passing the request to Generator, which then returns the dynamically created media to the servlet (*not* the browser). The servlet can then do any number of things with the media, including sending it to the browser for display, saving it to the file system, logging the file size, and so on. Although this technique is more complex than the first two, it's also more powerful.

Creating Generator data sources using middleware

Regardless of which middleware and data type you employ, you must perform the following steps to create a Generator data source using middleware:

1. Retrieve data. Your data can come from any source, including HTML form, database, or text file.

2. Format data for Generator. This includes escaping appropriate characters and putting the data into a format that Generator can use.

3. Send data to Generator. You will usually send your data though the URL or command line. You can also have Generator retrieve the data.

We will revisit these steps in each of the following sections and examples.

SENDING DATA THROUGH THE URL

In this section you'll learn how to use middleware to retrieve, format, and then send data to Generator though the URL. In the following example, we'll first create a PHP page that retrieves data submitted by a user through an HTML form; then, based on that data, we'll create a small Flash-based weather application. The page will format the data into a Column data source and then send that data to Generator through the URL when calling the Generator template. The Flash movie will consist of a Replicate action on a movie clip that will display weather information for each day of the week.

 Although our example is in PHP, you can use the same basic code for ASP, Cold Fusion, and JSP; only the syntax will differ . You'll find all of the files for this example on the accompanying CD, along with Cold Fusion, ASP, and JSP versions of the code.

> One thing to keep in mind when passing data through the URL to Generator is that some browsers limit the amount of data that can be sent—unfortunately, that amount varies significantly among browsers and browser versions. So, although this doesn't mean you cannot send data through the URL, it does mean that you need to test your application. If everything is processed on the server side, you probably won't have to worry about this limitation; see "The Generator wrapper" later in this chapter for an example of how to do this.

The following code retrieves and formats the data for Generator:

```php
<?php
    define("NUMDAYS", 7);
    $days = array("Monday", "Tuesday", "Wednesday", "Thursday",
                "Friday", "Saturday", "Sunday");
    $graphics = array("Sunny", "Cloudy", "Partly Sunny", "Rain",
                "Snow", "Wind", "none");
```

```php
$message = "Enter scrolling message here";
$messageURL = "";

$dailyHighs = array("85", "82", "87", "87", "80", "81", "89");
$dailyLows = array("62", "63", "60", "59", "65", "68", "62");
$dailyGraphics = array("Sunny", "Cloudy", "Rain", "Sunny",
                        "Cloudy", "Sunny", "Cloudy");
$dailyForecast = array("", "", "", "", "", "", "");

if($submit != "")
{
    $message = $HTTP_POST_VARS['message'];
    $messageURL = $HTTP_POST_VARS['messageURL'];

    for($i = 0; $i < NUMDAYS; $i++)
    {
        $dailyHighs[$i] = $high_[$i];
        $dailyLows[$i] = $low_[$i];
        $dailyGraphics[$i] = $graphic_[$i];
        $dailyForecast[$i] = $forecast_[$i];
    }
}

$dailyData = "day, forecast, high, low, graphic \\n";

for($i = 0; $i < NUMDAYS; $i++)
{
    $dailyData .= "\"" . $days[$i] . "\"" . ",";
    $dailyData .= "\"" . formatForGenerator
                    ($dailyForecast[$i]) . "\"" . ",";
    $dailyData .= "\"" . $dailyHighs[$i] . "\"" . ",";
    $dailyData .= "\"" . $dailyLows[$i] . "\"" . ",";
    $dailyData .= "\"" . $dailyGraphics[$i] . "\"";
    $dailyData .= "\\n";
}
?>
```

Now let's take a closer look at that code to determine precisely how it functions:

The first thing our code does is initialize all of the default values of our data and then store the data within arrays and variables. If this is the first time a user is viewing the page, the data will be sent to the template for use as the default values of the HTML form.

```
$days = array("Monday", "Tuesday", "Wednesday", "Thursday",
              "Friday", "Saturday", "Sunday");
$graphics = array("Sunny", "Cloudy", "Partly Sunny", "Rain",
              "Snow", "Wind", "none");

$message = "Enter scrolling message here";
$messageURL = "";

$dailyHighs = array("85", "82", "87", "87", "80", "81", "89");
$dailyLows = array("62", "63", "60", "59", "65", "68", "62");
$dailyGraphics = array("Sunny", "Cloudy", "Rain", "Sunny",
              "Cloudy", "Sunny", "Cloudy");
$dailyForecast = array("", "", "", "", "", "", "");
```

If we were working on an application that did not require user input from a form, this is where we would gather the data to use in the template. In most cases this information would be retrieved from a database; then, instead of looping through arrays (see the next batch of code), we'd simply loop through the result set. However, we're not using a database example here because we want to concentrate on how to format and use the data for Generator.

Once we set the default values of our data, we'll check to see if the user has submitted data to be used.

```
if($submit != "")
{
    $message =
formatForGenerator($HTTP_POST_VARS['message']);
    $messageURL =
formatForGenerator($HTTP_POST_VARS['messageURL']);

    for($i = 0; $i < NUMDAYS; $i++)
    {
        $dailyHighs[$i] = $high_[$i];
        $dailyLows[$i] = $low_[$i];
        $dailyGraphics[$i] = $graphic_[$i];
```

```
            $dailyForecast[$i] = $forecast_[$i];
        }
    }
```

If the user has submitted data ($submit != ""), we'll place that information into our arrays and variables for later use; if not, we'll simply use the default values that we set above. (If your application does not require user input, this section is not necessary.)

Now that we know which data to send to the Generator template, we need to convert it to Generator Column format: You do this by looping through the data and creating a string variable that contains a data source in a Column format. (If you had retrieved your data from a database, you would loop through the result set instead of the arrays.)

First, we'll create a variable to hold our data source as we build it.

```
$dailyData = "day, forecast, high, low, graphic \\n";
```

Note that we made the data source's initial value equal to the Column Header fields of the data source we were creating. Your Generator template as well as the Generator object you're using will determine the names of your header fields. Generator reads the "\n" (PHP removes the first "\") at the end of the line as a line return, and uses it to determine that the row has ended.

We're now ready to loop through our data and build the data source, looping once for each day of the week. If your data is contained in a result set, you will loop until you reach the end of the result set.

```
for($i = 0; $i < NUMDAYS; $i++)
{
    $dailyData .= "\"" . $days[$i] . "\"" . ",";
    $dailyData .= "\"" . formatForGenerator
                   ($dailyForecast[$i]) . "\"" . ",";
    $dailyData .= "\"" . $dailyHighs[$i] . "\"" . ",";
    $dailyData .= "\"" . $dailyLows[$i] . "\"" . ",";
    $dailyData .= "\"" . $dailyGraphics[$i] . "\"";
    $dailyData .= "\\n";
}
```

In PHP, the $dailyData .= "new data" code adds the data on the right to the data contained in the variable on the left.

Appending data to a variable

PHP/Perl	`dailyData .= "new data here";`
Java/JSP (without StringBuffer)	`dailyData += "new data here";`
Java/JSP (using StringBuffer)	`StringBuffer dailyData = new StringBuffer();` `dailyData.append("new data here");`
ASP	`dailyData = dailyData & "new data here"`
Cold Fusion	`<cfset dailyData = dailyData & "new data here">`

This basically adds "new data here" to the end of whatever the variable $dailyData currently equals, and then copies the value back into $dailyData.

Note that we've enclosed all of the values in the data source in double quotes: This allows us to use commas and line returns within our data. As a general rule, you should always surround your data with double quotes—unless you're certain that commas or line returns cannot be inserted into that data. For example, both the day and daily graphic values come from a Select box, where the user can only choose from a predefined list of values. Because users cannot type in their own values, you would be safe not enclosing those values in double quotes.

Also notice that we've inserted a comma after every value outside the double quotes. Generator will use this comma to determine the end of the current set of data. If you place the comma inside the double quotes, Generator will see the comma as part of the data and consequently not know when to move to the next item of data.

The $dailyForecast[] variable is passed to the formatForGenerator() method before its value is added to the data source. The formatForGenerator() method formats the string for Generator, escaping any characters that might confuse Generator. Here's the code for that method:

```
function formatForGenerator($string)
{
    $tempString = str_replace("\\", "\\\\", $string);
    return str_replace("\"", "\\\"", $tempString);
}
```

Basically, this method searches the string for double quotes (") and back-slashes (\); if it finds either, it places a backslash in front of the character. However, the above example's use of backslashes is a bit confusing: Because the backslash also serves as the escape character for PHP (and Perl and Java/JSP), we have to escape the backslash that is escaping this character—thus, the multiple backslash characters above. First PHP will remove one of them; then Generator will remove one of them, then—voila!—the character we wish to see will be displayed!

In this example, the function is included within the PHP page. If you were using Java or JSP, you would probably want to create a Generator utility class to contain this method. If, on the other hand, you were using Cold Fusion, you would use a custom tag. All of these files are included on the CD-ROM.

When the loop has finished executing, the `$dailyData` variable will contain our entire data source. We now have three variables that we will pass to Generator.

- `$dailyData` = Contains a Generator column data source that will be used by a Replicate action in the Generator template.

- `$message` = The message that will scroll across the bottom of the template.

- `$messageURL` = The URL where the user will be taken when he or she clicks the scrolling message.

Two steps remain: First, since we're sending the data through the URL, we must URL-encode the data. Second, we need to create the string that calls the Generator template and passes the data to it. We can do both simultaneously.

Let's take a look at the relevant portion of the HTML code that calls the Generator template and displays the resulting Flash movie:

```
weather.swt?message=<?php
print(urlencode($message))?>&messageURL=<?php
print(urlencode($messageURL))?>&dailyData=<?php
print(urlencode($dailyData))?>
```

This snippet of code is contained within the HTML tags required to display whatever media Generator creates. If the file being generated is a Flash movie, the code will be contained within OBJECT and EMBED tags; if it's an image, it will be included within IMG tags.

The name of our Generator template is weather.swt. The question mark ("?") following our template name in the above example signifies that we're sending data (in name/value pairs) along with the template name. An ampersand ("&") separates each name/value pair. Finally, we print out the values of our data. The data will be accessible within the Generator template by the name defined in the URL.

The urlencode() method is used in PHP to URL-encode the string passed to it. We pass all of our data to this method and then print the URL-encoded data out on the URL. Note that we are only encoding the data, not the entire URL string. If you encode the entire string, your URL will not pass the correct data.

How to URL-encode data in different languages

PHP	urlencode(String);
Java/JSP	java.net.URLEncoder.encode(String);
ASP	Server.URLEncode(String)
Cold Fusion	URLEncodedFormat(String)
Perl/CGI	use CGI; CGI::escape(String);

To Generator, the resulting data source in the $dailyData variable looks like this:

```
day, forecast, high, low, graphic
"Monday","","85","62","Sunny"
"Tuesday","","82","63","Cloudy"
"Wednesday","","87","60","Rain"
"Thursday","","87","59","Sunny"
"Friday","","80","65","Cloudy"
"Saturday","","81","68","Sunny"
"Sunday","","89","62","Cloudy"
```

Inside the FLA there's a Replicate action whose data source will be filled in by the contents of the $dailyData variable. You do this by placing a Generator variable preceded by a pound sign (#) into the replicate's data source section:

```
#{dailyData}
```

The above is replaced by the contents of the $dailyData variable that's passed in. The pound sign (#) preceding the Generator variable tells Generator that the variable contains the data source's data, not just a path to a file or URL containing the data source.

Let's take another look at the three steps that our code carries out:

1. Retrieves data. Our code does this in two ways: On a user's first visit to the page, it creates arrays with default values; on subsequent visits, it retrieves the user-submitted data from the form.

2. Formats data for Generator. This happens when the code loops through the data and creates the column data source for Generator.

3. Sends data to Generator: This occurs when we create the URL that calls the Generator template. We send the data, in Name/Value format, through the URL to Generator.

To recap: The user requests the PHP page. The page formats some hard-coded data into a Generator Column data source. A URL pointing to the Generator template and containing the Generator data is then constructed. The page is then sent to the browser, which requests Generator for the template, passing the data through the URL. Generator processes the template and returns a Flash movie to the browser, which is then displayed to the user.

MIDDLEWARE AS A GENERATOR DATA SOURCE

Generator can also point to a middleware page as its data source. The middleware then collects, formats, and returns the data to Generator in either Column or Name/Value format—an extremely flexible technique since it allows you to reap the benefits of middleware while avoiding the problems of sending data through the URL.

You retrieve and format data in almost exactly the same fashion as in the previous example—with two differences: First, the resulting page will return a Generator data source; it will not be intermixed with HTML. (Since we'll be returning plain text, not HTML, we'll need to set the correct content type.) Second, Generator will retrieve the data from the page (instead of having the data sent to it through the URL). In essence, Generator will act just as if it were loading a text file for its data source.

The following simple example uses almost exactly the same FLA as we used in the previous section. The middleware is an ASP page that contains some hard-coded arrays of data. Our only change to the FLA will be to alter the replicate's data source from a variable to point directly to the ASP page. This is because we're no longer passing the data source to Generator but rather telling Generator to retrieve the data source. The ASP page will then format the data and return a Generator Column data source.

We've included JSP, Java servlet, PHP, and Cold Fusion versions of the code on the accompanying CD-ROM.

Here's the code for our ASP page:

```
<%
    option explicit

    Const NUMDAYS = 7

    dim days(7), graphics(7), dailyHighs(7), dailyLows(7),
    dailyGraphics(7), dailyForecast(7)

    days(0) = "Monday"
    days(1) = "Tuesday"
    days(2) = "Wednesday"
    days(3) = "Thursday"
    days(4) = "Friday"
    days(5) = "Saturday"
    days(6) = "Sunday"

    graphics(0) = "Sunny"
    graphics(1) = "Cloudy"
    graphics(2) = "Partly Sunny"
    graphics(3) = "Rain"
    graphics(4) = "Snow"
    graphics(5) = "Wind"
    graphics(6) = "none"
```

```
dailyHighs(0) = "85"
dailyHighs(1) = "82"
dailyHighs(2) = "87"
dailyHighs(3) = "87"
dailyHighs(4) = "80"
dailyHighs(5) = "81"
dailyHighs(6) = "89"

dailyLows(0) = "62"
dailyLows(1) = "63"
dailyLows(2) = "60"
dailyLows(3) = "59"
dailyLows(4) = "65"
dailyLows(5) = "68"
dailyLows(6) = "62"

dailyGraphics(0) = "Sunny"
dailyGraphics(1) = "Cloudy"
dailyGraphics(2) = "Rain"
dailyGraphics(3) = "Sunny"
dailyGraphics(4) = "Cloudy"
dailyGraphics(5) = "Sunny"
dailyGraphics(6) = "Cloudy"

dailyForecast(0) = "Sunny and clear with temperatures
                   rising. Highs in the mid 80s."
dailyForecast(1) = "Sunny early then becoming cloudy. Highs
                   in the lower 80s."
dailyForecast(2) = "Rain with highs in the upper 80s."
dailyForecast(3) = "Cloudy early, becoming sunny by midday.
                   Highs in the upper 80s."
dailyForecast(4) = "Clouds moving in early with temperatures
                   in the lower 80s."
dailyForecast(5) = "Sunny and pleasant. Highs in lower 80s."
dailyForecast(6) = "Cloudy and very muggy. Highs near 90."

dim dailyData
dailyData = "day, forecast, high, low, graphic" & VBCRLF
```

```
dim j
for j = 0 to (NUMDAYS - 1)
    dailyData = dailyData & chr(34) & days(j) & chr(34) & ","
    dailyData = dailyData & chr(34) &
                formatForGenerator(dailyForecast(j)) &
                chr(34) & ","
    dailyData = dailyData & chr(34) & dailyHighs(j) &
                chr(34) & ","
    dailyData = dailyData & chr(34) & dailyLows(j) & chr(34)
                & ","
    dailyData = dailyData & chr(34) & dailyGraphics(j) &
                chr(34)
    dailyData = dailyData & VBCRLF
next

response.contentType = "text/plain"

response.write(dailyData)
%>
```

As you can see, most of the code simply defines the values of the arrays, which contain the weather data for each day of the week. Although you would normally retrieve the code from a database (or from another data source) rather than hard-code it in the file as we have done here, hard-coding allowed us to concentrate on how to format the data for Generator.

Our first section of code is straightforward; we simply created a number of arrays with data for each day of the week.

```
dim days(7), graphics(7), dailyHighs(7), dailyLows(7),
dailyGraphics(7), dailyForecast(7)

days(0) = "Monday"
days(1) = "Tuesday"
days(2) = "Wednesday"
days(3) = "Thursday"
days(4) = "Friday"
days(5) = "Saturday"
days(6) = "Sunday"
```

```
graphics(0) = "Sunny"
graphics(1) = "Cloudy"
graphics(2) = "Partly Sunny"
graphics(3) = "Rain"
graphics(4) = "Snow"
graphics(5) = "Wind"
graphics(6) = "none"

dailyHighs(0) = "85"
dailyHighs(1) = "82"
dailyHighs(2) = "87"
dailyHighs(3) = "87"
dailyHighs(4) = "80"
dailyHighs(5) = "81"
dailyHighs(6) = "89"

dailyLows(0) = "62"
dailyLows(1) = "63"
dailyLows(2) = "60"
dailyLows(3) = "59"
dailyLows(4) = "65"
dailyLows(5) = "68"
dailyLows(6) = "62"

dailyGraphics(0) = "Sunny"
dailyGraphics(1) = "Cloudy"
dailyGraphics(2) = "Rain"
dailyGraphics(3) = "Sunny"
dailyGraphics(4) = "Cloudy"
dailyGraphics(5) = "Sunny"
dailyGraphics(6) = "Cloudy"

dailyForecast(0) = "Sunny and clear with temperatures
                    rising. Highs in the mid 80s."
dailyForecast(1) = "Sunny early then becoming cloudy. Highs
                    in the lower 80s."
dailyForecast(2) = "Rain with highs in the upper 80s."
```

```
dailyForecast(3) = "Cloudy early, becoming sunny by midday.
                    Highs in the upper 80s."
dailyForecast(4) = "Clouds moving in early with temperatures
                    in the lower 80s."
dailyForecast(5) = "Sunny and pleasant. Highs in lower 80s."
dailyForecast(6) = "Cloudy and very muggy. Highs near 90."
```

The only difference between this data and that used in the previous section's example is that in the prior example we initialized default values whereas here we've initialized the values that will be used every time.

Now that we have our data, we need to loop through and convert it into a format that Generator can use. Once again, we'll do so in the same way as in the previous section.

```
dim dailyData
dailyData = "day, forecast, high, low, graphic" & VBCRLF

dim j
for j = 0 to (NUMDAYS - 1)
    dailyData = dailyData & chr(34) & days(j) & chr(34) & ","
    dailyData = dailyData & chr(34) &
                formatForGenerator(dailyForecast(j)) &
                chr(34) & ","
    dailyData = dailyData & chr(34) & dailyHighs(j) &
                chr(34) & ","
    dailyData = dailyData & chr(34) & dailyLows(j) & chr(34)
                & ","
    dailyData = dailyData & chr(34) & dailyGraphics(j) &
                chr(34)
    dailyData = dailyData & VBCRLF
next
```

As you can see from the above, we created a variable (dailyData) to hold our data source as we built it. The first data we placed in the variable comprised the column headers. We then looped through the data arrays (once for each day of the week) and began to build our data source. We wrapped all of our data in double quotes and passed the dailyForecast data through the formatForGenerator()method—not really necessary in this example since we already knew our data's values; however, we did so here to demonstrate how and where you would call the method. Finally, we inserted a comma after each value.

If you look closely, you'll notice one difference between the code in this loop and that from the loop in the previous section: In the previous example, we ended each row of data with a \n, which Generator reads as a line return. In this example, however, we inserted an actual line return (in ASP, you can do this with the VB Script constant VBCRLF). The main reason we did this is that it makes it easier to debug the code because you can connect to the page via a Web browser and view a well-formatted data source. While you *can* end each row of data by sending \n to Generator, as in the previous section, it will be more difficult to view the data source through a Web browser this way.

How to add a line return using middleware

Java/JSP/PHP/Perl	\n
ASP	VBCRLF, chr(10)
Cold Fusion	chr(10)

The formatForGenerator() method is the same as in the previous section.

```
function formatForGenerator(data)
    data = replace(data, "\", "\\")
    formatForGenerator = replace(data, chr(34), "\" &
                            chr(34))
end function
```

The above method places a backslash in front of double quotes (chr(34)) and backslashes.

Once the loop has executed, we have a variable (dailyData) containing our entire Generator Column data source. All we have to do now is write that data source to whatever requested the ASP page (in most cases this will be either a Web browser or Generator). However, first we have to set the content type so that whatever is calling the ASP page knows that we are sending back plain text rather than HTML.

```
response.contentType = "text/plain"
```

Setting content type in middleware

ASP	`response.contentType = "text/plain"`
Java servlet	`javax.servlet.http.HttpServletResponse.setContentType ("text/plain");`
JSP	`<%@ page contentType="text/plain"%>`
PHP	`Header("Content-Type:text/plain");`
Cold Fusion	`<cfcontent type="text/plain" />`
Perl/CGI	`print "ContentType:text/plain\n";`

Once we've set the content type, we then write out the contents of our data source.

`response.write(dailyData)`

If you open this page with your Web browser, you should get the following content:

```
day, forecast, high, low, graphic
"Monday","Sunny and clear with temperatures rising. Highs in the
        mid 80s.","85","62","Sunny"
"Tuesday","Sunny early then becoming cloudy. Highs in the lower
        80s.","82","63","Cloudy"
"Wednesday","Rain with highs in the upper 80s.","87","60","Rain"
"Thursday","Cloudy early, becoming sunny by midday. Highs in the
        upper 80s.","87","59","Sunny"
"Friday","Clouds moving in early with temperatures in the lower
        80s.","80","65","Cloudy"
"Saturday","Sunny and pleasant. Highs in lower
        80s.","81","68","Sunny"
"Sunday","Cloudy and very muggy. Highs near
        90.","89","62","Cloudy"
```

Generator treats this data source the same way it treats data sources from text files: It simply loads the data and then uses it on whatever object is calling the data source (in this case, a Replicate action).

This powerful (though simple) technique allows you to leverage the capabilities of whatever middleware you're using to fully extend Generator.

The code used in this technique carries out the same steps we outlined at the beginning of this chapter.

1. Retrieves data: In this case the data is already present in the form of hard-coded arrays.

2. Formats data for Generator: Just as in the previous section, this technique loops through and creates a Generator Column data source, escaping whatever characters Generator requires to be escaped.

3. Sends to Generator: We write out our newly created data source to whatever called the ASP page (which in most cases will be Generator).

THE GENERATOR WRAPPER

The Generator wrapper is a Java servlet that handles requests for one or more Generator templates. Instead of having your Web page or application call Generator and a Generator template directly, it will call the Generator wrapper, which in turn will call Generator. This gives you more control and flexibility over the entire process—from passing data to Generator to controlling the output of the file being dynamically created.

Although you can write the wrapper in any language that allows you to manipulate a file's raw bytes, most people use Java servlets because they make it easy to work with input and output streams in Java.

To demonstrate how the Generator wrapper works, we will once again build a small weather application using the same FLA we employed in the first section of this chapter. However, instead of having the Web page load the Generator template, the application will point to our Generator wrapper servlet, which will then format our weather data into a Column data source and pass it to the Generator template via the URL.

Because both Generator and the Generator wrapper will be executed on the server side, we don't need to worry about the amount of data being sent through the URL. Generator will take the template (and its data) and return a Flash movie to the servlet (not the browser). Once the Generator wrapper receives the bytes of the generated Flash movie, we'll send the file back to the browser (to be displayed to the user) and then enter the size of the generated file into a log file.

Take a look at the following examples of the functionality you can add to Generator by using this powerful technique:

Input

- Large, multiple data sources can be sent through the URL.
- Data can be received from new sources (for example, XML).
- Data can be filtered before it's sent to Generator.
- Frequent caching can be employed to improve performance.
- Data can be posted to the servlet.

Output

- Frequently used Generator templates can be cached to improve performance.
- Information about the generated media (such as file size) can be logged.
- Media can be output to multiple places—for example, to the browser (for display) or saved to a file system or cache.
- New types of output are allowed (for example, WBMP).
- Offline-only Generator media (Mac and PC executables, image maps, etc.) can be created in online mode.
- Different templates can be used, depending on request types. (You could, for example, send one template for requests coming from Pocket PCs, one for Palm Pilots, and one for Web browsers.)

These are just a few examples, but they should give you a good idea of how flexible and useful this technique can be.

Here's the code for our GeneratorWrapper servlet:

```
package com.markme.generator.generatorwrapper;

import javax.servlet.http.HttpServlet;
import javax.servlet.http.HttpServletRequest;
import javax.servlet.http.HttpServletResponse;

import javax.servlet.ServletOutputStream;
import javax.servlet.ServletException;
```

```java
import java.io.IOException;
import java.io.File;
import java.io.InputStream;
import java.io.BufferedInputStream;
import java.io.ByteArrayOutputStream;
import java.io.FileWriter;

import java.net.URL;
import java.net.URLEncoder;

import java.text.DateFormat;
import java.util.Date;


public class GeneratorWrapper extends HttpServlet
{

    private String templateURL;
    private String logFilePath;
    public static final int NUMDAYS = 7;

    public void init()
    {
        templateURL = "http://localhost/book/weather.swt";
        logFilePath = "c:\\file_sizes.log";
    }

    public void doGet(HttpServletRequest request,
                      HttpServletResponse response)
        throws ServletException, IOException
    {

        String message = "Enter scrolling message here";
        String messageURL = "";

            String[] days = {"Monday", "Tuesday", "Wednesday",
                             "Thursday", "Friday", "Saturday",
                             "Sunday"};
```

```
        String dailyHighs[] = {"85", "82", "87", "87", "80",
                               "81", "89"};
        String dailyLows[] = {"62", "63", "60", "59", "65",
                              "68", "62"};

        String dailyGraphics[] = {"Sunny", "Cloudy", "Rain",
                                  "Sunny", "Cloudy", "Sunny",
                                  "Cloudy"};

        String[] dailyForecast = new String[NUMDAYS];
        dailyForecast[0] = "Sunny and clear with temperatures
                           rising. Highs in the mid 80s.";
        dailyForecast[1] = "Sunny early then becoming cloudy.
                           Highs in the lower 80s.";
        dailyForecast[2] = "Rain with highs in the upper
                           80s.";
        dailyForecast[3] = "Cloudy early, becoming sunny by
                           midday. Highs in the upper 80s.";
        dailyForecast[4] = "Clouds moving in early with
                           temperatures in the lower 80s.";
        dailyForecast[5] = "Sunny and pleasant. Highs in
                           lower 80s.";
        dailyForecast[6] = "Cloudy and very muggy. Highs
                           near 90.";

        StringBuffer sb = new StringBuffer("day, forecast,
                          high, low, graphic \\n");

        for(int i = 0; i < NUMDAYS; i++)
{
sb.append("\"" + days[i] + "\"" + ",");
sb.append("\"" + formatForGenerator(dailyForecast[i])
         + "\"" + ",");
sb.append("\"" + dailyHighs[i] + "\"" + ",");
sb.append("\"" + dailyLows[i] + "\"" + ",");
sb.append("\"" + dailyGraphics[i] + "\"");
sb.append("\\n");
}
```

```java
String queryString = templateURL + "?dailyData=" +
URLEncoder.encode(sb.toString()) + "&message=" +
URLEncoder.encode(message) + "&messageURL=" +
URLEncoder.encode(messageURL);

        URL template = new URL(queryString);

InputStream in = new
BufferedInputStream(template.openStream());

response.setContentType("application/x-shockwave-flash");
ServletOutputStream toBrowser = response.getOutputStream();

byte[] readBuffer = new byte[1024];
ByteArrayOutputStream out = new ByteArrayOutputStream();

for (int i = in.read(readBuffer); i != -1; i =
in.read(readBuffer))
{
    out.write(readBuffer, 0, i);
}
byte[] fileBytes = out.toByteArray();

int fileSize = fileBytes.length;

toBrowser.write(fileBytes, 0, fileSize);
toBrowser.close();

        File log = new File(logFilePath);

        log.createNewFile();

        FileWriter fo = new FileWriter(log.getAbsolutePath(),
                                true);

        fo.write(this.getTimeStamp() + " : file size : " +
                fileSize + "\n");
        fo.close();
```

```java
    }

    private String formatForGenerator(String string)
    {
        char[] charArray = string.toCharArray();
        StringBuffer tempBuffer = new StringBuffer();

        for(int i = 0; i < charArray.length; i++)
        {
        if(charArray[i] == '\"')
        {
            tempBuffer.append("\\\"");
        }
        else if(charArray[i] == '\\')
        {
            tempBuffer.append("\\\\");
        }
        else
        {
            tempBuffer.append(charArray[i]);
        }
        }
        return tempBuffer.toString();
    }

    private String getTimeStamp()
    {
        Date now = new Date();

        DateFormat time = DateFormat.getTimeInstance
                        (DateFormat.MEDIUM);
        DateFormat date = DateFormat.getDateInstance
                        (DateFormat.SHORT);
        return date.format(now) + " " + time.format(now);
    }
}
```

The first section of code we'll examine is the init() method:

```
public void init()
{
    templateURL = "http://localhost/book/weather.swt";
    logFilePath = "c:\\file_sizes.log";
}
```

Called the first time the servlet is loaded, this method will initialize two variables: The variable templateURL contains the entire path to the Generator template used by our servlet, and logFilePath points to the log file to which we will be writing the size of the generated file. As a rule, you shouldn't hard-code file paths within your servlet code: Not only does it become difficult to change paths, it also makes your code platform specific. Normally, these values would be passed in through the Servlet Context or retrieved from a config file. We're hard-coding the values here so that we can concentrate on the Generator-related code.

The servlet in this example only works with one Generator template—the template defined in the templateURL variable. In most cases this will be fine since you can create servlets that are very specific to the template they work with. However, if you wanted to create a more generic Generator wrapper, you could pass in the template to be used through the URL when you call the servlet. If you were to store all of the templates in the same directory, you could use code similar to that below to dynamically determine which template to use.

```
String templateBase = "http://localhost/templates/";
String template = request.getParameter("template");
String templateURL = templateBase + template;
```

You would probably want to check and make sure that the template name was actually passed in.

This approach is useful if you want all of your templates to pass through the servlet. An even more generic approach would be to instruct your servlet engine to pass all requests for Generator templates to the Generator wrapper, which would then override some objects and become more tightly integrated with the Generator server.

Although we don't cover the above more advanced and complicated technique here, we do include an example—along with complete commented source code—on the CD-ROM in the Chapter 8 folder.

When the servlet is called from a Web browser, the doGet() method is automatically run. If you want to be able to post to the servlet, you need to put your code inside the doPost() method.

The first thing the doGet() method does is create some arrays and variables that will be used as the data for the data source. Since this is the same code we used in the previous examples, we won't go over it again here. It is, however, important to reiterate that you would normally retrieve the data from a more dynamic data source such as a database or XML.

After we initialize our data, we'll loop through it and create a Generator Column data source.

```java
StringBuffer sb = new StringBuffer("day, forecast, high, low,
                                    graphic \\n");

for(int i = 0; i < NUMDAYS; i++)
{
    sb.append("\"" + days[i] + "\"" + ",");
    sb.append("\"" + formatForGenerator(dailyForecast[i]) + "\""
            + ",");
    sb.append("\"" + dailyHighs[i] + "\"" + ",");
    sb.append("\"" + dailyLows[i] + "\"" + ",");
    sb.append("\"" + dailyGraphics[i] + "\"");
    sb.append("\\n");
}
```

This is the same code we used in previous examples. Notice, however, that we ended each line by sending a \n to Generator (Java removes the first backslash). Again, Generator will use the \n to determine when it has reached the end of each row of data.

When this loop has finished executing, we have a StringBuffer that contains our entire Column data source. We can now construct the URL that points to and passes our data to the Generator template. First, we'll convert the StringBuffer into a string and URL-encode it. Then, we'll add this URL-encoded string to the end of the templateURL variable, along with the message and messageURL name/value pairs initialized above.

```java
String queryString = templateURL + "?dailyData=" +
                    URLEncoder.encode(sb.toString()) +
                    "&message=" + URLEncoder.encode(message) +
                    "&messageURL=" +
                    URLEncoder.encode(messageURL);
```

The queryString variable now contains the entire URL pointing to the Generator template that we will be using.

The URL in the queryString object is then used to create a Java URL object.

```
URL template = new URL(queryString);
```

```
InputStream in = new
BufferedInputStream(template.openStream());
```

Calling the openStream() method on the URL object makes the request for the Generator template, passing along the data for the template. We store the media sent back from Generator in a BufferedInputStream object. We can then read the bytes of the generated media from the BufferedInputStream.

Before the bytes can be written to the browser, however, we need to do a couple things: First, we must tell the browser what type of file we're sending it (in our case, a Flash movie); we do this by setting the content type for our response.

```
response.setContentType("application/x-shockwave-flash");
```

Of course, if you're requesting a media type other than Generator, you'll have to set the appropriate content type for that media (see table below).

Content types for Generator media

Flash	application/x-shockwave-flash
JPEG	image/jpeg
GIF	image/gif
PNG	image/png
QuickTime	video/quicktime

Next, we need to get an output stream from the Response object so that the bytes of the Flash movie can be sent back to the browser.

```
ServletOutputStream toBrowser = response.getOutputStream();
```

We should now be able to read all of the bytes of the media created by Generator. Next, we'll create a ByteArrayOutputStream object to store the bytes as we read them.

Thanks to Christian Cantrell (http://www.sparkshop.com) for this section of code.

```
byte[] readBuffer = new byte[1024];
ByteArrayOutputStream out = new ByteArrayOutputStream();

for (int i = in.read(readBuffer); i != -1;
    i = in.read(readBuffer))
{
    out.write(readBuffer, 0, i);
}
byte[] fileBytes = out.toByteArray();
```

This code loops through the file's bytes and stores them in a ByteArrayOutputStream object. Once we've read all of the bytes of the generated media and stored them in the ByteArrayOutputStream, we'll get a byte array of the bytes from the ByteArrayOutputStream (`out.toByteArray()`); we'll store that array in the `fileBytes` variable.

We'll then use the byte array to get the file's size and to write the bytes to the browser. First, we'll get the size and store it in the `fileSize` variable.

```
int fileSize = bigBytes.length;
```

Then, we'll send the file's bytes to the browser (where they're to be displayed) by writing them to the ServletOutputStream.

```
toBrowser.write(bigBytes, 0, fileSize);
toBrowser.close();
```

Once we've written all of the bytes to the browser, we'll close the ServletOutputStream (`toBrowser.close()`). At this point, the Generator-created Flash movie will have been sent back to the browser (or whatever called the Servlet).

All that's left to do now is log the file size of the media created by Generator—an easy task since we've stored the file's size in the `fileSize` variable.

First we'll create a File object that points to the log file we defined in the `init()` method.

```
File log = new File(logFilePath);
log.createNewFile();
```

Next, we'll call the `createFile()` method on the File object. This method will create the log file if none exists. (It does nothing if a log file already exists.)

All that's left to do now is create a FileWriter object to write to our log file. We'll pass a True value to the constructor so that when we write to the file, it will append the new data to the end of the existing file (as opposed to overwriting the existing entries).

```
FileWriter fo = new FileWriter(log.getAbsolutePath(), true);
fo.write(getTimeStamp() + " : file size : " + fileSize +
        "\r\n");
fo.close();
```

Finally, we'll call the Write method on the FileWriter object and pass our log entry to be written to the log file.

The log entry consists of four items. First we call the `getTimeStamp()` method that is contained within our Servlet. This simply returns the current date and time on the server. Next we add " : file size : " to the string to make the log easier to read. After that we print out the size of the file that is stored in the `fileSize` variable. Finally, we add a line return (\r\n) at the end of our entry so each log entry will be contained on its own line. The write method writes this entire string to the log file. Once we have written the log entry to the log file, we close the connection to the file and the Servlet is finished.

POINTS TO REMEMBER

- Middleware is any programming language that can be used to manipulate and format data, and then make that data available to Generator. Examples of middleware include JSP, ASP, PHP, and Cold Fusion, as well as client-side languages such as JavaScript, Flash 4 and 5, and ActionScript.

- Generator and middleware are common companions in most data-driven Web applications.

- Generator uses middleware as the conduit for passing data through the URL string. It also uses middleware directly as a data source in a Generator-friendly way.

- Generator uses middleware to retrieve, format, and send data.

- The Generator wrapper is a Java servlet that handles requests for one or more Generator templates. Instead of having your Web page or application call Generator and a Generator template directly, it can call the Generator wrapper, which in turn calls Generator.

- The Generator wrapper gives you control and flexibility over the entire process—from passing data to Generator to controlling the output of the file being dynamically created.

PART 3:
DEPLOYMENT

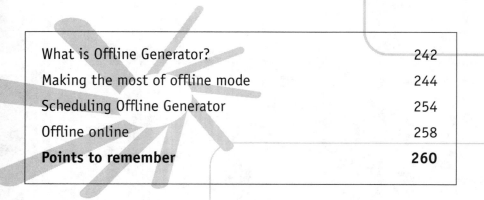

CHAPTER 9

GENERATOR OFFLINE

UP TO NOW, WE HAVE BEEN FOCUSING ON HOW TO USE GENERATOR IN ONLINE mode, where it is called from a Web server. However, Generator can also be used in offline mode in which it is run from the command line. By using the offline component of Generator, developers can process templates without burdening their Web servers or batching content on a regular basis. In this chapter, we'll explore the various ways you can put offline mode to use, as well as show you how to use Offline Generator in an online fashion.

WHAT IS OFFLINE GENERATOR?

Offline mode relies on the executable component of Generator, called *Generate*. For PC users, this is basically a DOS application (generate.exe) that can run directly from the MS-DOS command line or from a batch or scripting environment such as an MS-DOS batch file.

In both the Enterprise and Developer editions, Offline Generator is included as part of the application. Although the Developer edition can serve Web requests (one at a time), it's typically used in offline mode. In this mode, a user or batch process invokes the Generate application; Generator loads the template, reads the data source, and merges media; and the Generate application then returns the file—in SWF, GIF, PNG, JPEG, or QuickTime format—to the file system. The Web server can then serve this output file just as it would any other file.

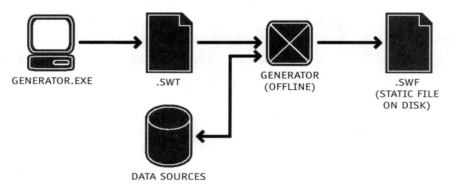

GENERATOR.EXE   .SWT   GENERATOR (OFFLINE)   .SWF (STATIC FILE ON DISK)

DATA SOURCES

Offline everywhere

Let's set up our system so that at any DOS prompt, we can invoke Generator. (This will come in handy when creating batch files for a PC environment since it will keep those files smaller, and thus more manageable.) To do so, Windows 98 and 2000 users would specify the Generator path in your system Path in Properties > (Advanced, Win 2000 users only) > Environment Variables of My Computer and then set the environmental variables there as well. In the Prompt field, they would then enter the following:

```
C:\Program Files\Macromedia\Generator 2;
```

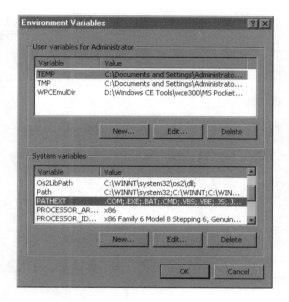

(Or wherever else Generator resides on your machine.)

To test your work, open a DOS command prompt. (The Program files usually include a link to the command prompt; if not, type cmd in the Run dialog in the Windows Start menu.)

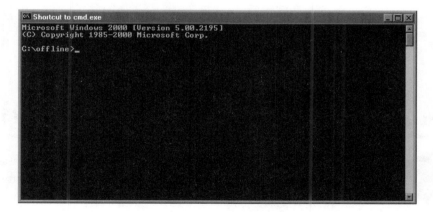

After you get to a DOS prompt, type generate. Since we did not pass any command-line switches, you'll see a list of the available switches.

```
Shortcut to cmd.exe                                             _ □ ×
Microsoft Windows 2000 [Version 5.00.2195]
(C) Copyright 1985-2000 Microsoft Corp.

C:\offline>generate
Macromedia Generator Version 2.1.0g6 Developer Edition - August 28, 2000
Copyright (C) Macromedia 2000. All rights reserved.

Usage: generate [options] <filename.swt>

Options:
    -help                     displays usage text
    -swf <filename.swf>       output a Flash movie
    -gif <filename.gif>       output a GIF movie
    -png <filename.png>       output a PNG image
    -qtm <filename.mov>       output a Quicktime 4.0 movie
    -jpg <filename.jpg>       output a JPEG image
    -txt <filename.txt>       output text within the movie
    -smap <filename.map>      output a server-side image map
    -cmap <filename.map>      output a client-side image map
    -cmapname <name>          set client-side image map tag name
    -xwin32 <filename.exe>    output a Win32 projector
    -xmacppc <filename.hqx>   output a Mac PPC projector
    -debug <1|2|3>            specifies the debug log level
    -log <filename.txt>       specifies the debug log file
    -param <name> <value>     specifies a named parameter
    -pngBitDepth <8|24|32>    specifies the bit depth with a PNG
                              image should be rendered
    -defaultsize <w> <h>      specifies the default width and height
                              of outputted images
    -embed "<message>"        inserts the specified message into the
                              flash movie
    -font <path>              specifies the location to search for
                              Generator external font files.
Filename:
    Flash template file (.swt) to process.

C:\offline>_
```

To automate testing and production, it's a good idea to create a shortcut to CMD.exe and specify a working directory to start in. For our examples we've created a directory on the C drive called Offline.

> Unlike the authoring extensions, the offline mode of Generator does not run on Macs.

MAKING THE MOST OF OFFLINE MODE

Now that we've set up our environment for offline processing, let's create some Offline Generator content. The first thing to do is move all of the files from the CD's Chapter 9 folder into a folder on your computer. Then from your DOS prompt change to the folder which contains your files.

The examples here are derived from the Flash-based charting and advanced data-source example we created in Chapter 6. If you've skipped ahead, though, it's OK: We've included the .swt so that you can dive right into offline processing.

Creating Flash movies

The SWF format is the most popular form of Generator output. To generate a Flash movie (SWF), you must use the -swf option to tell Generate what type of file you want. The following command creates the Flash movie yahoo.swf from the template yahoo.swt:

```
generate -swf yahoo.swf yahoo.swt
```

If you don't set your system to use "generate from any command prompt," you'll need to add the Generate location as well as the output location:

```
C:\progra~1\Genera~1\generate -swf
```

If you do not run the command from the same directory that contains your templates, then you will have to use an absolute path to the templates.

When you open the newly created .swf, you should see the chart information that resides in the data1.txt, data2.txt, and the datasource.txt text files.

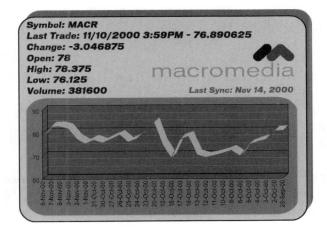

To send to standard output (useful when employing CGI scripts), use the following command:

```
generate -swf - yahoo.swt
```

The second hyphen (-) indicates that the movie should be written not to file but to standard output.

If you try this in a DOS environment, the entire .swf will be written to the DOS prompt—interesting but not very useful. Use this option only when you need to output the generated file to standard output.

Creating GIF, JPEG, PNG, and QuickTime files

Using the same template, we're now going to create GIF, JPEG, PNG, and QuickTime files. As you might imagine, once you've created the template, you don't need to republish within Flash. In fact, you can create all sorts of output formats without even having Flash installed (which is why you can create Flash on Linux and Solaris systems).

To create a GIF, use the following syntax:

```
generate -gif yahoo.gif yahoo.swt
```

To create a JPEG, use the following syntax:

```
generate -jpg yahoo.jpg yahoo.swt
```

To create a PNG, use the following syntax:

```
generate -png yahoo.png yahoo.swt
```

If you need to specify the bit depth of the PNG file use the –pngBitDepth option.

```
generate -png yahoo.png yahoo.swt –pngBitDepth 24
```

Valid values for the option include 8, 24, and 32.

To create a QuickTime file, use the following syntax:

```
generate -qtm yahoo.mov yahoo.swt
```

The compression parameters and image settings are stored inside the template when you publish your movie. However, if you need to dynamically specify them then you can use the following offline options:

```
-defaultSize [width] [height]
```

This allows you to specify the height and width of the generated file.

```
generate -png yahoo.png yahoo.swt –defaultSize 100 150
```

```
-bgColor [color]
```

This allows you to specify the background color of the generated file. Valid values include Web-safe color names (blue), Web hexadecimal values (#000000), and regular hexadecimal values (0x000000).

```
generate -png yahoo.png yahoo.swt –bgColor blue
```

```
-exactfit
```

This makes the generated image exactly fit the dimensions defined within the template. If the ratios of the image and of the template are not the same, then the image may be distorted. The property does not take parameter.

```
-font
```

This specifies the directory in which Generator will search for any external font files used in the template.

```
generate -png yahoo.png yahoo.swt –font c:\fonts
```

Extracting text from movies

One of offline mode's neatest tricks is its ability to extract all of a movie's text and insert it into a text file. This is especially handy since Flash won't let you index its text for use with search engines. However, if you use Generator's offline mode to collect all the text from a movie, you can then place that text as a comment in an HTML file or include it in your meta tags.

To create a text file containing a movie's text, use the -txt option.

The following command creates text:

```
generate -txt yahoo.txt yahoo.swt
```

Keep in mind that the above command can only extract text that has been displayed or generated; it cannot extract chart values or ActionScript text.

When you open the text file created (yahoo.txt), you should see the following:

```
Symbol: MACR Last Trade: 11/10/2000 3:59PM - 76.890625 Change:
-3.046875 Open: 78 High: 78.375 Low: 76.125 Volume: 381600 60
70 80 90 8-Nov-00 7-Nov-00 6-Nov-00 3-Nov-00 2-Nov-00 1-Nov-00
31-Oct-00 30-Oct-00 27-Oct-00 26-Oct-00 25-Oct-00 24-Oct-00
   23-Oct-00
20-Oct-00 19-Oct-00 18-Oct-00 17-Oct-00 16-Oct-00 13-Oct-00
   12-Oct-00
11-Oct-00 10-Oct-00 9-Oct-00 6-Oct-00 5-Oct-00 4-Oct-00 3-Oct-00
2-Oct-00 29-Sep-00 Sync: Nov 14, 2000
```

Creating image maps

Offline Generator can also create both server- and client-side image maps.

Server side vs. client side

Because most graphical browsers support server-side image maps, they've become the de facto standard on the Web. As their name implies, however, they rely on a server to interpret each click and serve up the appropriate HTML file, making them a bit slower than their client-side cousins.

Although not as widely supported, client-side image maps are preferred by savvy graphical surfers because they save the client's browser extra queries to the server as well as provide the ability to trigger and coordinate JavaScript events.

Creating a server-side image map

To create a server-side image map, use the -smap option. For example, the following command creates a server-side image map (yahoo.map) from yahoomap.swt:

```
generate -smap yahoo.map yahoomap.swt
```

If you open the yahoo.map file, you'll see the following line of code:

```
rect  http://www.yahoo.com 258,78 516,139
```

Each line of the image-map file can contain a definition of a single polygonal-shaped region and a corresponding URL. The regions are defined by (x,y) coordinates within your image. A set of coordinates makes a point, and you need two points— the top left corner and the bottom right corner—to describe a rectangle.

Linking the server-side image map to the HTML file

Now we're ready to begin working on the actual HTML document. Take a look at the HTML syntax for calling a server-side image map:

```
<a href="/cgi-bin/imagemap/yahoo.map"><IMG SRC="yahoo.gif"
ismap width=560 height=440 border=0></A>
```

There are three important points here:

1. The `<a href>` tag points to the server-side image-map file, which in turn targets multiple URLs based on region.

2. The `/cgi-bin/imagemap/` prefix is added to the relative path name of your image map file. (The prefix `/cgi-bin/imagemap/` represents a program your server uses to interpret image maps—fairly standard procedure, though archaic servers may vary.)

3. The `ismap` keyword within the `<img>` tag alerts your browser that the image has a corresponding map on the server. (You may still, of course, include any other image tag modifiers you wish.)

We call the image map from our HTML file using the following code:

```
<a href="/cgi-bin/imagemap/yahoo.map"><IMG SRC="yahoo.gif"
ismap width=560 height=440 border=0></A>
```

 In order for server-side image maps to work, you must have a program, usually a CGI program, installed on your server to interpret the coordinate from the image map.

Creating a client-side image map

To create a client-side image map, you must use both the -cmap and the -cmapname options. The -cmap option outputs a client-side image map; the -cmapname option sets the client-side image map tag name. When you create a client-side image map, you must specify an image map tag name. The following example creates the client-side image map movie.map with the tag name mapname from movie.swt:

```
generate -cmap yahoo.map -cmapname yahoomap yahoomap.swt
```

You must include client-side image maps manually in the HTML code or process them with server-side includes.

If you open the yahoo.map file, you'll see the following line of code. This is where the invisible button was placed inside the template.

```
rect http://www.yahoo.com 258,78 516,139
```

Using a client-side image map with an HTML file

Both types of image maps share a similar data structure; they just differ in syntax: Instead of writing `rect`, Generator specified `shape="rect"`; instead of writing `yahoo.html`, it wrote `href="yahoo.html"`. (Note that to remain compatible with 2.0 browsers, Generator includes the comma [","] between the coordinate pairs when creating a client-side image map.)

Client-side map created:

```
<MAP NAME="yahoomap">
<AREA COORDS="258,78,516,139" HREF="http://www.yahoo.com"
TARGET="_blank">
</MAP>
```

Bandwidth issues aside, a significant advantage of client-side image maps is that they allow users to preview URLs before following a link. In server-side image maps, the status bar at the bottom of the browser only displays coordinate points when the user mouses over the image. In contrast, client-side image maps automatically display the target URL of the region that's being moused over.

So where should you place the image map within your HTML file? As far as we know, there's no best place for a <map> within your HTML file. We've seen people put them between </title> and </head>, between </head> and <body>, and between </body> and </mymap/html>. We've also seen image maps happily embedded within the <body> and </body> tags, which leads us to believe that <map> declarations can hide anywhere. It may help you to think of these regions of your HTML document as secret rebel bases, ideal perhaps for hiding a ragtag fleet of <area> tags.

Creating projectors

You can even use offline mode to create Flash projectors for both Mac and PC platforms, allowing users to simply double-click the movie to play it even if they don't have Flash installed. To create a projector, use one of the following options:

- -xwin32 <filename.exe> (to create a Win32 projector)

- -xmacppc <filename.hqx> (to create a Mac PPC projector)

The following command would create a projector for Windows 32-bit systems:

```
generate -xwin32 yahoo.exe yahoo.swt
```

The following command would create a projector for Mac PPC systems:

```
generate  -xmacppc yahoo.hqx yahoo.swt
```

Controlling the projector

If you're creating templates to deploy projectors, you may need to specify FSCommands to control the player. Within Flash, you can specify the following (remember: you can use Generator variables or type them in as expressions):

1. **To add an FSCommand, select the frame, button instance, or movie-clip instance to which you will assign the action.**

2. **Choose Window > Actions to display the Actions panel.**

3. **In the Toolbox list, click the Basic Actions category to display the basic actions, then select FSCommand action.**

4. **In the Parameters pane, choose one of the following options to control the stand-alone player from the Commands for Standalone Player pop-up menu:**

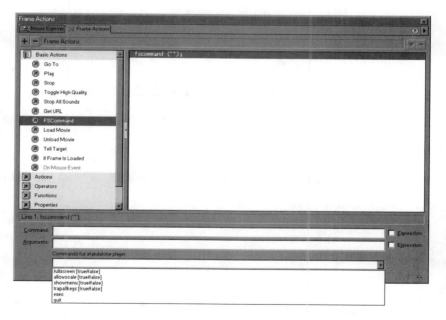

- Exec. Use this option to start an application from within the projector. In the Arguments text box, enter the path to the application.

- Fullscreen [True/False]. Use this option to control the projector view. In the Arguments text box, enter True for a full-screen view or False for a normal view.

- Allowscale [True/False]. Use this option to control the movie's scaling. In the Arguments text box, enter True to scale the animation with the player or False to display animation without scaling.

- Showmenu [True/False]. Use this option to control pop-up menu items. In the Arguments text box, enter True to display the full set of right-click menu items or False to hide the menu bar.

- Quit. Use this option to close the projector.

Creating more than one file from a single command

Generator allows you to create multiple files from a single command. For example:

```
generate -swf  yahoo.swf -gif yahoo.gif movie.swt
```

creates a Flash movie and a GIF file from the same template.

Specifying parameters

You can use the -param option to pass variables to a template that employs parameters. For example, the following command passes "datasource.txt" as the value for the datasource variable:

```
generate -swf yahoowd.swf yahoowd.swt -param datasource
datasource.txt
```

In the above example we used a template with a variable in the Generator Environment Settings called {datasource}. This allows us to pass any new data source via offline mode without opening our Flash movie.

Setting the debug message level

As Generator processes template files, it displays messages listing errors, warnings, and data sources encountered during processing. You can use the -debug option to specify the level of detail you wish to track in the log file during processing. The detail levels are as follows:

- 1. Logs errors.

- 2. Logs errors and warnings.

- 3. Logs errors, warnings, and data sources.

The following command creates a Flash movie called yahoo.swf from yahoo.swt and displays all messages, and data sources encountered by Generator when the template was processed.

```
generate -swf yahoo.swf -debug 3 yahoo.swt
```

Creating a log file

Using the -log option, you can create a log file that contains data about how your template was processed.

The following command logs all of the output from the debug option to a log file called logfile.txt.

```
generate -swf yahoo.swf -log logfile.txt -debug 3 yahoo.swt
```

This generates a Flash movie (SWF) and creates a log file with a debug level of 3 (logs all errors, warnings, and data sources) from a Generator template (yahoo.swt).

Undocumented message embedding

Offline Generator also has the undocumented ability to embed a string of uncompressed, unencrypted text within a .swf. We're not sure exactly why you would want to do this, but to embed a text string inside the .swf, use the following syntax (and keep in mind that it won't ever be displayed in Flash):

```
generate –swf yahoo.swf –embed "this is a secret message"
yahoo.swt
```

The parameters are as follows:

`-embed "<message>"` inserts the specified message into the flash movie.

If we crack open our .swf with a text or hex editor, you'll see the following string in the first line amongst a few thousand garbled characters:

```
FWSh3  x x  ˆo   Cÿÿÿÿ    this is a secret message
```

SCHEDULING OFFLINE GENERATOR

Now that we've gone over the Generate components that pass the settings and parameters to your Generator template, let's take a look at how to create a batch file (.bat) to save these settings. Batch files—which contain sequences, or *batches*, of commands—are useful for storing sets of commands that are always executed together: You simply enter the name of the batch file instead of entering each command individually.

Simple batch files do not require any special programming skills: Typically all you need to know are a few simple DOS commands.

Creating a batch file

In your favorite text editor let's create a .gif from the yahoo.swt file. In the text editor type the following:

```
generate -gif yahoo.gif yahoo.swt
```

Save the file and call it yahoo.bat. Place this file in the same directory as your template.

Now, when you double-click the file, a DOS window will quickly flash, and in the output directory you'll find a newly created .swf. If you wanted to automate this process and schedule the batch file to run every minute, you would use the Task Scheduler, which we describe below.

Windows' Task Scheduler

By using Window's Task Scheduler, you can schedule a batch file to run when it's convenient for you. With Task Scheduler—which runs in the background whenever you use Windows—you can schedule tasks to run daily, weekly, monthly, or at specified times (such as at system startup).

Using Task Scheduler

If Task Scheduler is installed on your system, you will find it in the My Computer folder. If it is not installed, you can install it from your Windows installation CD.

To use Task Scheduler, double-click the Scheduled Tasks folder in My Computer. Then double-click Add Scheduled Task. Now follow the instructions in the Add Scheduled Task wizard.

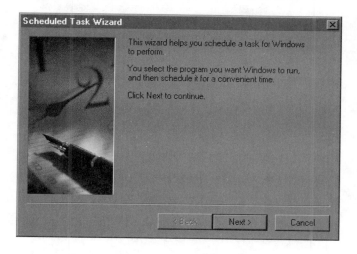

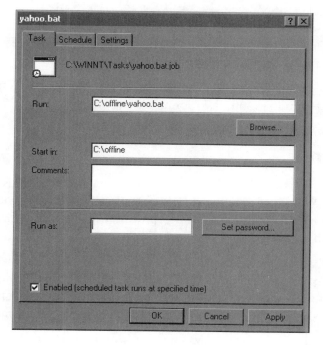

Our setting will invoke the Generate application every day at 3:34 a.m. by running the yahoo.bat file we created.

If you want to schedule more advanced settings, select "Open advanced properties for this task" for more setup options.

Cron

Cron is a UNIX command for scheduling future jobs—usually those that are executed periodically (for example, a notice that's sent out each morning). A cron is also a daemon process, which means it runs continuously in the background, waiting for specific events to occur.

Daemons perform specified operations at predefined times or in response to certain events. Although *daemon* is a UNIX term, other operating systems also support for them (though they sometimes call them by other names; Windows, for example, refers to daemons as System Agents and services).

Typical daemon processes include print spoolers, e-mail handlers, and other programs that perform administrative tasks for the operating system. The term comes from Greek mythology, in which daemons were guardian spirits.

Crontabs

A crontab is a program that allows users to create jobs that will run at a given time. Each user has his or her own crontab, and the entire system has a crontab that can only be modified by those with root access.

This file's syntax is very rigid: Each file contains six fields, each of which is separated by a space. The first five fields specify when the command is to be run; the sixth field is the command itself. The first five fields are as follows:

- Minute. Represents minutes after the hour (0-59).
- Hour. Uses the 24-hour format (0-23).
- Day. Represents day of the month (1-31).
- Month. Represents month of the year (1-12).
- Weekday. Represents day of the week (0-6; the 0 refers to Sunday).

Asterisks (*) indicate that commands are to be run in every instance of the value of the field. For instance, an asterisk in the Month field would mean the command should be run every month. In addition, multiple events can be scheduled within a field by separating all instances with commas (with no space between).

Options

- crontab -e. Edits the current crontab or creates a new one.
- crontab -l. Lists the contents of the crontab file.
- crontab -r. Removes the crontab file.

Creating a crontab for use with Generator

You create your crontab from the command line by typing `crontab -e`.

After you have done that, insert the following lines and save the file.

```
# this is comment about the job
1 * * * * /usr/local/generator_2/generate
-swf /home/phil/public/flash/yahoo.swf
/usr/local/apache/htdocs/generator/yahoo.swt
```

This job will run every minute after the hour and create a new .swf. To get more details on the crontab function, type `man crontab`.

The above example assumes that your default text editor is `vi` (type `:q` to save the file).

OFFLINE ONLINE

There are many ways to run Offline Generator in an online fashion. We've included a few popular methods as well as a custom COM object that you can use for the same purpose.

Server-side includes

If you know ASP, you're probably also familiar with server-side includes (SSIs). For those of you who aren't, here's a brief overview.

SSIs—which are not limited to ASP—provide a way of including content in your Web page. You can embed an SSI in standard HTML; however, you will need to save the file as a SHTML file. All SSIs do is look for and execute certain instructions.

SSIs provide a good way of executing CGI scripts and .exe files—a fact that interests us because Generate is an .exe.

Using SSI to execute offline.exe

The code for executing Generator is as follows:

```
<!-- #exec gen="/generator/generator.exe" -->
```

You will need to define a logical path to the Generator file (shown here as generator). You can pass any parameters you want to the Generator file, just as you would normally.

You can also execute a batch file or CGI script (for example, by accessing a Perl script in the Scripts directory).

The main drawback of this method is that you can't include any ASP (or PHP, etc.) code with the SSI:

```
<!-- #exec gen="//generator.exe" -->
```

Due to the way SSI works, it passes requests by the client for SSI to the SSI interrupter before the ASP interrupter and so any ASP code is treated like normal text.

StarFish

StarFish is an easy-to-use yet powerful COM component for Generator that allows you to run Offline Generator from your Web pages. You can use it with Active Server Pages, Cold Fusion, and PHP, as well as languages such as Visual Basic and C++.

StarFish basically allows developers to place batch file info into an HTML or server page. The example below uses StarFish from within an ASP page:

```
<HTML>
<HEAD>
<TITLE>Untitled</TITLE>
</HEAD>
<BODY>
<%
dim gen
set gen = Server.CreateObject("StarFish.offline")
gen.AddPath ("D:\Program Files\Macromedia\Generator 2\")
gen.AddTemplate ("D:\mystuff\Neptune\StarFish\examples\
                simple2\test2.swt")
gen.AddType ("swf")
gen.AddFileType ("D:\mystuff\Neptune\StarFish\examples\
                simple2\test2.swf")
gen.AddParam1Name ("test1")
gen.AddParam1Value ("andrew")
gen.AddParam2Name ("test2")
gen.AddParam2Value ("emma")
gen.AddParam3Name ("test3")
gen.AddParam3Value ("tom")
gen.AddParam4Name ("test4")
gen.AddParam4Value ("terry")
gen.AddParam5Name ("test5")
gen.AddParam5Value ("mary")
gen.RunGen
%>
</BODY>
</HTML>
```

In the Goodies folder on the CD, we've included StarFish (along with complete instructions for the program and sample files).

POINTS TO REMEMBER

- Offline mode is basically a DOS-like application that allows developers to quickly update content by "batching" commands.

- With offline mode you can create all the formats available in the Publish setting (for example, SWF, JPEG, GIF, PNG, MOV, EXE, and HQX). The only format that cannot be automated is the Real Player format.

- Offline mode also allows you to automate logging, text output, and client- and server-side image maps.

- Offline mode can be used with many common scheduling applications such as Windows Task Manger for Window and cron for UNIX-based systems.

- By creating batch files or crontabs, you can store the command switch needed to output the desired format on a regular basis.

- By using COM objects and other Web server extending utilities, developers can invoke Offline Generator in much in the same way as Online Generator.

CHAPTER 10

THE GENERATOR ADMINISTRATION SERVLET AND CACHING

THE GENERATOR ADMINISTRATION SERVLET—ONLY AVAILABLE WITH THE Generator Enterprise Edition—provides real-time feedback on server load and types of content served; it also displays information about your system and Web server. By using it, you can make changes to your resources and Generator settings (including cache settings), as well as get information on graphics (including type, response time, and size), which the servlet provides in a printable HTML report.

The Administration Servlet also allows you to configure caching which is one of the most advanced features of Generator Enterprise edition. Caching allows Generator to maintain copies of frequently used resources in memory in order to provide increased performance.

Because the Administration Servlet has a browser-based interface, you can administer Generator from a local or remote machine—basically anywhere you can connect to your server! In this chapter we'll take an in-depth look at the Administration Servlet and caching.

Note: The Administration Servlet and caching are features only available with the Enterprise edition of the Generator server. If you have Generator Developer Edition, you may safely skip this chapter.

THE GENERATOR ADMINISTRATION SERVLET

The Administration Servlet provides a user interface for setting administration and caching properties for Generator. It also displays information about your system, your Web server, and the files served by Generator. The information in the Administration Servlet panels is recorded in the generator.properties file located in the properties folder at the root of the Generator installation folder.

Using the Administration Servlet

You must have Generator 2 Enterprise Edition and a Web server installed and running to access the Administration Servlet. The first time you log in to the Administration Servlet, you'll want to create a permanent log-in name and password.

Note: The Administration Servlet requires a Flash 4 (or greater) plugin. You must have the plugin installed before you can use the Administration Servlet.

If you are using iPlanet on Solaris then you must enter the following lines to iPlanet's rules.properties file before being able to use the Generator Administration Servlet:

```
/servlet/GenAdmin=GenAdmin
/__Admin__Logon__.swt=Generator
/__Admin__Message__.swt=Generator
/__Admin__Service__.swt=Generator
```

To log in to the Administration Servlet:

1. *Start your Web server and Generator.*

2. *Start your Web browser and enter the following:*

`http://localhost/servlet/GenAdmin`

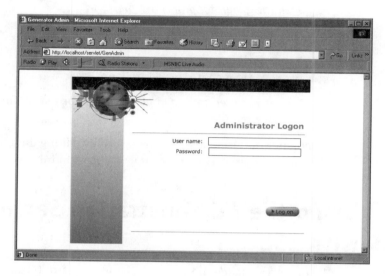

The Administration Servlet Log-On page will be displayed.

3. *The first time you log in enter* Admin *for the log-in name and your Generator 2 serial number for the password. The password entry is case sensitive.*

4. *Click "Logon."*

The Administration panel Information page will be displayed, which means you've successfully entered the Administration Servlet.

5. *To create a permanent log-in name and password, click Admin in the Navigation bar on the left side of the screen.*

6. *In the Admin panel fields enter your new log-in name and password, then retype your password for confirmation.*

7. *Click Apply.*

The next time you log in to the Administration Servlet, use your new log-in name and password.

To change your log-in name and password using the generator.properties file:

1. *Open the properties folder at the root of the Generator 2 installation folder.*

2. *Open the generator.properties file.*

Look for the following lines:

```
com.macromedia.generator.adminPassword=
com.macromedia.generator.adminUserName=
```

3. *The current user name and password will be listed. Change the value and save the file.*

Changing your user name and password by editing the generator.properties file is the same as changing it using the Administrator panel.

Using the Administration Servlet with SSL

If you have installed the latest release of Generator (Generator 2 Release 3), then you cannot use the Administration Servlet over SSL.

To use the Administration Servlet with SSL, Generator 2 users must first download and run the updater for Generator 2 Enterprise Edition (Release 2) (future versions will likely include this functionality). Next, you will need to edit your generator.properties file. For UNIX distributions of Generator, this file should be located in <generator parent>/generator/properties. On Windows, this file will be located in Program Files\Macromedia\Generator 2\properties.

Add the following line to the generator.properties file:

```
AdminHTMLtype=https
```

When using the Administration Servlet with Internet Explorer, you may have to click the Refresh button to see updates.

Netscape browsers do not support use of the Administration Servlet with SSL. What's more, iPlanet Web Server users won't be able to use the Administration Servlet with SSL in *any* browser. To use the Administration Servlet with an iPlanet Web Server, you must use a Netscape browser without SSL (since use of the Administration Servlet with Internet Explorer is not supported on the iPlanet Web Server).

INFORMATION PANEL

The first panel you'll encounter upon logging in to the Application Servlet is the Information panel, which displays the following (current) information about your Generator installation:

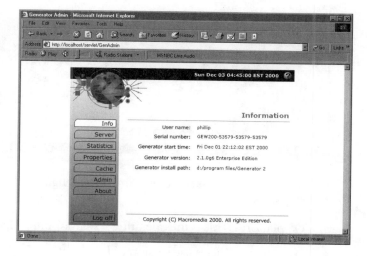

- User name. This is the name of the user currently logged into the Administration Servlet.

- Serial number. This is the Generator installation serial number.

- Generator start. This represents the time at which you launched Generator in conjunction with your Web server. Start time affects the information displayed in the Generator Statistics panels as well as the information written to the HTML file generated by clicking the Report button. Stopping and restarting Generator (and whatever servlet engine you're running) will update this time, reset the values on the Generator Statistics panel to zero, and erase the information currently recorded in the Generator Statistics Report file.

- Generator version. Represents the version of Generator currently running.

- Generator install path. Lists the folder in which Generator is installed.

SERVER ENVIRONMENT PANEL

The Server Environment panel displays the following information about the Generator server environment:

- Servlet engine. This represents the servlet engine currently running Generator.

- OS platform. This is the operating system running Generator.

- Java version. This is the version of Java Runtime Engine used by Generator.

- Server name. This is the name of the Web server.

- Server port. This is the port used by the Web server. In TCP/IP and UDP networks, a port is the endpoint of a logical connection. The port number identifies the type of port. For example, Port 80—which is usually used for HTTP traffic—is what's usually displayed.

- Thread count. This is the number of concurrent threads (requests) that Generator is currently processing. Click your browser's Refresh button to view current thread count information.

What is a thread? In programming, a thread is a part of a program that can execute independently of other parts. Operating systems that support multithreading enable programmers to design programs whose threaded parts can execute concurrently. Generator Enterprise Edition—as you may have already guessed—is a multithreaded application that can support thousands of simultaneous threads. Basically, this means that Generator can do more than one thing at a time, allowing it to process and serve templates faster, especially under high loads.

GENERATOR STATISTICS PANEL

You can view statistics about each file type supported by Generator (Flash, GIF, JPEG, PNG, and QuickTime) by clicking the buttons at the bottom of the Generator Statistics panel. The displayed statistics represent those compiled since you last started Generator. Stopping and restarting Generator (and whatever servlet engine you're running) resets the values on the Generator Statistics panel to zero. You can generate a printable report containing statistics for all file types by clicking the Report button.

The displayed statistics apply only to the file type indicated by the highlighted button.

- Requests. This represents the number of requests for files of this type served by Generator.

- Average size. This represents the average size (in kilobytes) of requested files (Flash, GIF, JPEG, PNG, and QuickTime).

- Max size. This represent the largest file (in kilobytes) of this type served by Generator.

- Average time. This represents the average time (in milliseconds) it took Generator to process requests for files of this type.

- Max time. This represents the longest amount of time it took Generator to process a request for a file of this type.

- Report button. This button generates a printable HTML file listing Generator statistics for all file types as well as the maximum number of concurrent threads processed in the current session.

SERVLET PROPERTIES PANEL

The information you enter in the Servlet Properties panel is recorded in the generator.properties file and determines how Generator processes requests for information. This section requires an understanding of your Web server's capabilities and of the files accessed by Generator.

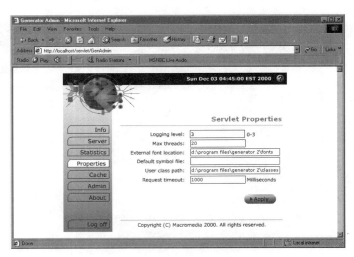

You can also adjust all of these settings by manually editing the appropriate property in the generator.properties file in the Generator 2\Logs directory.

Logging Level

The logging level determines how much information will be written to the Generator.log file, located in the Generator 2\Logs directory. Valid values are 0 (off), 1 (errors), 2 (warnings), and 3 (verbose).

While you're developing your applications, it's good practice to set logging to Level 3 (verbose). This writes all data gathered from data sources to the log to help troubleshooting and development. As development progresses, you may want to switch to Level 1 (errors) or 2 (warnings): This way, errors would only be displayed when they prevent Generator from performing an expected task.

In a production (as opposed to testing) environment, you should either turn off logging or set it no higher than Level 1 to conserve system resources and hard disk space. (We'll cover cache logging—which you set on the Global panel—later in the chapter.)

When you're ready to deploy your application, the lower the logging level the better the application will perform, although any performance hit will be minimal. If Generator needs to marry database data with Flash templates as well as generate a verbose log, resources will be taxed and, over time, an extremely large log file will be created.

To change Logging Level in the Properties file:

1. *Open the properties folder at the root of the Generator 2 installation folder.*

2. *Open the generator.properties file.*

3. *Look for the following line(s):*

```
com.macromedia.generator.loggingLevel=
```

The current logging level will be listed. The logging level integer can range from 0 to 3, as described above.

4. *Enter a value, then save the file.*

Changing the logging level by editing the generator.properties file is the same as changing it via the Administrator panel.

Max Threads

Max Threads represents the maximum number of templates, or *threads,* that can be processed at the same time. The number you enter here should correspond to your Web server's capabilities and the volume of traffic it handles. If you were to set Max Threads too low, visitors could receive a 503 or Service Unavailable message when attempting to access your site. If, on the other hand, you were to set Max Threads at a level that exceeded your Web server's capabilities, you could possibly get slow request-response times.

To change Max Threads in the Properties file:

1. *Open the properties folder at the root of the Generator 2 Installation folder.*

2. *Open the generator.properties file.*

3. *Look for the following line(s):*

```
com.macromedia.generator.maxThreads=
```

The current Max Thread value will be listed; the max threads integer must be greater than 1.

4. *Enter a value, then save the file.*

In Chapter 9, we give you the scoop on tuning up Generator.

Changing Max Threads by editing the generator.properties file is the same as changing it via the Administrator panel.

Note: On Windows with JRun 2.3.3, the Max Thread property is limited to a maximum of 5 threads, regardless of what the property is set to. This was due to performance and stability issues with JRun that were encountered when allowing a higher Max Thread count. Updating to Generator 2 (Release 3) will alleviate this issue, since this version uses JRun 3.

External Font Location

External Font Location is the folder where your external font files are stored. The path to the fonts folder at the root level of the Generator program directory is entered by default.

You should place the fonts used by your templates in this folder rather than in the directory for each template. By storing all of your fonts in one folder, you conserve disk space, make it easier to manage your fonts, and make it possible for Generator to process requests more quickly.

To change External Font Location in the Properties file:

1. *Open the properties folder at the root of the Generator 2 installation folder.*

2. *Open the generator.properties file.*

3. *Look for the following line(s):*

`com.macromedia.generator.fontPath=`

The current directory path location of the fft files (external font files) will be listed.

4. *Enter a value, then save the file.*

Changing External Font Location by editing the generator.properties file is the same as changing it via the Administrator panel.

Default Symbol File

This specifies a Generator template that contains symbols to be used for labels in charts and tables.

Usually we create our own External Symbol file and specify its name and location within our templates. Unless your Generator installation will always contain the same type of labels for charts and tables, it's best to use individual external symbol files to keep Generator "clean."

To change the Default Symbol file in the Properties file:

1. *Open the properties folder at the root of the Generator 2 installation folder.*

2. *Open the generator.properties file.*

3. *Look for the following line(s):*

`com.macromedia.generator.defaultSymbolFile=`

The current Default Symbol File will be listed.

4. *Enter a value, then save the file.*

Changing the Default Symbol File by editing the generator.properties file is the same as changing it via the Administrator panel.

User Class Path

User Class Path specifies the folder where your Java data-source classes are stored. If left blank, Generator will default to the classes folder at the root level of the Generator application folder; this is the setting most developers use.

To change User Class Path in the Properties file:

1. *Open the properties folder at the root of the Generator 2 installation folder.*

2. *Open the generator.properties file.*

3. *Look for the following line(s):*

com.macromedia.generator.userClassPath=

The current User Class Path will be listed.

4. *Enter a value, then save the file.*

Changing User Class Path by editing the generator.properties file is the same as changing it using the Administrator panel.

Request Time Out

Request Time Out specifies the amount of time (in milliseconds) that will elapse before a Service Unavailable message is returned when a request has been issued over max threads. For example, if Max Threads is set at five and six requests are made simultaneously, one of the six requests will be put on hold for whatever amount of time you enter here. If the other requests are processed within that time, the sixth request will be processed. If the server remains busy, the request will not be processed.

To change Request Time Out in the Properties file:

1. *Open the Properties folder at the root of the Generator 2 installation folder.*

2. *Open the generator.properties file.*

3. *Look for the following line(s):*

com.macromedia.generator.requestTimeout=

The current Request Time Out file will be listed; the integer is in milliseconds.

4. *Enter a value, then save the file.*

Changing Request Time Out by editing the generator.properties file is the same as changing it via the Administrator panel.

In Chapter 9, we give you the scoop on tuning up Generator.

GENERATOR CACHING

One of the most powerful features of Generator Enterprise Edition is its caching abilities. Generator can cache frequently used media and templates, allowing Generator to retrieve and serve media and/or templates from memory or the file system as opposed to always remaking the same content or retrieving frequently used content. This can greatly increase the speed with which Generator can process templates and thus can increase the amount of traffic that Generator can serve.

The Cache Settings panel is where you enable and configure Generator caching. The configuration you choose will depend on your Web server's capabilities, your system's hard disk space and memory, and the types of files you plan to process. Of course, as with all of the other settings in the Administration Servlet, you can also set all of the caching properties in the generator.properties file.

You must enable and configure each of the Generator caches (Request, Font, Media, and File) separately. The default setting for all caches is Off. The Global panel settings apply to all of the caches.

You can also dynamically specify caching settings through the URL requesting the templates. Cache parameters set in the URLs for individual files require that the cache be turned on. Setting the Force cache setting to True caches all files in that cache regardless of cache parameters in the URL of individual files. Expire parameters specified in the URL override the Expire After setting.

The following diagram shows Generator caching flow.

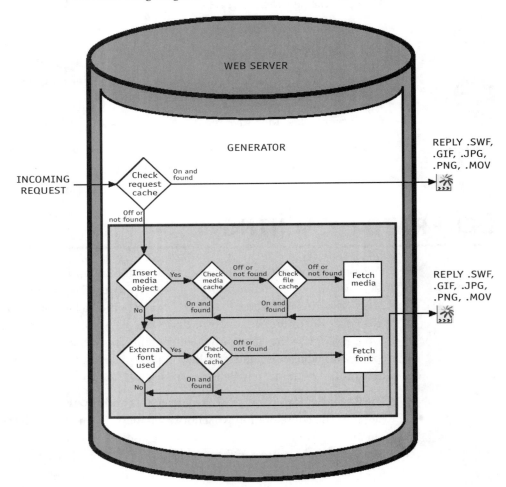

How It Works

Generator's caching has two types of caching: caching in memory and caching to the file system. Memory caching is faster than the disk caching. The memory cache is divided into three separately configurable sections: request, media and font. Each is configured separately, but they all work together in determining when cached content is used for a template.

If the caching feature is not enabled (Max Size set to 0 for all caches), Generator will not use caching and will completely process and retrieve all media and templates each time they are requested.

Generator processing with all caches enabled

If all of the cache types (request, media, font) are enabled then Generator will see if the template is cached in the request cache. If it is, then it stops processing the template and returns the file from the cache to the user. If it is not, then it looks for parts of the template in the media, font, and file caches. Any media it finds in those caches that are needed by the template are then used to process the template. Any media required but not found in the caches is then requested from its original source. Once all of the media has been retrieved, the template is processed and returned to the user.

While this is the least system-intensive cache setting, you need to be careful not to cache data that needs to be updated on each request (for example, account information or real-time stock data).

For example, let's say that you have a template that dynamically inserts an image into a template. When Generator processes the template, it first searches the cache to see if it has already loaded the image and stored it in the cache. If it has, then Generator simply loads the images from the cache. Otherwise, it requests the image from the file system or URL; a process that is extremely slow compared to retrieving it from the cache. Once Generator retrieves the image for the first time, it places it into the cache, so that future requests for the same image can be processed much faster. Using the cache in a situation like this can dramatically decrease Generator's response time.

Request cache

The Request cache saves (or *caches*) and serves entire template (SWT) files. If the Request cache is enabled when a template is processed for the first time the resulting file is stored in the request cache. Subsequent requests for the template are served directly from the cache and are not re-processed by Generator.

Font cache

The font cache saves font information from external font files into a cache. The first time that a font file is used by a template it is retrieved from the file system and then placed into the cache. All subsequent requests for the font file by a template are served from the font cache and not from the font file.

The Font cache should be enabled whenever possible since fonts are seldom changed.

Media cache

The Media cache saves and serves files (such as images) from memory. This is the fastest of the Generator caches. If media and file caching are both enabled, Generator checks the Media cache first, with the File cache acting primarily as a backup.

File cache

The File cache saves and serves files (such as images) from the disk. If media caching is enabled, Generator only searches the File cache if the request cannot be processed from the Media cache. If file caching is not enabled, or if the file is not in the File cache, Generator fetches the file from the disk on the local or external network (as specified in the file's URL).

CACHE SETTINGS PANELS

You can activate caching and set and modify how it works via the Cache panel in the Administration Servlet. By default, all the caching for Generator is turned off (Max Size set to 0 in the cache panel in the Administration Servlet).

As described earlier, each cache type has its own settings. They can be accessed in the Administration Servlet by clicking on the respective cache setting tab at the bottom of the page on the cache panel in the Administration Servlet.

Max Size

This determines the maximum size of the cache in kilobytes. If this is set to 0, then caching will not be enabled.

When setting this property, be sure to take into account the amount of memory that can be used by the Web server as well as the amount of data that you wish to cache. If you set the Maximum Size setting too high, data may be written and retrieved to the file system, significantly decreasing performance.

Recycle

This determines how the data in the cache is recycled. If this property is set to True, the oldest data in the cache will be deleted to make room for the newest data. If it is set to False, data will not be deleted from the cache. Once the cache is full (determined by the size set in Max Size) then no more data will be added to the cache.

Expire After

This setting determines how long (in seconds) data will be stored in the cache before it is removed.

Expire After can also function as a content management system: If you have a project such as a financial application that uses regularly refreshed data, you can specify how many seconds should be cached before making a new cache entry. This is similar to updating the template in offline mode at regular intervals.

Cache Force

Setting the property to True caches all requests, regardless of any settings in the URL. Set this property to False if you want to determine what is cached via the URL for the request or by setting the appropriate cache settings for objects in the Generator panel when creating the template.

Check Modified

If this property is set to True, Generator will first check to see whether there is a newer version of the cached media or template before it serves data from the cache. The most recent version will be served. If this is set to False the data will always be served from the cache.

Use Index File

You can only set Use Index File for File cache. Enter True to re-create the disk cache at startup. Enter False to clean out the cache directory and create a new disk cache each time Generator is restarted. Make sure to click Apply before exiting each panel.

MODIFYING CACHE SETTINGS

Each panel in the Administration Servlet has entries in the generator.properties file; in the next section we've provided the value descriptions of each property. Although we suggest you use the Administration Servlet to ensure that the settings are valid, some users prefer to edit the property files directly.

The Request, Font, Media, and File cache settings can be modified by editing the generator.properties file. To modify any of these settings:

1. *Open the properties folder at the root of the Generator 2 installation folder.*

2. *Open the generator.properties file.*

3. *Look for the property that you want to modify. A complete description of all properties is listed in the next section.*

The current value will be listed.

4. *Enter a new value, then save the file.*

5. *You need to restart the Servlet engine running Generator before the new settings will take effect.*

Note: A description of each property can be found in their respective sections above.

Request Cache panel settings

Max Request Cache Size

com.macromedia.generator.requestCacheMaxSize=

Max Request Cache Size is set in kilobytes and must be greater than zero.

Recycle Request Cache

com.macromedia.generator.requestCacheRecycle=

The values are True or False.

Request Cache Expiration

com.macromedia.generator.requestCacheDefaultExpiration

Expiration time is expressed in seconds and must be greater than zero.

Force Request Cache

com.macromedia.generator.requestCacheForce

The values are True or False.

Font Cache panel settings

Max Font Cache size

com.macromedia.generator.fontCacheMaxSize

This setting is expressed in kilobytes and must be greater than zero.

Font Cache Recycle

com.macromedia.generator.fontCacheRecycle

The values are True or False.

Font Cache Expiration

com.macromedia.generator.fontCacheDefaultExpiration

Expiration time is expressed in seconds and must be greater than zero.

Force Font Cache

com.macromedia.generator.fontCacheForce

The values are True or False.

Check Font Cache Modification

com.macromedia.generator.fontCacheCheckModifiedSince

The values are True or False.

Media Cache panel settings

Max Media cache size

com.macromedia.generator.mediaCacheMaxSize

This setting is expressed in kilobytes and must be greater than zero.

Media Cache Recycle

com.macromedia.generator.mediaCacheRecycle

The values are True or False.

Media Cache Expiration

com.macromedia.generator.mediaCacheDefaultExpiration

Expiration time is expressed in seconds and must be greater than zero.

Force Media Cache

com.macromedia.generator.mediaCacheForce

The values are True or False.

Check Cache Modification

com.macromedia.generator.mediaCacheCheckModifiedSince

The values are True or False.

File Cache panel settings

Max File Cache size

com.macromedia.generator.fileCacheMaxSize

This setting is expressed in kilobytes and must be greater than zero.

Recycle File Cache

com.macromedia.generator.fileCacheRecycle

The values are True or False.

File Cache Expiration

com.macromedia.generator.fileCacheDefaultExpiration

Expiration time is expressed in seconds and must be greater than zero.

Force File Cache

com.macromedia.generator.fileCacheForce

The values are True or False.

Check File Cache Modification

`com.macromedia.generator.fileCacheCheckModifiedSince`

The values are True or False.

Load File Cache Index File

`com.macromedia.generator.fileCacheLoadIndex`

The values are True or False.

Using URL parameters to set caching preferences

You can dynamically specify whether a template or media file is cached and when it expires by specifying cache parameters in the URL. There are two valid Generator cache parameters: the Request cache parameter `grc= true/ false` and the Media cache parameter `gmc= true/ false`. You would use the Request parameter in URLs that point to the template file and the Media parameter with URLs in Insert Template commands (when creating or editing a template).

If you set Force Cache to True, all of the templates and media files used by Generator will be cached, regardless of the parameter specified in the URL. If you set Force Cache to False, only templates and files that specify `gmc=true` or `grc=true` in the URL will be cached.

There are two valid Generator expire parameters: the Request expire parameter `gre= true/ false` and the Media expire parameter `gme= true/ false`. You would use the Request parameter in URLs that point to the template file and the Media parameter with URLs in Insert Template commands (when creating or editing a template). If you don't specify an expire time in the URL, the Expire After time you set on the Cache Settings page will determine when the cached file expires. When two settings conflict, True always overrides False.

The following URL, for the GIF file zoo.gif, is set to True for Media caching and will expire after 90 seconds—even if Force Cache is set to False, and Expire After is set for 30 seconds.

`http://www.foo.com/zoo.gif?gmc=true&gme=90`

The URL below, for the JPG file moon.jpeg, is set to True for Media caching and is not given an expire time. This file will be cached whether Force Cache has been set to True or False, and it will automatically expire at the Expire After time. If an Expire After time is not set, the cached image will never expire and will be used to process template requests even if the data source has been updated. To avoid serving stale or outdated files, you should enter an Expire After value.

```
http://www.foo.com/moon.jpeg?gmc=true
```

The following URL, for the SWF file tree.swf, is set to False for Request caching. If Request caching is enabled, files with a True parameter of this type will be cached; however, this file will not. Because the file will not be cached, no Expires parameter is needed.

```
http://www.foo.com/tree.swf?grc=false
```

GLOBAL CACHE SETTINGS PANEL

The information entered in the Global Cache settings panel applies to all of the caches. Remember: You must click Apply before exiting the panel.

Logging Level

This determines the amount of information written to the cache.log file located in the Logs directory. Valid values include 0 (off), 1 (errors), 2 (warning), and 3 (verbose).

Log Cycle

This determines the amount of time in minutes that you want the cache.log file to log information. By default, this is set to zero.

Max Cycled Logs

This determines the maximum number of cache.log files that will be created. Once the limit is reach, the oldest file will be deleted to make room for the newest.

Flush

This button deletes all the cache.log files.

Log Hits

This saves the number of hits for cached items to the cache.log file. This allows you to see how often data is served from the cache.

Expire After

This setting determines how long (in seconds) data will be stored in the cache before it is removed.

Force

Setting the property to True caches all requests, regardless of any settings in the URL. Set this property to False if you want to determine what is cached via the URL for the request or by setting the appropriate cache settings for objects in the Generator panel when creating the template.

Reset

Clicking the Reset button restores the default settings for the cache.

Modifying the Global settings in the Properties file

Note: A description of each property can be found in their respective sections above.

Cache Logging Level

`com.macromedia.generator.cacheLoggingLevel`

This specifies the logging level for the cache. Valid values include 0 (off), 1 (errors), 2 (warning), and 3 (verbose).

Cache Log Cycle

`com.macromedia.generator.cacheLogCycle`

This specifies the Log Cycle in seconds greater than zero.

Max Cache Log Files

`com.macromedia.generator.cacheLogMaxFiles`

This specifies the Max Cycled Logs property and must contain a number greater than zero.

POINTS TO REMEMBER

- Generator Enterprise Edition has a one-stop control panel that you can use to manage, modify, and administrate Generator.

- The Generator Administration Servlet is basically a front end for the generator.properties file.

- Generator can cache files, requests, media, and fonts to greatly improve the performance and scalability of your Web applications.

CHAPTER 11

OTHER DEVELOPMENT TOOLS

EVERY DEVELOPER HAS A TOOLBOX OF GOODIES HE OR SHE USES TO HELP automate workflow and tasks. In this chapter we'll introduce you to a few of the tools we like to keep around as part of our super help utility belt.

USING DREAMWEAVER WITH GENERATOR

Macromedia's popular Dreamweaver Web-site creation tool offers every-thing you need to develop professional-looking Web sites. Whether you use the program's visual layout tools or its text-editing environment, its intuitive user interface makes it easy to add Generator objects and perform quick HTML editing even if you're not an HTML coder. Dreamweaver ships with an Insert Generator Object, works with the Exchange just like Flash, and is tightly integrated with both Flash and Generator.

You can download a 30-day trial version of Dreamweaver from the follow-ing Web site:

http://www.macromedia.com/software/dreamweaver/download/

Inserting Generator objects with Dreamweaver

To insert a Generator object in your HTML page using Dreamweaver 3+:

1. *In the Document window, place the insertion point where you want to insert the object.*

2. *Click the Generator button in the Objects panel.*

3. *In the dialog box that appears, select a Generator template (.swt) file.*

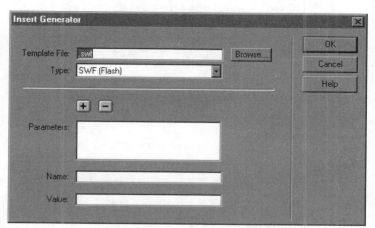

4. *If desired, click the Plus (+) button to add a "name=value" parameter pair.*

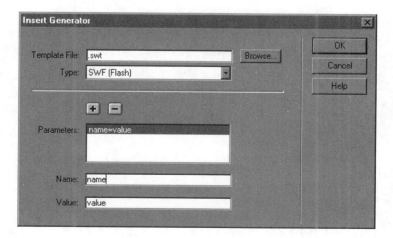

5. *Enter a name for the parameter in the Name field and a value for the parameter in the Value field. Repeat this step for each parameter.*

6. *To remove a parameter, select it in the Parameters list and click the Minus (-) button.*

7. *When you finish entering parameters, click OK to insert the Generator object. You can also select the output type from the pop-up list.*

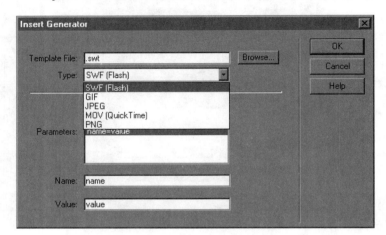

To edit the parameters after the Generator object has been inserted, use the HTML Source inspector.

Generator attempts to obtain values to plug into the template from a database file; if no database file is available, the server uses the "name=value" pairs you supplied here when inserting the object.

 Besides hard coding name/value pairs in the HTML document, you can also use middleware to add dynamic content to your Flash movies. See Chapter 8 to learn more about using middleware with Generator.

EXTENSIONS AND THE MACROMEDIA EXCHANGE FOR FLASH

Extensions are software you can add to Macromedia applications to enhance their capabilities. Macromedia offers several types of extensions: Dreamweaver and UltraDev extensions, for example, include everything from HTML code that you can add to the Objects panel and the Insert menu, to JavaScript commands that you can add to the Command menu, to new behaviors, Property inspectors, and floating panels. Flash 5+ extensions include Smart Clips you can use to build projects, reusable

ActionScript code snippets, additional symbol libraries, and even customized Generator objects. All Macromedia applications that support Macromedia Extension Manager can use font extension packages that install fonts to your hard disk.

The Macromedia Exchange Web site (http://www.macromedia.com/exchange) serves as a repository for many kinds of extensions—both those created by Macromedia and those created by third-party developers. If you want to use one of the extensions found on the site, you can download it with your Web browser and then install it using Macromedia Extension Manager.

Macromedia Exchange for Flash is the place to get easy-to-install extensions, learn how to get the most out of them, and even create your own. Each extension has its own page that includes the extension, a short description, user reviews, and a discussion group where you can post questions and get support.

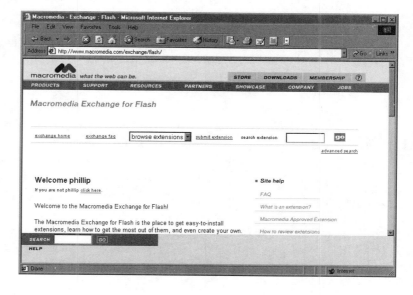

Macromedia Extension Manager, which is available for download from the Exchange, allows you to install, manage, and delete the extensions you've downloaded from the Exchange. Once you've downloaded and installed Extension Manager, you can access it from within Flash 5 by selecting Help > Manage Exchange Items.

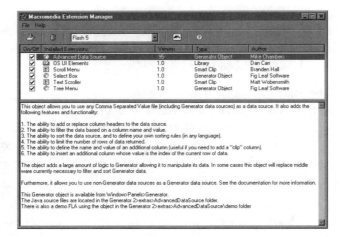

The free Extension Manager is available at the following Web site:

`http://dynamic.macromedia.com/bin/MM/exchange/flash/`
`em_download.jsp`

Once you've downloaded and installed Extension Manager, you can begin downloading extensions from the Exchange:

`http://www.macromedia.com/exchange/flash/`

As a recent addition to the Exchange, Macromedia Exchange for Flash has opened the door to myriad new and helpful extensions and objects for Flash and Generator. And because most of the extension developers provide fully commented files and documentation, the Exchange has become an excellent learning resource as well. If you're about to start a project that requires a custom Generator object or complex ActionScripting, check the Exchange first: There's a good chance a portion of your work already exists there—and at the very least you're likely to find an example that will inspire you.

See Chapter 6 for a discussion of custom objects available from the Exchange.

Installing extensions

Downloading and installing extensions from Macromedia Exchange is easy: Simply go to the Flash Exchange, browse through the Generator Objects section (which contains user-created custom Generator objects), and download the extension you're interested in. When you click an extension's name to download it, you may have two choices, depending on your Web browser:

POINTS TO REMEMBER

- The Flash player is currently supported in dozens of devices and appliances as well as many forthcoming next-generation systems such as cell phones and set-top boxes.

- Flash developers are now designing applications and content for a wide range of mediums and devices.

- With new devices come new caveats: From colors palettes to fonts, supporting devices is almost as complicated as supporting hundreds of browsers if the applications aren't built properly.

- Personalized, frequently updated content and applications are what most device users employ and where Generator meets the challenge of providing content.

- With proper planning, most dynamic Flash content and applications can run on myriad platforms and devices.

- Using detection built right into ActionScript, many of the device environment variables can be determined so that you can provide a better user experience and ensure your application's success.

CHAPTER 13

GENERATOR FOR VIDEO

BY LICENSING MACROMEDIA'S FLASH PLAYER AND BUILDING IT INTO QuickTime, Apple has made it possible for Flash 3 content to be played back interactively in QuickTime 4 movies. By using Flash with QuickTime, you can add navigational controls, text effects, animation, titling, alpha transparency, and more to your QuickTime movies. You can also add content to QuickTime without actually modifying the QuickTime movie.

In this chapter we'll explore the many ways you can use Flash and Generator in conjunction with QuickTime. We'll also create an Internet news video with Generator charts, custom navigation, controls, and URLs.

FLASH AND QUICKTIME

Because Flash supports the importing of QuickTime movies, you can import and display QuickTime movies inside the Flash authoring environment, adding vector graphics, animation, interactivity, and even data-driven graphics from Generator. And because QuickTime supports the importing of Flash movies, you can then export the entire file into a single QuickTime movie that now includes your added Flash content. And because the Flash content you added is now a layer in the QuickTime movie, you can take advantage of Flash's transparency effects when creating menus and text so that the video actually shows through the Flash elements. And by using Generator, you can even further enhance your QuickTime movies.

Flash's ability to create a QuickTime movie that contains Flash elements makes it easy for Web developers to incorporate compact, distinctive Flash interface elements into QuickTime movies—functionality that can add enormous value. For example, you can give users DVD-like random access movie controls as well as add text and graphics that help convey your movie's message. You can even replace the default QuickTime movie playback controls with custom vector based controls of your own design.

Another benefit of using Flash and Generator with QuickTime is that the combination allows you to protect your content by embedding watermarks and links to specified Web sites.

Combining Flash with QuickTime is also a good way to protect your interests when users start trading your files on their own. Because you can easily brand the video and even embed Web links, you can release your enhanced video out to the wide open Internet confident that any unintentional distribution that takes place will actually help your interests, not hurt them. By using Flash and Generator with QuickTime, you can overlay high-quality streaming video with Macromedia Flash interfaces that stream over the Internet to provide broadband-quality interactive Web experiences. You can even deliver ads and custom messages (all within the familiar development environment of Flash) as Generator churns out assets for your video.

SNOWBOARDING EXAMPLE
ON MACROMEDIA'S SITE
THAT USES FLASH AND
QUICKTIME.

While QuickTime movies can contain Flash movies, Flash movies cannot contain QuickTime movies. However, you can use a series of JPG images or Insert Jpg Generator objects that resemble video along with a sound-track to simulate video inside Flash. When you're in the Flash authoring environment, try importing a small QuickTime movie and then exporting it as a series of JPG images. Then reimport the images and add a sound-track that you've extracted with QuickTime. We've included an example of this technique, called "videoflash," on the CD-ROM in the Chapter 13 folder. However, there are important limitations with this technique. It can result in extremely large file sizes, playback on slower computers can be a little erratic, and the quality is typically low due to the large amount of JPG compression required to keep the file size under control. However, if the video you want to bring into Flash is small in size and short in length, and if quality isn't of paramount importance, this technique might be just what you need.

If you've explored the Flash 5 CD-ROM, you will have found a Flash-enhanced QuickTime movie in the Goodies folder that we created for Macromedia. The demo includes sophisticated DVD-like controls, water-marks, custom navigation, playback controls, and links to Web sites.

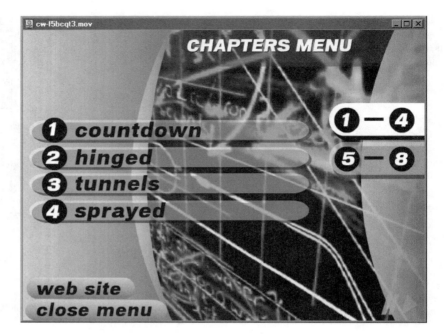

In our next lesson, we'll use some of the assets we created in the previous chapters to enhance a QuickTime video for a simulated Internet news broadcast. We'll insert a Generator stock chart and watermarks, enhance the shape of the video, and create custom playback controls for the QuickTime movie.

INSTALLING QUICKTIME

Now is a good time to install QuickTime (if you haven't already) since you won't be able to do these lessons without it. You can download a free version from the following URL:

http://www.apple.com/quicktime/download/

Both the Mac and PC platforms support QuickTime, which means you can share your movie with any of the 50 million users who have a QuickTime Player—regardless of their platform.

Windows QuickTime requirements:

- A Pentium-based PC-compatible computer
- At least 16MB of RAM
- Windows 95, Windows 98, or Windows NT 4.0 system software
- A Sound Blaster–compatible sound card and speakers
- Direct X version 3.0 or later (recommended)

Mac QuickTime requirements:

- A PowerPC processor–based Macintosh computer
- At least 16MB of RAM
- Mac OS 7.5.5 or later

Supported Web browsers (Mac and Windows):

- America Online 3 or later
- Microsoft Internet Explorer 3.x or later
- Netscape Navigator 3.x or later

QuickTime Pro

We encourage you to get the Pro version of QuickTime ($30): First, it eliminates the screen that pops up periodically and annoyingly reminds you of the Pro version's features. That screen can really get old if you do a lot of work with QuickTime. And second, the QuickTime Pro license also unlocks a full suite of editing tools. Some developers use these tools to do almost all of their QuickTime editing for use with Flash. QuickTime Pro is a good tool to have around for opening files (it supports more than 200 formats) and for doing some quick editing.

With QuickTime Pro, you can play back full-screen video; resize movies; create streaming movies; work with more than 30 audio, video, and image formats; and create, open, edit, and save movies and audio—all of which you can accomplish using familiar operations such as copy and paste.

For more information on QuickTime, visit the following Web site:

```
http://www.apple.com/quicktime/specifications.html
```

Things you can't do

The most important limitation is that QuickTime 4 only supports Flash 3 movies so you'll need to dust off your knowledge of the tellTarget command because no advanced ActionScripting is allowed here. But even within the world of Flash 3, there are additional limitations. QuickTime 4 allows you to do everything you can with Flash 3 except for the following:

- You can't use a Keyframe action to trigger a Get URL action in the exported QuickTime movie.

- You can't use the Load Movie action to place external SWF files into the current Flash movie.

- The cursor does not always turn into a hand when passing over buttons so be mindful of this – use obvious rollover states to compensate.

- You can't use "mask" layers to mask QuickTime content.

- You can't use Generator variables to insert dynamic data for authoring, and you can't use Generator to automate the process of "merging" a Flash layer with QuickTime. However, don't be too concerned about this: We'll show you how to work around this limitation.

> QuickTime 5 may provide some of these capabilities. When we wrote this, the beta version of QuickTime 5 included Flash 4 support. Visit the Apple QuickTime site to find out the latest.

HOW IT'S DONE

On the accompanying CD-ROM, we've included some video that you'll need to put on your hard drive. Copy vnews.mov from the Chapter 13 folder and place it in a folder you created for this lesson.

1. *Open Flash and create a new movie (File > New).*

2. *Create six layers and name them, from bottom to top, "video,"
    "vector news," "navigation," "stock chart," "frame," and "actions."*

3. *Save the Flash movie in the same directory as vnews.mov.*

Importing and using video in Flash

1. *Click the first frame of the "video" layer and then import the
    QuickTime movie (File > Import). Select the QuickTime movie.*

You'll notice that the first frame of the video occupies one frame on the
stage and that the library contains your movie, as shown in this figure.

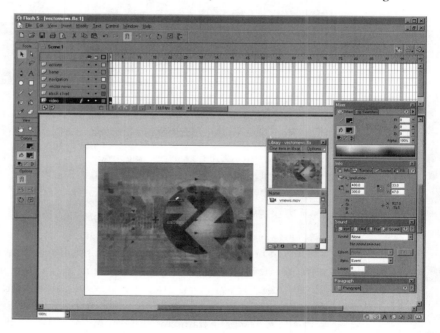

If you plan to share your Flash files (.fla's) with video assets, you'll need to
modify the path when you reopen the file on another system. You can do
this by highlighting the video library item, clicking the properties icon, and
then specifying the new path. Until you make that modification, you'll just
see a big *X* on the stage.

2. *Open the Info panel (Window > Panels > Info) and get the width and height of the movie.*

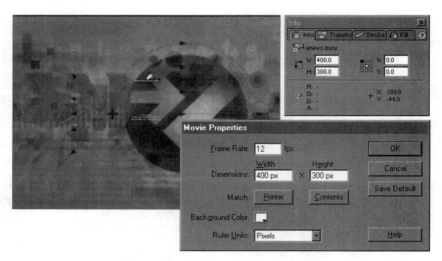

3. *Modify the movie so that it's the same size as the QuickTime movie (Modify > Movie). Set the background to black.*

You can position the movie by dragging it so that it fits inside the stage or by using the Info/Align panels. You can also place content in a Flash border around your QuickTime movie. However, for this example, we want to keep the video fairly standard.

Exit Flash briefly and open the "vnews" QuickTime movie. Double-click the file and note the total number of seconds listed (Movie > Get Info, second pull-down list, time). In the case of our movie, that number is 43:05. To calculate the number of frames that you need to insert so that the movie will play in Flash, multiply that number (43:05) by the movie frame rate. Since the frame rate for our movie is 12, we'll need approximately 517 frames in the Flash movie. The formula is as follows:

```
Number of seconds in QuickTime x frame rate =
Number of frames needed to display the entire video in Flash
```

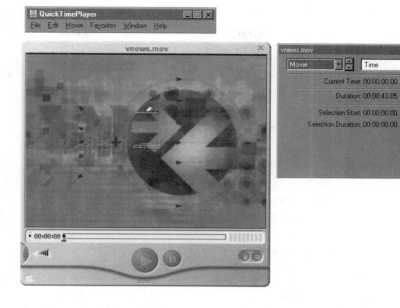

4. **Close the video and pop back into Flash. Add a frame on Frame 516 in the "video" layer.**

Because this process isn't exact, you should move the frame around: If you see a box containing an *X* instead of the video, you may need to delete frames.

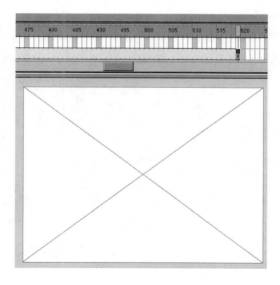

5. *Click and hold the pink-box playback head/indicator on the timeline and scrub along the Flash movie to see a preview of the video we just imported.*

Adding Flash and Generator content to video

Next, we'll add a stock chart.

In Chapter 6 we created a stock chart for viewing on a PDA or Web browser that displayed the values for a day on NASDAQ. Now we're going to export this file for our QuickTime video. (If you're not progressing through this book in order and thus haven't created the chart yet, don't worry: We have a chart ready to go for you in the Chapter 13 folder.)

1. *Add a keyframe on Frame 38 of the "chart" layer. Find mychart.png in the Chapter 13 folder on the CD-ROM and import this file into Flash in the "stock chart" layer on Frame 38. The chart should span the time-line up to Frame 517.*

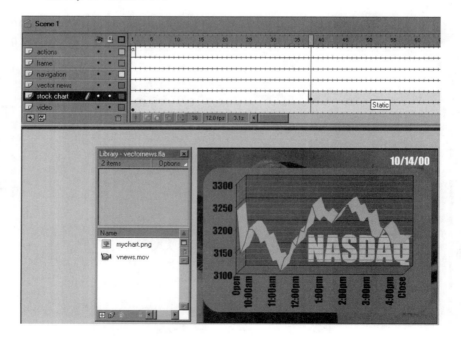

We've used a PNG here. Since your results may vary, it's a good idea to try importing a SWF but to have a PNG ready to use if the SWF doesn't work properly. For reasons of size and scalability, it's always best to use a SWF; however, when that won't work, PNG is the next best format.

2. **Resize and position the chart in the upper right corner of the stage so that we can still see our newscaster. Scrub along the timeline to see how it looks.**

3. **Select the chart and make it a symbol (Insert > Symbol). Name the movie clip "chart." Add a keyframe to Frame 61.**

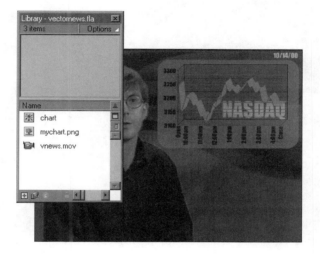

4. **Click the span of the chart on the timeline—from Frame 38 to Frame 61—and create a motion tween (Insert>Create Motion Tween) to make the chart fade.**

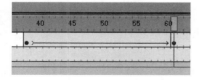

5. **Click the first frame of the chart on the "stock chart" layer (Frame 38) and pull up the Effects panel (Window > Panel > Effects). Set alpha to 0. Move along the timeline to see how it looks.**

6. Add a keyframe to Frame 38 in the "vector news" layer.

Using the Rectangle tool, create a black box that covers about one-twelfth of the stage. Now, using the Text tool, create some white text in the same layer on the black box. For our example, we're going to brand our video with the text *vector news*. Once you create the text, select the text box and break it apart (Modify > Break Apart).

7. Select and delete each chunk of broken-up text.

This will allow you to see through to the video.

8. In the "actions" layer, add a keyframe in Frame 1, and add a play action.

Although we can only access Flash 3 actions, it's still possible to create a highly interactive and compelling movie.

If you're worried about using Flash actions that you shouldn't, go to the Publish settings (File > Publish Settings) and in the Flash tab set the version to Flash 3. The Actions panel will then only allow you to access Flash 3–specific actions.

Now let's see what our movie looks like: Testing the movie from within Flash will only preview the SWF; to preview your QuickTime movie, you must publish it.

Before you test your movie, you should be aware that the authoring environment can be a touch unstable when using QuickTime in Flash. It is a very memory-intensive task. If you have a beefy machine (that is, one with at least 128MB of RAM), you 're probably OK. If not, we suggest you allocate more memory to Flash (Mac) and that you save your work often.

9. Go to the Publish settings (File > Publishing Settings) and select the QuickTime movie (.mov).

10. *Click the QuickTime tab and use the following settings:*

Now publish! You'll notice our movie plays without the QuickTime controller. We now need to add some navigation—but how to control a QuickTime movie with Flash?

Adding interactivity to video

Close the QuickTime movie and hop back into Flash: We're now going to add a few simple buttons in the "navigation" layer for our example, starting in Frame 38. If you're not comfortable creating Play and Pause buttons, or if you have trouble following the instructions here, open vectornews.fla in the Chapter 13 folder.

Make sure to create a large hit area on each of your buttons so that the user doesn't have to position the mouse cursor precisely over each button to play, rewind, or pause the movie.

1. *After you've created your Play and Pause buttons, position them as follows:*

2. *Place an action in the Play button.*

```
on (release) {
    play ();
}
```

3. *Add a Stop action in the Pause button.*

```
on (release) {
    stop ();
}
```

4. *Add a Goto action in the Rewind button:*

```
on (release) {
    gotoAndPlay (1);
}
```

These actions will control the QuickTime movie just as they would a regular Flash movie.

Instead of having the Rewind button go to the first frame, add a Get URL action:

```
on (release) {
    getURL ("http://www.peachpit.com", "_blank");
}
```

5. **Highlight the Play and Pause buttons in the Effects panel (Window > Panel > Effects). Set the alpha to 30 percent so that you can see through the controls**

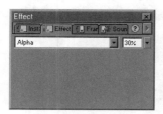

6. **Republish your movie to make sure everything is working (File > Publish).**

If the Play, Pause, and Rewind buttons aren't causing your QuickTime movie to behave as expected, compare your file with the included .fla in the Chapter 13 folder on the CD-ROM.

This video would be more exciting if it weren't just a square, and we can use Flash to change the shape of the video.

7. **Lock all but the "frame" layer.**

Create a black rectangle with the same dimensions as the stage. Then create a rectangle of another color with a corner radius of 30 and place it on the stage so that only the upper left corner of the previous rectangle shows through. Highlight and delete the rectangle you just created, leaving just the corner.

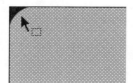

Publishing your video for the Web

Now let's publish! Use (File > Publish Settings) and select HTML (.html). Click the HTML tab. From the Template pull-down list, select QuickTime. Publish and view the movie by going to the folder where the file is saved and opening the HTML file that was created when you published the movie.

The video now looks like it's part of the page rather than just a square box with default controls.

If your results aren't what you expected, compare your work with the sample files included in the Chapter 13 folder.

Try adding other types of Flash content such as animations, menu systems, and banner ads. Just remember that you can only access the version of Flash that QuickTime supports.

POINTS TO REMEMBER

- You need QuickTime in your bag of tricks not just for the production value it provides but also for its usefulness in creating highly interactive video.

- QuickTime 4 supports Flash 3. Later versions of QuickTime will likely support newer versions of Flash. At the time of our writing, the beta version of QuickTime 5 included Flash 4 support.

- You can create custom controls, navigation, links, transparencies, and many other effects with Flash support for QuickTime. You can also take advantage of Generator-created assets (such as charts and graphs) to create information-packed video.

- Using Flash to enhance video may streamline some video production. For example, it's much easier and more cost-effective to add a Flash layer than to use time-consuming tiling, video recompression, and high-end video tools.

- Test frequently and save often. You're asking your machine to do some intensive processing; video and vectors will result in lost work if you're not proactive.

PART 4:
ADVANCED
TOPICS

CHAPTER 14

THE GENERATOR SDK AND API: EXTENDING GENERATOR

BY USING GENERATOR'S SOFTWARE DEVELOPMENT KIT (SDK), DEVELOPERS can extend the application's functionality by creating their own objects. If a company needs custom Flash-based applications, it can easily create the objects in Java and add them to the Generator Object panel for all designers/developers to use.

In this chapter, we'll explore the power and flexibility of the Generator SDK by showing you how to work with it and then building a couple of custom objects.

THE GENERATOR SDK

The Generator SDK (included in the latest version of the application) provides an application programming interface (API) to Generator. Written in Java, the API allows users to extend Generator's functionality by creating custom Generator objects.

You don't need to know Java or write your own objects to take advantage of the SDK. Indeed, this chapter is useful even if all you want to do is download and install objects.

If you're interested in creating custom objects, this chapter covers the basics—from installing the Java development kit (JDK) and creating a Config file to building an advanced Insert Text object. Keep in mind, however, that if you do want to create your own objects, you should have at least a basic knowledge of Java programming.

Installing and configuring Java

Before you can begin creating objects, you need to install a JDK on your computer. You can download one from Sun's site at http://java.sun.com, or you can use a third-party Java development IDE (such as Borland's JBuilder or Symantec's Visual Cafe). For this chapter, we're going to assume that you're using Sun's JDK along with a text editor (such as Notepad) to edit your files.

Once you've downloaded the JDK, run the setup program and follow the prompts. If you're unsure about some of the options, just accept the defaults. Jot down the path where Java is installed because you'll need this information later in the setup. When the installation program is complete, you'll need to set some environment variables for your operating system. In Windows 95 and 98, you do this by editing the autoexec.bat file (normally found on your C: drive). In Windows NT and 2000, you set these variables by right-clicking the My Computer icon on your desktop and selecting the Properties>Advanced tab>Environment Variables button.

You will need to set or edit your Classpath and Path environment variables.

Classpath

The Classpath variable tells Java where to find the classes used in Java programs. The Classpath variable can have more than one Path value as long as a semicolon separates each entry. Be sure to include in your Classpath variable the path to the flashgen.jar file in the Macromedia\Generator 2\classes directory. It should look something like the following:

```
CLASSPATH=" c:\Program Files\Macromedia\Generator 2\classes\
        flashgen.jar
```

Depending on where Generator and the authoring templates are installed on your machine, your Classpath variable may vary slightly.

Path

The Path variable tells your operating system where to find programs it's asked to run. Although it's not essential that you edit this variable, doing so makes it a bit easier to work with Java. The examples in this chapter assume that you've edited the Path variable so that it points to the directory bin inside your Java install directory. If the default path was used when you installed Java, you should add the following to your class path:

```
c:\jdk1.2.2\bin.
```

If you downloaded a different version of the JDK, your directory path may vary slightly.

After you've made these changes, reboot your computer to ensure that they take effect and then open a Command Prompt window (Start Button>Run: command) and type in **java -version**. When you do so, you should see something that resembles the following:

```
C:\>java -version
java version "1.2.2"
Classic VM (build JDK-1.2.2-004, native threads, symcjit)
```

If you don't see something similar to this, or if you get an error stating that the command is not recognized, make sure your Path variable points to the bin directory in your Java install directory.

COMPILING YOUR FIRST OBJECT

By default, the Generator installation program will create a directory in c:\Program\Files\Macromedia\Generator 2. (Your install directory may be slightly different.) This directory includes the following subdirectories, which will be important when working with the SDK:

- api_docs: Containing all of the SDK documentation, this directory is a valuable resource for creating objects.

- classes: This directory contains all of the compiled Java files that Generator needs to run. This is where you'll place your compiled custom objects.

- extras: This directory contains example Generator objects and their associated files. It contains both compiled code and source code so that you can view and edit the examples.

In addition, you'll find a subdirectory in your Flash directory (usually c:\Program Files\Macromedia\Flash 4) called generator\template. This is where you'll store the configuration files (.def's) for your Generator object (see below).

Once you've set up your Classpath variable, you're ready to compile one of the example objects that come with the authoring templates. Look in the extras directory and open the insertbox.java file in your Java editor. Note the following lines of code at the top of the file:

```
import com.macromedia.generator.api.*;
import com.macromedia.generator.app.*;
```

These lines import the Generator classes (located in the flashgen.jar file) that allow you to access Generator's API. When you set your Classpath, you're telling your compiler where to find these classes.

We're finally ready to compile. If you're using Sun's JDK, run "javac" and tell it where the insertbox.java file is located. Open the command prompt and run the following command:

```
javac "c:\Program Files\Macromedia\Generator 2\
extras\insertbox.java" -d "c:\Program Files\
Macromedia\Generator 2\classes"
```

The first part, "javac," runs the Java compiler. The first argument tells the compiler which Java file (.java) to compile. The third argument ("-d" and the file path) tells the compiler where to put the compiled file. If you don't set this argument, the compiled file will be placed in the same folder as its source. If you're in the extras directory, you don't need to provide the complete path to the insertbox.java file. If you're using another compiler, you should compile the file into the classes directory.

The error you're most likely to receive at this point is that the compiler cannot find the Generator classes—probably because of a problem with your Classpath variable. Recheck your Classpath and try recompiling. If you can't run "javac," make sure the path to your Java install directory\bin is set in your computer's Path environment variable (as discussed earlier in this chapter). If you receive any other errors, you need to make sure you installed the Java JDK correctly.

If you don't get any errors, you've successfully compiled the file. Take a quick look at your classes directory: You should see a file named insertbox.class. If you don't see this file, make sure you told your compiler the correct location to place the file, then recompile.

Understanding the Config file

Each object you compile or create must have a corresponding DEF file if you plan to use it within Flash. This file adds your object to Flash and creates a menu that allows you to pass values to the object. The configuration files are stored in your Flash 4\generator\template directory.

Open up the insertbox.def Config file located in the extras directory.

```
/* This is the definition file for the insertbox example
   referenced in the SDK documentation.
 * The definition file creates the UI for the Generator Object
   in the Object palette and Generator inspector.
 * Create a [Value] field for each parameter that you wish to
   define for the object in the Generator inspector.
 */
```

```
[Begin_Command]
    Name        InsertBox
    Type        1
    Token       insertbox
    Resource    Generator.Rsrc
    ResID       304

Value sections removed

[End_Command]
```

The Value sections have been removed from the file that we reproduced above. Each Config file must contain a `[Begin_Command]`/`[End_Command]` pair, along with the following header fields: Name, Type, Token, Resource, and ResId. In addition, the Config file can contain any number of Value fields as well as comments. Beginning with /* and ending with */, comments are the same as in Java and cannot be nested.

Let's take a look at each header field.

- [Begin_Command]: Delineating the start of the Config file, this field must appear before any other fields (except comments).

- [End_Command]: Delineating the end of the config file, this field must appear after all other fields (except comments).

- Name: This is the name of the object as it will appear within Flash.

- Type: This is always 1.

- Token: This is the name of the object's .class file, and it must be unique. If the compiled object is called insertbox.class, you'll enter **insertbox** (dropping the ".class"). Flash uses the Token field to determine which Java classes to use for the object.

- Resource: This is always Generator.Rsrc.

- ResId: This determines which icon will be associated with your object in the Generator Object window in Flash. Valid values are numbers between 300 and 321.

The rest of the Config file consists of Value sections. These sections—each of which starts with `[Value]`—allow the user to define and pass data to the Generator object through the Generator Inspector window within Flash. Although they're not required, most objects will contain at least one Value field.

A Value section contains a number of fields, some required and some optional. The following represents a simple Value section:

```
[Value]
    Name        Width
    Type        Number
    Token       width
    DValue      1000
    HelpString  Specifies the width of the button. Units are
                1/20th of a pixel.
```

Value section fields:

- **Name:** This name will appear for the Value field in the Generator Inspector; it should tell the user what the field represents.

- **Type:** Specifies data type for the current Value section. There are five valid Value field types—Browse, List, Number, String, and ColorList—each of which either allows the user to enter a different data type or provides a specialized interface.

- **Browse:** This field provides a window that users can employ to browse through a file's file system—useful for specifying data sources.

- **List:** This allows the user to select a value from a list of options. The values for the list are specified with the ValueList tag, and the default value is specified with the DValue tag (see below). For example, you could change the Width Value field above to use a List box:

```
[Value]
    Name        Width
    Type        List
    Token       width
    DValue      1000
    ValueList   250
    ValueList   500
    ValueList   750
    ValueList   1000
    HelpString  Specifies the width of the button. Units are
                1/20th of a pixel.
```

This would present the user with a list of four options (250, 500, 750, 1000), with 1000 selected as the default.

- **Number:** The Number field tells Generator that it should expect to receive a number, not a non-numeric character.

- **String:** The user can enter any sequence of characters in this field.

- **ColorList:** This field allows the user to enter color values (choosing from those on the automatically provided color palette). Any valid method of representing a color in Generator (color name: "black," hexadecimal value: "0x000000," Web hexadecimal value: "#000000") can be used as a value here.

- **Token:** This field—which should be unique to the Config file—sets the name that the Generator object will use to access the section's value (see below).

- **DValue:** This is the default value of the Value field that will be displayed to the user. If the user does not change the value, this is what will be passed to the Generator object.

- **HelpString:** This is a string that's displayed to the user each time he or she selects the Value field. You should use this string to describe what the field represents, the values it can accept, and any other instructions that might be useful.

All Config files must be placed within the Macromedia\Flash 4\generator\templates directory or subdirectories. If a Config file is not placed into this directory, its object will not be available within Flash.

Flash may crash if you have a Generator object with no Value section, or if all of the Generator Panel Value sections are empty. If your object doesn't require Value sections, you may need to create a fake section to prevent Flash from crashing. Simply create a Value section with a default value. Make sure the Token value is different than the other values in the .def (see below for more information).

USING CUSTOM GENERATOR OBJECTS IN FLASH

Now that we've covered the Config file basics, let's use the Insertbox object in Flash.

1. *Open Flash and create a new Flash file.*

2. *Ensure that the Generator Template (.SWT) box is checked in File>Publish Settings. Also, make sure that the Generator Object panel (Window>Generator Objects) and Generator Object Inspector (Window>Inspectors>Generator) are open.*

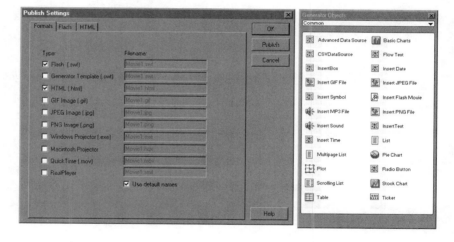

You should see an Insertbox object on the Generator Object panel.

If you don't, make sure that you copied the insertbox.def file into the correct directory.

3. *Click and drag the object into the Flash movie.*

4. *When you select the object on the workspace, its configuration parameters will appear on the Generator tab of the Object Inspector.*

These fields are determined by the object's Config file, and their values are passed to the Generator object when the Flash file is created. You may place both values and Generator variables into these fields. For now, do not change any of these values.

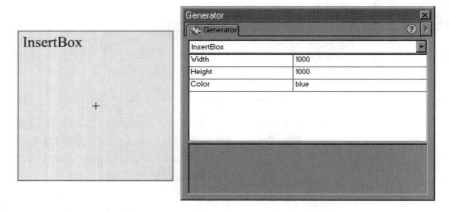

5. **Select Control>Test Movie or press Ctrl-Enter to preview your Flash movie. You should see a rectangle in your movie. If you don't, make sure that you enabled Generator in the Publish Settings window.**

6. **Now go back and change some of the properties in the Inspector window.**

7. **Preview the file again and notice how the changes affect the Flash movie. The box is being built dynamically based on the settings passed to it through the Inspector Window.**

Congratulations! You've successfully compiled, installed, and used a Generator custom object. You can now compile and install custom objects, and you're on your way to creating your own objects.

A quick note about security: When you download an object from the Internet, you don't always have to compile it. If the object is already compiled, you can simply place its .class file in the Macromedia\Generator 2\classes directory, and place its Config (.def) file in the Macromedia\Flash 4\generator\template directory.

However, as with other programs downloaded from the Internet, you should be cautious about using custom objects unless they come from a trusted source (such as Macromedia) or are included with the object's source code. A malicious programmer could conceivably disguise a harmful program as a Generator object. If an object comes with its source code, you should look over the code and then compile the object yourself. That way you can make sure it's not doing anything harmful.

Creating an advanced Insert Text object

Now that you know how to compile and install objects, you're ready to create a Generator object from scratch. The object we'll create here will give users advanced control over dynamically inserting text into Flash movies via Generator.

Although Generator allows users to insert text dynamically in Flash movies (by simply setting and replacing text variables within the template), it can be difficult and tedious to dynamically set the *attributes* of that inserted text. (You must dynamically determine which of the multiple movie clips to load.) The object we create, however, will allow us to dynamically insert text *and* specify some of its attributes, including font type, size, color, alignment, and transparency. This makes it much easier for users to dynamically insert and customize text with Generator, and it gives us the opportunity to show you how a custom object works.

To begin the process, create a new text file in the extras directory and name it InsertText.java (be sure to match the case precisely). This file will contain the Java code for the object.

Although we'll go through the code section by section here, we won't discuss portions of it that aren't vital to understanding how the object works. You may view all of the source code with comments on the CD-ROM.

First, we need to import the packages we plan to use in our code:

```
import java.util.Properties;
import com.macromedia.generator.api.*;
import com.macromedia.generator.app.*;
```

The first line above imports a Java class required by the SDK; the next two Import statements make the Generator API available to us. After we declare our Import statement, we can declare our class.

```
public class InsertText extends GenericCommand
{
}
```

Our class, InsertText, extends the GenericCommand class contained within the Generator API. All custom objects must extend GenericCommand and must contain a doCommand() method that Generator calls when executing the object. The doCommand() method is synonymous with the main() method when running a command-line Java program.

The doCommand method must have the following signature:

```
public void doCommand(FlashEnvironment fEnv, Script script,
                      Context context, int cmdIndex,
                      Properties params)
{
}
```

The arguments that Generator passes enable the object to access the Flash file, its environment, and the name/value data pairs set by the user. These arguments also provide methods that allow the object to dynamically modify the template. Let's look at each of the arguments passed in by Generator when the object is processed:

- **FlashEnvironment fEnv:** This object manages the way the custom object is processed. It contains methods that allow you to log errors, send messages to the authoring environment, and process scripts.

- **Script script:** The Script object represents a timeline or symbol in Flash. All templates contain at least one script representing the main timeline. Scripts can contain other scripts, just as movie clips can contain other movie clips within Flash. The Script object that's passed in represents the main timeline of the Generator template.

- **Context context:** This object stores the Generator name/value pairs present in the current template's environment. These name/value pairs can come from any valid data source. They can also be sent to the template through the URL or command line.

- **int cmdIndex:** This represents the index of the current Generator object in the template and is used to reference the object from a number of other classes and methods.

- **Properties params:** This contains the entire set of name/value pairs entered by the user in the Generator Inspector window for the custom object.

Using just the code above, we could compile and install the object. Of course, if you installed the object in Flash, it wouldn't do anything even though it contains all of the required code to create a Generator object. The object's real code is contained in the doCommand method.

First, we need to get a reference to the Generator object that the user placed in the template. We do this by retrieving its script from the main timeline's script.

```
Script clip = script.getCommandScript(cmdIndex);
```

Remember that cmdIndex is the index of the current object in the template. The getCommandScript() function takes the index and returns the Script object for that index. We will store this as a variable called "clip."

We're now ready to add the code that will ultimately insert our text. Our code follows the following steps:

1. **Create a Text object and set its attributes.**

2. **Create Color and Font objects, set their attributes, and pass them to the Text object.**

3. **Create a Matrix object and set the text's position within the template.**

4. **Insert the Text object in the template.**

Don't worry if some of the above terms don't make sense now; we'll cover them in detail later in the chapter.

Almost all Generator objects and methods throw the GeneratorApiException when something goes wrong. Of course, if a method throws an exception, it must be caught. We'll show the "try/catch" block in the first snippet of code below, but for brevity's sake we'll omit it in all subsequent code examples.

If you're unsure whether you need to catch the exception, consult the SDK documentation or view the source code on the CD-ROM.

First, we need to create a Text object that will contain our actual text and its attributes:

```
Text insertText = null;
try
{
    insertText = new Text();
}
catch(GeneratorApiException gae)
{
    fEnv.logError("problem creating text object : " + gae);
    return;
}
```

This creates a new Text object that represents text in a Flash movie. In the "catch" block, you'll notice the fEnv.logError() method call: Depending on the user's settings, this method call will log errors and pass them to the Output window in the Generator authoring environment. Extremely useful for debugging, this method works in the same way that System.out.println() does for debugging in Java console programming.

Just creating a Text object, however, doesn't actually insert text into the movie: You must first set a number of attributes such as font type and text string. To set font type, we need to create an instance of the Font class, set some of its attributes, and then pass it to our Text object:

```
Font font = null;
String fontName = getStringParam( context, params,
                              "fontType", "Arial" );

boolean bold = getBoolParam( context, params, "bold");
Boolean italic = getBoolParam( context, params, "italic");
```

There are a number of important things going on here, including our first example of how to access the data the user defined in the object's Inspector window:

```
String fontName = getStringParam( context, params,
                              "fontType", "Arial" );
```

The first two objects passed to the getStringParam method ("context," "params") contain the environment and object variables present in the movie. The third argument determines which value will be retrieved (this argument should match a token name from the Config file). The last argument is the default value returned if the token cannot be found or if the user left the field blank. This method, which makes it easy to retrieve the values set by the user, is employed extensively for creating custom objects.

There are two other methods, getIntParam() and getBoolParam, that are similar to getStringParam except that they return "int" and Boolean values, respectively. The getBoolParam does not take a default value but returns False if its value cannot be found.

Now that we've retrieved the font values, we can create a new Font object and pass the user-defined values to it.

```
    font = new Font();
    font.setFont(fontName, bold, italic);
```

The first line creates a new Font object, while the second line sets the attributes of the Font object. The first argument sets which font to use, while the second and third arguments are Boolean values that determine whether the text should be bold and italic.

Once we've created our Font object, we'll pass it to our Text object:

```
InsertText.setFont(font);
```

We then need to set other attributes of our Text object, such as the size and color of the displayed text:

```
int fontSize = getIntParam( context, params,
                            "fontSize", 12 ) * 20;
InsertText.setSize(fontSize);

Color fontColor = null;
fontColor = new Color();
fontColor.setRGBValue(getStringParam( context, params,
                        "fontColor", "#000000" ));
InsertText.setColor(fontColor)
```

This code simply sets properties on the Text object just as we set them above. Generator measures units in *twips*, with each twip equal to one-twentieth of a pixel. Because the size set by the user is measured in pixels, we need to convert that number to twips by multiplying it by 20. We also need to create a new Color object and pass it to the Text object in the same manner that we created the Font object.

Because we want our object to allow the user to specify the width of the text field (which determines the amount of text that can appear on one line before wrapping to the next), we must find out the width of the InsertText object that the user placed in the Flash movie. The default width is 102.4 pixels; however, the user can change this by scaling the object so that it's wider when placed in the movie.

```
int lineWidth = -1;
int lineHeight = -1;

Rect rect = script.getCommandRect(cmdIndex);
lineWidth = (rect.getXMin() * -1) + rect.getXMax();
lineHeight = (rect.getYMin() * -1) + rect.getYMax();

InsertText.setLineWidth(lineWidth);
```

First, we get a Rect object from the Generator object's script. A Rect object represents the area and width of an object, symbol, or script in the Flash movie. By retrieving the Rect object, we can determine the width of the Generator object in the movie and then set the text width to that same value. Note that we also get the line height and store it in a variable, which we'll use in our code below.

We also want to set the text's alignment relative to the width of the Text field we set above. The Text object contains four constants that define alignment: Left = 0, Right = 1, Center = 2, and Justify = 3.

We set these constants based on the value passed in by the user; however, we must first convert the user's input into the appropriate "int" value.

```
int alignment;
String textAlign = getStringParam( context, params,
                                   "alignment", "" );
if(textAlign.equals("right"))
{
    alignment = 1;
}
else if (textAlign.equals("center"))
{
    alignment = 2;
}
else if (textAlign.equals("justify"))
{
    alignment = 3;
}
else
{
    alignment = 0;
}

InsertText.setAlignment(alignment);
```

The above code determines what string the user has passed in and then sets the appropriate integer. We pass this to the Text object through the setAlignment() method.

We must now create a Matrix class to describe the inserted object's properties (for example, rotation, scale, and color). You can access these properties within Flash through the Transform Inspector window.

All of the methods used to insert objects in Generator templates take a Matrix class as one of their arguments. Thus, you almost always have to instantiate a Matrix object—even if you don't plan to use it. You may also notice that most of these same methods take two Matrix objects in their arguments. In most cases, you'll simply reference the same Matrix twice. However, you can also pass in two separate matrixes with different settings. Flash will tween any differences between the Matrixes over the number of frames specified when inserting the object.

By default, objects are inserted into the Flash movie at the center point of the Generator object in the movie. However, we want to insert our text at the top left corner of the object so that the user can more accurately place the text and set its width relative to the template. We do this by determining the object's center point and then setting the Text object's offset on the Matrix up and to the left so the text is placed in the top left corner.

```
Matrix matrix = null;

matrix = new Matrix();
script.setCommandMatrix(cmdIndex, matrix);
matrix.setXOffset((lineWidth / 2) * -1);
matrix.setYOffset((lineHeight / 2) * -1);
```

We're finally ready to place the text that will be displayed in the movie into our Text object. To do this, we get the user-set value of the text and pass it to the Text object—all of which can be accomplished with the following short line of text:

```
InsertText.setString(getStringParam( context, params,
                  "text", "" ));
```

If the user has left the Text field blank, we'll insert an empty string.

The last thing we need to do before inserting the Text object in the Flash file is set the transparency/alpha for the text field. We do this by setting the alpha on the script that represents our object:

```
int transparency = getIntParam( context, params,
                        "transparency", 100 );
script.setCommandTransparency(cmdIndex, transparency);
```

By now, our code snippet should begin to make sense. We get the transparency level passed in by the user, with 100 as the default, and pass it to the setCommandTransparency method for the script representing our Generator object.

Now that we've set all of the properties and attributes of our Text object, we can finally insert it in the Flash movie. To do so, we'll call the insertText method on the Generator Object's script:

```
clip.insertText(insertText, 0, 0, matrix, frameCount,
                matrix);
```

Each of the following arguments is passed into the method.

- **insertText:** This is the Text object we're inserting in the Flash movie.

- **First 0:** This is the layer of the Flash movie into which the text will be inserted.

- **Second 0:** This is the first frame in the Flash movie in which the text will appear.

- **First matrix:** This is the starting matrix for our text object.

- **frameCount:** This is the last frame in which the text will appear. FrameCount is a code-initialized "int" variable (not shown above) representing the total number of frames in the Generator object.

- **Second matrix:** This is the ending matrix for our text object. We use the same matrix as that used in the first Matrix field.

Once you've inserted the appropriate try/catch blocks as well as any other code left out above, you're ready to compile the object. Make sure to compile it into the classes directory. The command to compile the object should look something like the following:

```
javac "c:\Program Files\Macromedia\Generator 2\
extras\InsertText.java"  -d "c:\Program Files\
Macromedia\Generator 2\classes"
```

Chances are, you'll get some compiling errors caused by mistakes in your code. Simply fix the errors and recompile. Once the object is compiled, you'll need to make a Config file that will make it available within Flash and allow the user to set the attributes to be passed to the object.

Creating the InsertText Config file

Now that you've created and compiled the InsertText object, we need to create a Config file so that the user can set the object's attributes.

As with the above code, we won't list every Value field in the Config file; however, you can view the entire file on the CD-ROM in the Chapter 14 folder.

The first thing we need to do is insert [Begin_Command] and [End_Command] tags. All of the Config file's settings must appear between these tags. At the top of the file, just under the [Begin_Command] tag, we'll add the Header fields:

```
Name        Insert Text
Type        1
Token       InsertText
Resource    Generator.Rsrc
ResID       304
```

The Name field determines the object's name in the Generator object window in Flash. Although you can name it anything you want, it's a good idea to give it a name that describes its function.

The extremely important Token field tells Generator which object to use with the Config file. The value must match the name of our object minus the .class or .java extension.

As mentioned earlier, the Type and Resource fields always have the same values. Although we don't need to change the ResID value, you can view the different icons by entering values between 300 and 321.

Once all of the Header fields are complete, we can begin adding Value sections to our Config file.

```
[Value]
Name        Text
Type        String
Token       text
HelpString  The text that will be inserted into the movie.
```

The first Value section determines the actual text that will be displayed. Its type, String, has no default value and will be referenced within the object by "text."

```
[Value]
Name         Color
Type         ColorList
Token        fontColor
Dvalue       blue
HelpString   Specifies the color of the inserted text.
```

The next section allows the user to set the font's color. Its type, ColorList, has a default value of blue. Because this is a ColorList, a button will be created that causes a color palette to pop up from which the user can specify a color.

```
[Value]
Name         Type
Type         List
Token        fontType
DValue       Arial
ValueList    Arial
ValueList    Comic Sans MS
ValueList    Courier New
ValueList    Georgia
ValueList    Impact
ValueList    Lucida Console
ValueList    Tahoma
ValueList    Times New Roman
ValueList    Trebuchet MS
ValueList    Verdana
HelpString   Specifies the font type used.
```

The fontType Value section is a List type that allows the user to select the font type in which the text will be displayed. This section has a default value (DValue) of Arial, and it contains a number of fonts from which to choose. Notice that Arial appears twice, once as the DValue and once in the ValueList. This is necessary to allow users to reselect the default value once they've deselected it.

```
[Value]
Name         Bold
Type         List
Token        bold
```

```
DValue      false
ValueList   true
ValueList   false
HelpString  Specifies whether the text will be bold.
```

The final section we'll examine is the Bold field, which determines whether the text is displayed bold. This section is a List with False the default value. Note that in the object's Java code, you could use both getBoolParam() and getStringParam() to obtain its value. In this case, we'll use getBoolParam() because the method we're passing the value to requires a Boolean value.

You'll still need to add Value sections for fontSize, italic, transparency, line spacing, and alignment. You can create your own or look at the completed Config file on the CD-ROM. Just make sure that the Token values in the Config file match those in your object.

Once you've created the Config file, save it as InsertText.def and place it in the Macromedia\Flash\generator\templates directory. Any time you make a change to your object or its Config file you must restart Flash for the change to take effect. If Flash is open, close it and reopen it to load the new Config file. You can now use the custom object you created.

Using the Insert Text custom object

1. *Create a new Flash movie and set it as a Generator template by checking File>Publish Settings>Generator Template (.swt).*

2. *Open the Generator Objects window and drag the Insert Text object into the movie. If you don't see the Insert Text object, make sure you placed the object's Config file (InsertText.def) in the correct directory.*

   InsertText

3. *Once you've placed the object into the Flash movie, set its width by scaling its size.*

4. *You can then set all of the object's attributes in the Generator Inspector window. You may place both values and Generator variables in the Value fields.*

5. *Once you've set the object's values, preview the movie by pressing Ctrl-Enter. You should see your text with all of the settings that you specified. If nothing shows up or you receive an error message, make sure you filled in all of the object's properties in the Generator Inspector window, then make sure there are no errors in the object's code.*

If you continue to receive errors, compare your files with those on the CD in the Chapter 14 folder.

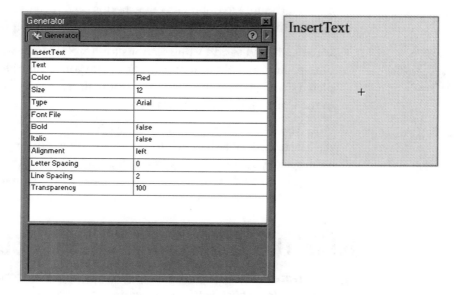

The custom Insert Text object is now complete and ready to use.

INSTALLING CUSTOM OBJECTS ON THE GENERATOR SERVER

Once you've tested and debugged your custom Generator object, you're ready to install it on a Generator server. All you have to do to install a custom object on a Generator server is copy that object's .class onto the server and place it in the Generator\classes directory. You will have to restart the server once you have installed it. Once the server has been restarted, Generator will be ready to process templates with the new object.

POINTS TO REMEMBER

- The Generator SDK allows Java developers to extend the functionality of Flash and Generator by creating their own Generator objects.

- Compiling and creating Generator Objects requires at least an intermediate knowledge of Java.

- Using custom Generator objects in Flash is the same as using the included objects with Generator.

- Installing custom objects on the Generator server requires copying the class files to the classes directory of the Generator server.

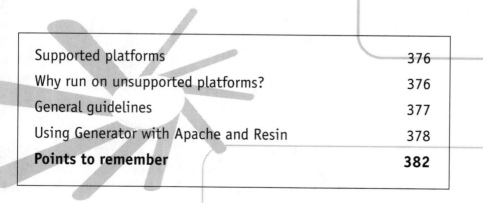

CHAPTER 15

INSTALLING AND RUNNING GENERATOR WITH CUSTOM CONFIGURATIONS

AS DISCUSSED EARLIER, MACROMEDIA SUPPORTS GENERATOR ON A NUMBER of operating systems and Web server/servlet-engine combinations. You can also set up Generator to work with servlet engines, Web servers, and even operating systems that Macromedia doesn't officially support.

This chapter describes the steps for installing Generator with Web servers and servlet engines that Macromedia doesn't support. We'll also take you step by step through the process of getting Generator to work with Apache and the Resin Servlet engine.

Generator is about 90 percent c++ code and 10 percent Java code. Although this may lead you to believe that getting Generator to run in an unsupported configuration would be difficult, such is not the case. This is because online Generator's code is written as a Java servlet. In fact, JRun and Netscape iPlanet are simply standard Servlet engines that run the Generator servlet.

SUPPORTED PLATFORMS

Officially, Generator will work on the following platforms:

- Windows with IIS/PWS and JRun
- Linux (x86) with Apache and JRun
- Solaris (Sparc) with Apache and Netscape iPlanet

You can also get Generator to run on just about any servlet engine or Java application server, including the following:

- Caucho's Resin
- BEA WebLogic
- IBM WebSphere

In addition, you can get Generator to run with unsupported Web servers such as Apache on Windows.

WHY RUN ON UNSUPPORTED PLATFORMS?

Why would you want to run Generator on an unsupported platform? That is actually a very good question, and in most cases, the answer is that you do not really need to. Generator runs fine as is.

However, it's not unusual for companies to invest a great deal of time and money in a particular platform. By using Generator with the existing platform, you can:

- Take advantage of tighter integration between your application and Generator

- Leverage your knowledge of the current platform

- Eliminate the worry of learning and supporting a new platform

- Take advantage of existing functionality (such as load balancing)

However, once again, most users will not have a compelling reason to run Generator in an unsupported configuration. If you don't have a need to run Generator on an unsupported platform, you can safely skip this chapter.

Keep in mind that Macromedia will not support Generator if you're running it in an unsupported configuration. Thus, if you run into problems, you're on your own.

GENERAL GUIDELINES

Regardless of which servlet engine/Web server you're attempting to install Generator under, you must do the following to ensure that it works correctly:

- Install and configure the Web server and servlet engine to work together. (This is beyond this chapter's scope; however, the documentation included with your Web server and servlet engine should show you how.)

- Add the Generator flashgen.jar file to your Servlet engine's Classpath.

- Install the Generator Servlet in your servlet engine.

- Specify the Generator Install Path to be used by the servlet.

- Instruct your Web server to pass all requests for Generator templates (.swt's) to the Generator server.

- Place Generator's c++ code in the operating system's path so that the servlet engine can locate it.

With the exception of the Administration Servlet—which won't work in unsupported configurations—Generator should work and perform just as if it were installed in a Macromedia-supported configuration.

USING GENERATOR WITH APACHE AND RESIN

This section describes how to install Generator to run with the Apache Web server and the Resin Servlet engine on both Windows and Linux.

Although we've configured the files and formatted the properties specifically for use with Resin, the steps described here can apply to any servlet engine. (You just need to locate the files and properties for whatever servlet engine you're using.)

As a robust, open-source Web server, Apache is the most popular Web server on the Internet. When used with the JRun Servlet engine, Generator supports Apache on the Linux and Solaris platforms. Generator does not support Apache on Windows.

You can find out more about Apache as well as download the latest version from the following URL:

http://httpd.apache.org/

Resin is an open-source servlet engine developed and maintained by Caucho. Like Apache, it's robust and flexible, and it works especially well as a development platform.

You can find out more about Resin as well as download the latest version from the following URL:

http://www.caucho.com/products/resin/

The following steps assume a basic knowledge of how to configure Java servlets.

1. *Download, install, and configure the Apache Web server.*

2. *Download, install, and configure the Resin Servlet engine.*

Make sure that Resin is configured to work with Apache correctly. The directory in which you install Resin will be referred to below as `<resin>`.

3. *Install the Generator server for your operating system.*

At this point it's not important that Generator works; you just want to make sure that the installation was successful. The directory in which you install Generator will be referred to below as `<generator>`.

Don't proceed to Step 4 until you're certain you've completed Steps 1 through 3.

4. ***Using a text editor, open the <resin>/conf/resin.conf file (the servlet-engine configuration file).***

5. ***Find the following tag: <web-app id='/'>.***

All of the Generator configuration tags we'll add fit within this tag.

Note that you can also create your own Web-app tag to contain the Generator tags; however, that task is beyond the scope of this chapter. The important thing to understand here is that the Web-app tag simply maps the scope of the tags relative to the Web server. Thus in this case, the tags we're adding apply to the entire Web server because the Web-app "id" tag is mapped to the root of the Web server (id='/').

6. ***Add the following tags:***

```
<classpath id='<generator>/classes/flashgen.jar'/>
<classpath id='<generator>/classes'/>
```

Remember to replace <generator> with the path in which you installed Generator.

The "classpath" tags tell the Servlet engine where to find the actual Java code used by the Generator Servlet.

7. ***Add the following tag:***

```
<servlet servlet-name='Generator' servlet-class='com.macromedia
  .generator.servlets.FlashGenerator'>
<init-param InstallPath='<generator>' />
</servlet>
```

Remember to replace <generator> with the path in which you installed Generator.

The first part of this tag maps the Generator Servlet, telling the servlet engine what to call the servlet (`servlet-name='Generator'`) and where it can find the files for the servlet (`servlet-class='com.macromedia .generator.servlets.FlashGenerator'`). The actual code for the servlet is contained in the flashgen.jar file that we set the "classpath" to point to in the previous step.

The init-param tag inside of the servlet tag is used to pass Name/Value pairs to the Generator Servlet. In this case, we're passing the InstallPath variable to the servlet. The value of InstallPath is the directory that Generator was installed into. Note that the variable name is case sensitive.

8. Finally, add the following:

```
<servlet-mapping url-pattern='*.swt' servlet-name='Generator' />
```

This tag maps any files that end in SWT (*.swt) to the servlet named Generator, which we specified in the previous step.

Anytime a Generator template (SWT) is requested from the Web server (Apache), that request will be passed to the servlet named Generator. Generator will then process the template and send the response to whomever requested the template.

9.   Save and close the resin.conf file.

10. Restart Resin.

If you get any errors, make sure your newly added tags don't contain any typos. Once you're able to start Resin without receiving errors, move on to the next step.

11.   You must now place Generator's c++ code where it can be found by programs on the computer (including the servlet engine).

- On Linux: In the <generator>/bin directory, there is a file called lib-jflashgen.so. Copy this file—which contains all of Generator's c++ code—into the /lib directory. You can also place a link from the /lib directory pointing to the libjflashgen.so file.

- On Windows: In the <generator>/bin directory there is a file called jflashgen.dll. Copy this file—which contains all of Generator's c++ code—into the c:\winnt\system32 directory (the directory name may vary slightly, depending on which version of Windows you're using).

12. Restart your computer.

This step may not be necessary if you're using Linux or Solaris.

13. **Copy the install_test.swt template from your <generator> directory and place it in the root of the Apache Web server.**

14. **Call the template through the Web server using your browser.**

You should see a message stating that the server is installed correctly.

The following is a list of possible errors and their meanings:

java.lang.ClassNotFoundException: This usually means that the "classpath" pointing to the flashgen.jar file has not been specified correctly. Go back to Step 7 and make sure you've entered the "classpath" correctly.

java.lang.UnsatisfiedLinkError: no jflashgen in java.library.path: The libjflashgen.so/jflashgen.dll file cannot be located. Make sure that you placed it in the correct location; go back to Step 12 and follow the instructions carefully. Also, if you didn't reboot your server, do so now.

Message stating that Generator has not been installed correctly: Make sure that you set the InstallPath param correctly in the resin.conf file (Step 8). You can also check the Generator.log file in the <generator>/log directory for more information on the problem.

POINTS TO REMEMBER

- Generator is able to run in a number of servlet engines and application servers, even though they are not supported by Macromedia.

- Most users do not need to run Generator in an unsupported configuration.

- Configuring Generator to run in an unsupported configuration involves installing the Generator servlet, placing Generator's c++ code where Generator can find it, and telling the Web server to pass all requests for Generator templates to the Generator server.

- If you run Generator in an unsupported configuration, you cannot receive support from Macromedia if you have a problem.

CHAPTER 16

OTHER TOOLS THAT DELIVER DYNAMIC FLASH CONTENT

GOOD AS IT IS, GENERATOR ISN'T THE BEST TOOL FOR EVERY CONCEIVABLE project. That's why in this chapter we take a look at some of the other tools for delivering data-driven Flash content. As a developer, you need to be familiar with all of the currently available tools so that you can help your clients choose the best ones for their projects. This chapter should serve as a good starting point to help you do just that.

THE OTHER GENERATORS

In this chapter, we've tried to present the available tools in the most neutral manner possible. We encourage you and your teams to look closely at these products, comparing not only features but also the level of support and certification each company provides. What, for example, happens at 1 a.m. when the server goes down? Is there an established developer community? Does the tool use existing standards like XML? Is it proprietary? It's important to consider all angles when selecting a tool for getting dynamic content into Flash.

Unless you have an application that needs to run on a very specific platform, we expect you'll use Generator in most situations. However, there are certain rare situations which make another tool more appropriate. For example, suppose you need to deliver data-driven PDFs on Mac OS X. In that case, you'd most likely want to use ReportMill.

Another thing to consider when selecting tools is openness. All developers can use the Flash file format and Generator API/SDK to extend Flash and Generator as needed. Not all other tools, however, allow this kind of (or any) prodding.

Finally, when choosing a new tool that may be used under heavy loads, ask the tool manufacturers what white papers or third-party testing they've completed. Theoretical performance and the fact that a tool runs on Linux doesn't mean it will survive a 14-day consecutive load.

SWIFT-GENERATOR

As a Generator-like Dynamic Flash content generator, Swift-Generator can dynamically replace texts, fonts, sounds, images, and movie clips in either a template file or a standard Flash file. You can also use it to dynamically change action parameters in frames or buttons. Like Generator, Swift-Generator requires only Flash as the authoring tool. But an important difference is that Swift-Generator can produce only Flash data—you can't create graphic formats other than Flash. You can use Swift-Generator as a CGI program, and you can also employ it off line with schedulers like Cron. Swift-Generator requires the proprietary Swift-Scripts and files (SWS) to replace variable content inside the Flash templates. Swift-Generator supports CGI parameters, text files, MySQL, and ODBC for database connectivity on some platforms. You cannot, however, create charts, graphs, and other Generator objects.

Supported Platforms

Linux x86

Linux MIPS (Cobalt)

Linux Alpha

Linux PPC

Windows (95/98/NT/2000)

FreeBSD

Solaris 2.6 (Sparc)

Solaris 2.8 (x86)

BSDi

Mac OS X (Unix)

Price

You can use Swift-Generator for free; however, if you use it on a Web site without registering (and paying for) it, you must display the product's logo. To remove the logo, you must register and pay a fee of $100 or 100 Euros. Each registration is valid for only one Web site.

Web site

http://swift-tools.com

Front-end user interface for Swift-Tools

http://swift-tools.com/swift-generator.html#3rd_party

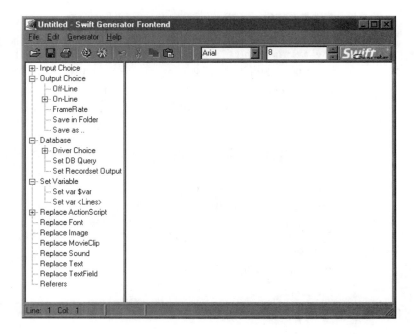

Swift-Tools also offers a front-end user interface that makes it possible to view and edit the Swift-Tools script files (SWS) on Windows machines.

Feature-by-feature comparison with Generator

Note: A few features were still unknown to the authors at the time of this writing.

Uses Flash as UI/ development tool: Swift: Yes uses proprietary language **Generator**: Yes

Server-side customizations: Swift: Yes **Generator:** Yes

Multiplatform support: Swift: Yes **Generator:** Yes

Multithreaded: Swift: Unknown **Generator:** Yes

Multiprocessor support: Swift: Unknown **Generator:** Yes

Symbol replacement: Swift: Yes **Generator:** Yes

Multiple language/encoding support: Swift: Unknown **Generator:** Yes

Text replacement: Swift: Yes **Generator:** Yes

Processed SWF files contain only used elements:
Swift: Yes **Generator:** Yes

Insert external images: Swift: Yes **Generator:** Yes

Customized Flash (SWF) movies: Swift: Yes **Generator:** Yes

Output as GIF: Swift: No **Generator:** Yes

Output as JPG: Swift; No **Generator:** Yes

Output as PNG: Swift: No **Generator:** Yes

Output as MOV: Swift: No **Generator**, Yes

Output as projector (Mac and PC): Swift: No **Generator:** Yes

Outputs image maps: Swift: No **Generator:** Yes

Output to multiple Flash versions: Swift: No **Generator:** Yes

Dynamic charts and graphs: Swift: No **Generator:** Yes

Scrolling tickers and lists: Swift: No **Generator:** Yes

External MP3 insertion: Swift: No **Generator:** Yes

Supports additional dynamically created objects:
Swift: No **Generator:** Yes

Replicate frames using database records: Swift: No **Generator:** Yes

Native database connections: Swift: Yes ODBC/MySQL **Generator:** Yes

Caching support: Swift: No **Generator:** Yes

Logging: Swift: Yes Error log only **Generator:** Yes

Transaction reporting: Swift: No **Generator:** Yes

Java API: Swift: No **Generator:** Yes

We also encourage you to check the Web site because new versions and features may have been added.

SwiffTools

SwiffPEG and SwiffEG Server are specialized tools, for inserting MP3 files into .swf's much like Generator does. SwiftPEG is a small Windows utility that allows users to select an MP3 to insert into a movie clip of an existing .swf (which does not stream). Once you've registered the application, you can use it to create a new .swf. You can specify a level, instance name, and spriteID.

SwiftPEG Server does the same thing as the regular version of SwiffPEG—but on the fly (for example, with an NT server). You can use SwiffPEG Server to upload MP3s to the server. SwiffPEG will then convert them as needed, on the fly and streaming.

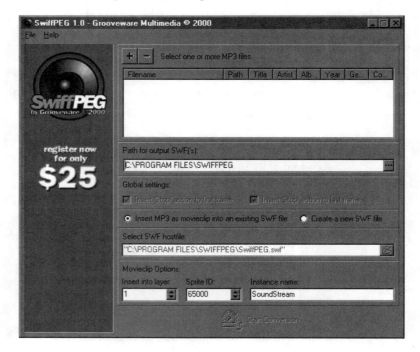

Supported platforms

Windows 95/98/NT/2000 only.

Price

$25

Web site

http://swifftools.com/stools/

Features

Since this tool is designed to do just one thing—insert MP3s—we won't provide a feature-by-feature comparison with Generator. If you need a tool for creating streaming MP3s and don't want to use Flash or Generator, this product can tackle that task.

We also encourage you to check the Web site because new versions and features may have been added.

FLASH TURBINE

ASP Flash Turbine, Flash Turbine Direct, and Linux Turbine are Dynamic Flash engines that can also add live content to Flash movies.

Turbine allows you to generate Flash movies with content obtained from a variety of sources (for example, text files, image files, ODBC-compliant databases, and so on). You can generate tables, lists, and charts from accessed content, and you can draw directly into Flash movies using the proprietary Draw Script language. You can also place text and movie clips, images included.

ASP Flash Turbine is a Dynamic Flash content generator that works from ASP scripts.

Direct Flash Turbine is the ISAPI version of the Turbine Dynamic Flash engine. Direct Turbine is aimed at users who don't need the scripting capabilities of ASP Flash Turbine but do need fast Dynamic Flash generation.

Linux Turbine is the Apache Web server version of Flash Turbine engine. It has the same features as ASP and Direct Flash Turbine.

Supported platforms

ASP Flash Turbine will run on Windows 2000, Windows NT 4.0 (SP3 or later), and Windows 95/98.

ASP Flash Turbine supports Internet Information Server (IIS), Personal Web Server (PWS) 4.0, and IIS 5.0.

Linux Flash Turbine is compatible with the Linux 2.2 operating system and Apache 1.3.6+, running on Intel-architecture machines.

Linux Flash Turbine runs on Red Hat 6.0+, SuSE Linux 6.1+, Turbo Linux 6.0, Debian 2.1+, and other popular Linux distributions.

Price

ASP Flash Turbine license: $395; Server Farm Pack (five licenses), $1,095.

Direct Flash Turbine license: $315; Server Farm Pack (five licenses), $915.

Linux Flash Turbine license: $355; Server Farm Pack (five licenses), $995.

Web site

http://www.blue-pac.com/

Feature-by-feature comparison with Generator

Note: A few features were still unknown to the authors at the time of this writing.

Uses Flash as UI/ development tool:
Flash Turbine: Yes Uses proprietary language **Generator:** Yes

Server-side customizations: Flash Turbine: Yes **Generator:** Yes

Multiplatform support: Flash Turbine: No **Generator:** Yes

Multithreaded: Flash Turbine: Unknown **Generator:** Yes

Multiprocessor support: Flash Turbine: Unknown **Generator:** Yes

Symbol replacement: Flash Turbine: Yes **Generator**: Yes

Multiple language/encoding support:
Flash Turbine: Unknown **Generator**: Yes

Text replacement: Flash Turbine: Yes **Generator**: Yes

Processed SWF files contain only used elements:
Flash Turbine: Yes **Generator**: Yes

Insert external images: Flash Turbine: Yes **Generator**: Yes

Customized Flash (SWF) movies: Flash Turbine: Yes **Generator**: Yes

Output as GIF: Flash Turbine: No **Generator**: Yes

Output as JPG: Flash Turbine: No **Generator**: Yes

Output as PNG: Flash Turbine: No **Generator**: Yes

Output as MOV: Flash Turbine: No **Generator**: Yes

Output as projector (Mac and PC): Flash Turbine: No **Generator**: Yes

Outputs image maps: Flash Turbine: No **Generator**: Yes

Output to multiple Flash versions: Flash Turbine: No **Generator**: Yes

Dynamic charts and graphs: Flash Turbine: Yes—Uses proprietary language **Generator**: Yes

Scrolling tickers and lists:
Flash Turbine: Yes—Uses proprietary language **Generator**: Yes

External MP3 insertion: Flash Turbine: No **Generator**: Yes

Supports additional dynamically created objects:
Flash Turbine: Yes—Uses proprietary language **Generator**: Yes

Replicates frames using database records:
Flash Turbine: Yes **Generator**: Yes

Native database connections: Flash Turbine: Yes—ODBC **Generator**: Yes

Caching support: Flash Turbine: Yes **Generator**: Yes

Logging: Flash Turbine: Yes—Errors only **Generator**: Yes

Transaction reporting: Flash Turbine: No **Generator**: Yes

Java API: Flash Turbine: No **Generator**: Yes

SAXESS WAVE (VISWEB)

Wave is a platform-independent Shockwave/Flash generator which is distinctive in that it has an XML interface. It uses a proprietary language, SWFML, which defines the XML form of the binary SWF format. Written entirely in Java, this tool is designed to convert any kind of XML-input data into Shockwave/Flash format (SWF).

This conversion ability is valuable due to expected widespread XSL transformation technology. The entire transformation language has been defined within the SWFML DTD. SAXESS also ships with a SVG-to-SWF converter.

Supported platforms

This tool appears to run anywhere the Java 2 platform is supported.

Price

Free

Web site

http://saxgate.saxess.com/visweb/

Features

Wave is designed to function exclusively as a conversion tool. If you have XML or SVG and want to use the SWFML DTD, this may be a tool worth exploring. Keep in mind, however, that conversion is all this tool does—at least for now. Flash and Generator support XML via the XML Object (Flash) and the XML Generator Object (Generator).

FORM2FLASH

Form2Flash makes use of HTML forms to change Flash movies in a very simplistic and limited way: It allows you to pass variables to SWF files along the URL to SWF movies via a form. Form2Flash is not a command-line tool; you can only use it as a CGI-bin application running on a Web server.

Supported platforms

Form2Flash is compatible with all Web servers on UNIX and Windows NT. The only requirement is that you have (access to) cgi-bin functionality on your Web server. A typical Form2Flash-installation consists of only two files: the executable and a configuration file. Form2Flash will work only when used as a cgi-bin program.

Price

Free (source code included)

Web site

http://www.kessels.com/Form2Flash/index.html

Features

For non-mission-critical applications that require only that text be replaced via a form, Form2Flash may be a good option. Typically, developers would use JavaScript to pass variables along the URL to a SWF. However, if for some reason your project requirements preclude relying on JavaScript, Form2Flash may be the tool for you. If you want to do anything besides replace text, however (and most developers do), you'll need to step up to Generator.

PopChart Image Server

PopChart Image Server Pro promotes easy integration with high-end Web application servers, as well as stability for high-traffic sites. The tool ships with a Java API, advanced image caching, load balancing, and patented data funneling technologies.

When reviewing other tools that support charting, compare their charting capabilities with those demonstrated in the charts in Chapter 6.

PopChart Image Server Pro uses a Java tool that runs on the server and generates dynamic images of charts and graphs that can be displayed in a Web browser as GIF (RLE), PNG, or Flash.

Supported platforms

PopChart Image Server can run on any Java-enabled platform.

Price

PopChart Image Server Pro and PopChart Builder, including one year of maintenance per server: $6,290.

Web site

http://www.popchart.com/

Feature-by-feature comparison with Generator

Note: A few features were still unknown to the authors at the time of this writing.

Uses Flash as UI/ development tool: PopChart: No **Generator:** Yes

Server-side customizations: PopChart: Yes **Generator:** Yes

Multiplatform support: PopChart: Yes **Generator:** Yes

Multithreaded: PopChart: Unknown **Generator:** Yes

Multiprocessor support: PopChart: Unknown **Generator:** Yes

Symbol replacement: PopChart: N/A **Generator:** Yes

Multiple language/encoding support:
PopChart: Unknown **Generator:** Yes

Text replacement: PopChart: N/A **Generator:** Yes

Processed SWF files contain only used elements:
PopChart: Yes **Generator:** Yes

Insert external images: PopChart: No **Generator:** Yes

Customized Flash (SWF) movies: PopChart: Yes **Generator:** Yes

Output as GIF: PopChart: Yes **Generator:** Yes

Output as JPG: PopChart: No **Generator:** Yes

Output as PNG: PopChart: Yes **Generator:** Yes

Output as MOV: PopChart: No **Generator:** Yes

Output as projector (Mac and PC): PopChart: No **Generator:** Yes

Outputs image maps: PopChart: Yes **Generator:** Yes

Output to multiple Flash versions: PopChart: Unknown **Generator:** Yes

Dynamic charts and graphs:
PopChart: Yes—Uses proprietary system **Generator:** Yes

Scrolling tickers and lists: PopChart: No **Generator:** Yes

External MP3 insertion: PopChart: No **Generator:** Yes

Supports additional dynamically created objects:
PopChart: Yes—Uses proprietary system **Generator:** Yes

Replicates frames using database records: PopChart: N/A **Generator:** Yes

Native database connections: PopChart: Yes **Generator:** Yes

Caching support: PopChart: Yes **Generator:** Yes

Logging: PopChart: Yes **Generator:** Yes

Transaction reporting: PopChart: Yes **Generator:** Yes

Java API: PopChart: Yes **Generator:** Yes

REPORTMILL

ReportMill uses a proprietary layout application to create placeholders for data, much like Flash does for Generator. This high-end page layout program creates sophisticated reports, templates, and visual displays of information in QuickTime, PDF, and Flash formats. Although Generator doesn't support PDF, we've found that most clients prefer to print from within Flash since it doesn't require an additional plug-in.

If your project needs to be deployed on Mac OS X or if it makes extensive use of WebObjects with support for PDF, this is a tool worth exploring.

Supported platforms

ReportMill is available for Windows NT and Mac OS X Server. The developer framework is available for these, and for additional platforms such as Solaris, HP/UX and OpenStep. A Java version of the framework is predicted to be released soon.

Price

Visit the Web site or call the latest ReportMill pricing. The related product, Web Objects, originally started at $50,000, but its price was reduced recently. Visit http://www.apple.com/webobjects/ for more information.

Web site

http://www.reportmill.com/

Feature-by-feature comparison with Generator

Note: A few features were still unknown to the authors at the time of this writing.

Uses Flash as UI/Development tool: ReportMill: No **Generator:** Yes

Server-side customizations: ReportMill: Yes **Generator:** Yes

Multiplatform support: ReportMill: Yes (NT and OSX) **Generator:** Yes

Multithreaded: **ReportMill:** Unknown **Generator:** Yes

Multiprocessor support: **ReportMill:** Unknown **Generator:** Yes

Symbol replacement: **ReportMill:** N/A **Generator:** Yes

Multiple language/encoding support:
ReportMill: Unknown **Generator:** Yes

Text replacement: **ReportMill:** N/A **Generator:** Yes

Processed SWF files contain only used elements:
ReportMill: Yes **Generator:** Yes

Insert external images: **ReportMill:** Yes **Generator:** Yes

Customized Flash (SWF) movies: **ReportMill:** Yes **Generator:** Yes

Output as GIF: **ReportMill:** No **Generator:** Yes

Output as JPG: **ReportMill:** No **Generator:** Yes

Output as PNG: **ReportMill:** No **Generator:** Yes

Output as MOV: **ReportMill:** Yes **Generator:** Yes

Output as projector (Mac and PC): **ReportMill:** No **Generator:** Yes

Outputs image maps: **ReportMill:** No **Generator:** Yes

Output to multiple Flash versions: **ReportMill:** Unknown **Generator:** Yes

Dynamic charts and graphs:
ReportMill: Yes—Uses proprietary authoring system **Generator:** Yes

Scrolling tickers and lists: **ReportMill:** No **Generator:** Yes

External MP3 insertion: **ReportMill:** No **Generator:** Yes

Supports additional dynamically created objects:
ReportMill: Yes—Uses proprietary authoring system **Generator:** Yes

Replicate frames using database records: **ReportMill:** N/A **Generator:** Yes

Native database connections: **ReportMill:** Yes **Generator:** Yes

Caching support: **ReportMill:** Yes **Generator:** Yes

Logging: **ReportMill:** Yes **Generator:** Yes

Transaction reporting: **ReportMill:** Yes **Generator:** Yes

Java API: **ReportMill:** Yes **Generator:** Yes

POINTS TO REMEMBER

- Developers are often asked to compare tools that perform similar functions to Generator as part of due diligence for clients, and Generator isn't the only game in town.

- While there are many tools that accomplish some of the functionality of Generator's features, features are not the only parts of a tool that make it desirable.

- When selecting a tool for getting dynamic content into Flash, you should consider all of the following: support, SDKs, open APIs, open formats, performance, scalability, and platform support. Let the demands of your project guide your choice.

- Although Generator is extremely powerful and flexible, there are some cases in which it may not be the best tool; thus, it's a good idea to know about the alternatives and the impact they might have on your project.

- New tools are always coming out. Be sure to check the provided links to ensure that the information contained in this chapter is accurate at the time of your reading.

CHAPTER 17

GENERATOR DEVELOPER RESOURCES

IN THIS CHAPTER YOU'LL FIND LISTS OF THE BOOKS WE KEEP ON OUR shelves as well as our bookmark links and the resources we use daily as professional Generator developers. Because Generator has an open architecture, developers who work with it must have multidisciplinary skill sets. We hope that the resources provided here inspire as well as teach.

Although some of the resources here may seem developer-specific, keep in mind that Generator requires a basic knowledge of the technologies involved. And since even designers are often asked to send Generator links to project teams and clients, our aim here is to keep you designing rather than searching the Web.

DASHBOARD

As a dynamically updated movie built into Flash 5, DashBoard provides direct access to the latest Flash and Generator resources from Macromedia and the Flash developer community. To access DashBoard, simply go to Help>Macromedia DashBoard.

The Macromedia
DashBoard in Flash 5.

GENERATOR WEB SITES

Flash and Generator go hand and hand; thus, the resources included here generally work well with both applications. We've also included links that team members often request, such as white papers, links to the authoring extensions, and FAQs.

Macromedia

http://www.macromedia.com/software/generator

At this URL, you'll find product info, reviews and awards, product resources, showcase, support and training, community, partners, related products, and downloads.

Macromedia Gallery

http://www.macromedia.com/software/generator/gallery/collection/

Macromedia Gallery contains case studies and links to a variety of Generator-developed Flash sites. Go here if you seek inspiration, or if you want to view projects similar to your own.

Generator Authoring Extensions

http://www.macromedia.com/software/generator/
download/extensions.html

Free, fully functional Generator authoring templates for Flash. These templates allow you to create, preview, and test Generator content.

Generator Maintenance Release Update

http://www.macromedia.com/software/generator/
download/maintenance_release/

This is the latest update to Generator. Make sure that you download and install this because it fixes some bugs and adds some functionality to Generator. Note that the updated authoring extensions will not work with the free trial edition of Generator.

Generator Support Center

http://www.macromedia.com/support/generator/

A great resource with tons of technotes, downloads, tutorials and information about Generator. This site usually posts three to four new technotes per week in the Generator section. If you get stuck while working with Generator, search the technotes here before you get too frustrated.

Generator Developer Edition free trial

http://www.macromedia.com/software/generator/trial/

After you've created your Generator content with the free authoring templates, test its performance with the free 30-day trial of Generator 2 Developer Edition.

Generator FAQ
http://www.macromedia.com/software/generator/productinfo/faq/

This information-packed Macromedia page has answers to many of the questions you'll be asked by clients and developers. Print it, memorize it, and sleep with it under your pillow!

Macromedia Flash / Generator Exchange
http://www.macromedia.com/exchange/flash/

This is the place to go to download new Generator objects and templates and Flash SmartClips.

MarkMe.com
http://www.markme.com

Probably the most extensive Generator resource site on the Web. Includes links to tutorials, forums, mailing lists, examples and FLAs as well an extensive list of Generator tips.

FlashKit
http://www.flashkit.com

This extremely popular community site includes source files, message boards, examples, and more. Macromedia trainers moderate the Generator message boards.

Were-Here.com
http://www.were-here.com

Has a very active Generator forum, as well as a few tutorials.

FlashGen
http://www.flashgen.com

This site includes several good tutorials and examples as well as a groovy full-screen Flash interface.

Generator Developers Network
http://www.gendev.net

Tutorials, source files, message boards, and examples are all available here. The site also includes several helpful tools for converting information to a Generator-friendly format (for example, Gen Code and ASCII Generator).

GenDev.net offers on-line tools such as GenCode and ASCII Generator for automating variables with ASP and ColdFusion

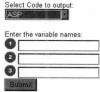

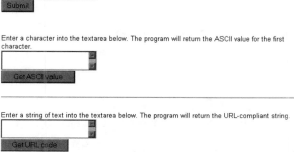

Helpful on-line URL encoding tool at GenDev.net

FlashLite

http://www.flashlite.net

This Flash and Generator resource site, run by Generator veterans, includes great articles, resources, and source files. Keep an eye on this site; there's always an interesting article or example file.

FlashMove

http://www.flashmove.com/gen/

This Flash and Generator resource site includes source files and message boards—all in a slick interface.

GENERATOR DATA SOURCES

In Chapter 15, we use news feeds from MoreOver to demonstrate the format Generator requires for lists and scrolling lists.

Generator can accept data in many forms, from Java classes to Oracle databases. In addition, a large number of news providers are beginning to format their data in XML as well as in a ready-to-use format for Generator. Either way, you can use the data to make extremely interactive and information-packed experiences.

MoreOver.com

http://w.moreover.com/categories/category_list_flashs.html

This site provides free news feeds preformatted for Generator.

GENERATOR NEWS GROUPS

Macromedia Generator

news://forums.macromedia.com/macromedia.generator

On this site, which is designed for both beginning and advanced Generator users, Macromedia engineers respond to questions on an almost hourly basis.

Macromedia Generator SDK

news://forums.macromedia.com/macromedia.generator.sdk

This group for users of the Generator SDK/API hosts discussions on developing, troubleshooting, and usage. When you need to dig deep, this is the place to go.

GENERATOR MAILING LISTS

Powerhouse Generator

http://chattyfig.figleaf.com/mailman/listinfo/powerhouse/

Generator mailing list run by Fig Leaf software that focuses on Generator-related questions and issues.

Flasher

http://www.chinwag.com/flasher/

This site provides an unmoderated discussion forum for Flash and Generator developers. Think carefully before you subscribe, however, because traffic can amount to 200 to 400 messages per day.

FlashCoders

http://chattyfig.figleaf.com/mailman/listinfo/flashcoders

Although the primary function of the FlashCoders mailing list is to provide an online community for Flash 5 programmers, Generator is often part of the discussions.

GENERATOR WHITE PAPERS

Macromedia Generator white papers describe in detail how Generator works as well as how it integrates with other technologies. On average, we get at least three requests per week for this link from team members and clients.

http://www.macromedia.com/software/generator/productinfo/whitepapers/

FLASH WEB SITES

Macromedia

http://www.macromedia.com/software/flash

This site contains product info, reviews and awards, product resources, showcase, support and training, community, Flash exchange, related products, and downloads. If it's Flash, it's here.

Macromedia Gallery

http://www.macromedia.com/software/flash/gallery/collection/

The Gallery contains case studies and links to a variety of Flash sites. Get inspired, and get funky.

Flash Deployment Kit

http://www.macromedia.com/software/flash/download/deployment_kit/

The Macromedia Flash Deployment Kit makes it easy for developers and first-time users to employ Flash content (SWF) on their Web sites.

Flash JavaScript Kit

http://www.macromedia.com/software/dreamweaver/
productinfo/extend/jik_flash5_index.fhtml

Are you deploying Flash and need to use JavaScript? By using Flash and JavaScript together, you can control the user's experience by manipulating Flash Player. To facilitate interface design, Flash Player uses JavaScript and HTML to interact with the browser. This kit helps automate that process with Dreamweaver.

Flash File Format FAQ

http://www.macromedia.com/software/flash/open/licensing/
fileformat/faq.html

This FAQ contains everything you need to know to make and license Frankenstein-like creations of Flash.

Were-here

http://www.were-here.com

This popular and useful Flash help site contains tutorials, discussion boards, and more.

FlashKit

http://www.flashkit.com/

This extremely popular community site includes source files, message boards, examples, and more. Macromedia trainers moderate the Generator message boards.

Moock.org

http://www.moock.org/webdesign/flash/

Colin Moock's great Flash resource site includes ActionScript, tutorials, JavaScript, and more.

Flashmagazine

http://www.flashmagazine.com/

The online Flashmagazine includes articles, tutorials, and interviews, along with a nice data-driven interface.

FlashLite

http://www.flashlite.net

On this Flash and Generator resource site—which is run by Generator veterans—you'll find great articles, resources, and source files. This is a good site to check frequently for interesting articles and example files.

Flashzone

http://www.flashzone.com

This Flash help site includes tutorials, discussion boards, and so on.

FlashPlanet

http://www.flashplanet.com/

This site includes resources, articles, tutorials, and more.

ShockFusion

http://www.shockfusion.com/gotflash.html

This free resource for Flash developers comes with a slick interface.

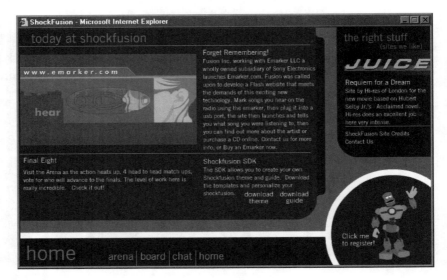

OpenSWF.org

http://www.openswf.org/

This site contains everything you need to know about the SWF file format.

FLASH NEWS GROUPS

Macromedia Flash

news://forums.macromedia.com/macromedia.flash

This group hosts discussions on installation, troubleshooting, and general usage.

FLASH MAILING LISTS

Flasher

http://www.chinwag.com/flasher/

This site provides an unmoderated discussion forum for Flash and Generator developers.

FlashCoders

http://chattyfig.figleaf.com/mailman/listinfo/flashcoders

The primary function of the Flashcoders mailing list is to provide an online community for Flash 5 programmers. However, Generator is often part of the discussions.

FLASH AND GENERATOR CLASSES

Macromedia University

http://macromedia.elementk.com/

Offering beginner and advanced online courses, Macromedia University offers affordable online Macromedia Flash 5 training.

UDA

http://www.uda.com

As the nation's premier new-media and Internet training company, United Digital Artists offers intensive, highly acclaimed courses and certificate programs for creative professionals who need Flash and Generator training.

Fig Leaf

http://www.figleaf.com

Fig Leaf's intensive classes take students through the complex world of advanced Flash and Generator programming. These are probably the most advanced Flash and Generator classes available.

FLASH AND GENERATOR EVENTS

One of the primary benefits of being Flash and Generator developers is the community it offers. Every year, Woodstock-like Flash and Generator events feature instruction by the industry's top talent. In coming years, we hope to see you at these events with your Generator projects!

Macromedia UCON

http://www.macromedia.com/macromedia/events/

UCON, Macromedia's user conference provides four days of intensive, comprehensive training led by the experts: Macromedia's engineers and developers.

FlashForward2001

http://www.flashforward2001.com

FlashForward2001 is jam-packed with keynotes, how-to sessions, in-depth site deconstructions, animation panels, and showcases of products, such as Flash, Generator, LiveMotion, that write to the Macromedia SWF file format. There's a good chance you'll meet this book's authors there!

FLASH BOOKS

Often programmers are eager to learn the Flash basics quickly and then dive right into Generator development. The books listed here should serve as excellent tutorials and references for even the savviest Flash developers.

ActionScript: The Definitive Guide

by Colin Moock
O'Reilly & Associates
ISBN: 1-56592-852-0

As the title implies, this is the definitive guide on ActionScript written by one of the top Flash developers in the world.

Flash 5! Creative Web Animation
by Derek Franklin and Brooks Patton
Macromedia Press
ISBN: 0-201-71969-X

This comprehensive guide to Flash 5 serves as a great companion to this book.

Flash 5 Magic
by David J. Emberton, J. Scott Hamlin
New Riders Publishing
ISBN: 0735710236

A concise book with great examples.

Flash Web Design
by Hillman Curtis
New Riders Publishing
ISBN: 0735708967

Flash instruction with a motion-graphics focus.

Flash 5 Bible
by Robert Reinhardt, Jon Warren Lentz
IDG Books Worldwide
ISBN: 0764533568

This book's name says it all.

OTHER SERVER-BASED TOOLS FOR DELIVERING DYNAMIC FLASH CONTENT

See chapter 16 for a description of each of these products and how they compare to Generator.

In Chapter 16 we explored each of the following products. As a Generator developer, you'll often be asked how these compare and contrast with Generator and which product is best suited for particular projects. Keep these sites handy.

Swift Generator

http://swift-tools.com

Swift-Generator is a dynamic Flash content generator.

Flash Turbine

http://www.blue-pac.com/

ASP Flash Turbine 4.1 is a dynamic Flash engine that will add live content to Flash movies.

SwiffTools

http://swifftools.com/stools/

SwiffPEG and SwiffEG Server insert MP3 files into SWFs much like Generator.

VisWeb

http://saxgate.saxess.com/visweb/

XML/XSL-to-SWF converter for the XML Flash developer.

Form2Flash

http://www.kessels.com/Form2Flash/index.html

Form2Flash uses html forms to change Flash movies in a simplistic way.

PopChart Image Server
http://www.popchart.com/

This dynamic charting server offers advanced charting capabilities.

ReportMill
http://www.reportmill.com/

Dynamic PDF and Flash. Very Generator-like.

JGenerator
http://www.flashgap.com

JGenerator is a dynamic Flash content generator. It tries to emulate the Macromedia Generator behavior and functionality. It is a completely different product than Macromedia Generator.

DEVICE RESOURCES

See Chapter 12 for creating data-driven content for mobile devices.

In Chapter 12, we created content for PDAs, set-top boxes, and Web phones. The following resources will help you prepare and deploy that content.

Developing for the UP.browser
http://www.phone.com/products/upbrowser.html

Once you've created data-driven graphics, you'll want to deploy them on cell phones that use specific phone browsers. Phone.com is the leading provider of the popular UP.browser. This site offers developer resources, source files, and discussion boards.

Supporting WAP
http://www.wapforum.org/

If you're embedding your data-driven graphics in WML pages (the language needed to deliver content via the Wireless Application Protocol, or WAP), look here for WAP information.

Gelon

http://www.gelon.net

This is a great site for testing your WML content after you've created data-driven graphics.

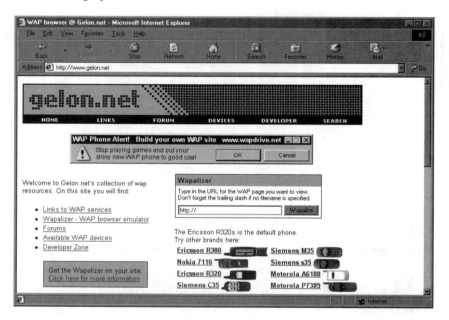

Creating content for AvantGo

http://avantgo.com/developer/reference/tutorials/
jumpstart/jumpstart.html

If you're deploying content to mobile devices using the AvantGo delivery software, this site has the guidelines you'll need to follow.

PROGRAMMING AND BACK-END RESOURCE WEB SITES

The following bookmarks come from people who earn their livings working on Generator sites. The fact that Generator is such an open, robust system means that you often need to know something about various middleware and back-end systems. We hope these resources help you as much as they've helped us with our Generator projects.

ASP Web sites

Microsoft

http://msdn.microsoft.com/workshop/server/

This one-stop resource for ASP and Microsoft technologies will come in handy if your project is ASP based.

Microsoft Web and Application Services

http://www.microsoft.com/windows2000/guide/server/features/appsvcs.asp

This is Microsoft's guide to the application development services needed to build integrated, component-based applications that take advantage of the Internet.

ASP Components and Objects

http://www.aspobjects.com

You can use these downloadable, searchable ASP objects to extend ASP for Generator-based projects.

ASP Today

http://www.asptoday.com

This site includes good hard-to-find information about ASP.

Active Server Corner

http://www.kamath.com

This site provides in-depth information on ASP and more.

Free ASP

http://www.aspfree.com

Free ASP components and tutorials.

Apache Web sites

Apache HTTP Server Project

http://httpd.apache.org/

The Apache Project site is a collaborative software development resource aimed at creating a robust, commercial-grade, feature-rich, and freely available source-code implementation of an HTTP (Web) server.

Apache SSL

http://www.apache-ssl.org/

Apache SSL is a secure Web server based on Apache and SSLeay/OpenSSL. If you're using Apache and Generator, and need to employ SSL for security, this is the place to go.

ColdFusion Web sites

Allaire

http://www.allaire.com/developer/referenceDesk/index.cfm

Allaire is the creator of JRun and ColdFusion, the servlet engine that ships with Generator. The ColdFusion Developer's center offers articles and developer forums.

FlashCFM

http://www.flashcfm.com

A very useful site focusing on using Flash with Cold Fusion.

iPlanet Application Server Web sites

iPlanet
http://www.iplanet.com/products/infrastructure/
app_servers/

This site is an excellent resource for iPlanet Application Server, the industry's first to achieve the rigorous J2EE certification. iPlanet is fully supported as a servlet engine with Generator.

Netscape
http://developer.netscape.com

Netscape's developer site includes tools, tutorials, and discussion groups.

Java

JGuru
http://www.jguru.com

This community-oriented developer site is devoted to advancing software technology and development via Java. If you're creating anything in Java for your Generator project, you'll find yourself visiting this site.

Sun
http://java.sun.com

This Web site is devoted to the various products that Sun supports and creates. If it's Java, it's here.

ServerSide
http://theserverside.com/home/index.jsp

This online community is dedicated to Enterprise JavaBeans (EJB) and the Java 2 Platform, Enterprise Edition (J2EE).

JavaScript

Website Abstraction

http://www.wsabstract.com/

This site includes tutorials, sample files, articles, and discussions about building JavaScript projects.

ECMA

http://www.ecma.ch

ActionScript is based on this organization's standards. This is a good place to go to determine whether certain JavaScript functions and methods are supported with Flash.

JSP Web sites

Sun

http://java.sun.com/products/jsp/

This is Sun's developer resource site for Java Server pages, supporting technologies, and products. Developers working on projects using JSP will find this site a great resource.

JGuru

http://www.jguru.com

This community-oriented developer site is devoted to advancing and improving software technology and development using Java.

JRun

Allaire

http://www.allaire.com/developer/jrunreferencedesk/

Allaire is the creator of JRun and ColdFusion, the servlet engine that ships with Generator. This site contains resources for JRun developers and users, including articles, technical papers, and case studies.

Linux

RedHat

http://www.redhat.com

This site includes community support as well as information on installing, configuring, and tweaking for RedHat Linux. If you need to deploy on Linux, this sites provides a good starting point.

Linux Documentation Project

http://www.linuxdoc.org/

This site is devoted to the open system of Linux documentation—from the basics to securing, installing, and administering Linux.

MySQL

MySql.com

http://www.mysql.com
http://www.mysql.com/information/links.html

This is the resource site for the open-source relational database management system.

Oracle

Oracle

http://www.oracle.com/ip/deploy/database/

This is Oracle's product and support hub for its database products.

DBASupport

http://www.dbasupport.com/dsc/ora8/

This site provides a one-stop source for Oracle database administration support and resources.

PHP

PHP.net

http://www.php.net

This site is devoted to development, documentation, and PHP support. If you're developing middleware applications with Generator and PHP, this is a good starting point for support.

PHP Builder

http://www.phpbuilder.com

This site is devoted to the creation of real-world PHP applications.

PHP Flash Functions

http://www.php.net/manual/ref.swf.php

This site contains documentation on PHP and creating Flash files via a libswf module.

Solaris

Sun

http://www.sun.com/solaris

This site provides support and development assistance for the Solaris Operating System.

SQL Server

Microsoft

http://www.microsoft.com/sql/

This site provides service and support for the MS SQL database product.

XML

IBM XML ZONE
http://www.ibm.com/developer/xml/

IBM's XML resource site contains articles, case studies, tutorials, discussion groups, and more.

JDOM
http://www.jdom.org

This site provides the information you need to build a complete Java-based solution for accessing, manipulating, and outputting XML data from Java code. If you're creating Generator objects and using XML, this is a popular API.

Apache XML Project
http://xml.apache.org

Home of Xerces (an XML parser for Java), this site provides information on producing commercial-quality XML solutions related to Apache.

World Wide Web Consortium

W3C.org
http://www.w3c.org

W3C develops interoperable technologies (specifications, guidelines, software, and tools) for the Web. This is a good place to go to keep abreast of emerging standards such as SVG and WML so that you can formulate long-term project strategies.

PROGRAMMING AND BACK-END RESOURCE NEWS GROUPS

http://www.dejanews.com/usenet

Since busy Generator developers rarely have time to read all of the news groups daily (except, of course, for the Generator ones), Deja news provides a quick way to search programming-related newsgroups for answers to specific questions.

PROGRAMMING AND BACK-END RESOURCE BOOKS

These are the books we have on the shelves directly above our desks. Although some of them are quite advanced, they offer a great deal of useful information. And because Generator works with so many systems and products, it would be difficult to encompass all of these topics in just one book.

ASP 3.0 Programmer's Reference
by Wrox Team, Dan Denault, Brian Francis, Matthew Gibbs, David
    Sussman, Chris Ullman
Wrox Press
ISBN: 1861003234

Mastering ColdFusion 4.5
by Arman Danesh, Kristin Aileen Motlagh
Sybex
ISBN: 0782127738

Learning Java
by Pat Niemeyer, Jonathan B. Knudsen
O'Reilly & Associates
ISBN: 1565927184

Beginning Java 2
by Ivor Horton
Wrox Press, Inc.
ISBN: 1861002238

Java in a Nutshell
by David Flanagan
O'Reilly & Associates
ISBN: 1565924878

Professional Java Server Programming - J2EE Edition
by Subrahmanyam Allamaraju, Andrew Longshaw, Daniel O'Connor,
   and more.
Wrox Press, Inc.
ISBN: 1861004656

Javascript: The Definitive Guide
by David Flanagan
O'Reilly & Associates
ISBN: 1565923928

Web Development with Java Server Pages
by Duane K. Fields, Mark A. Kolb
Manning Publication Co.
ISBN: 1884777996

Professional Java XML Programming with servlets and JSP
by Alexander Nakhimovsky, Tom Myers
Wrox Press
ISBN: 1861002858

Professional Php Programming
by Harish Rawat, Sascha Schumann, Chris Scollo, Jesus M. Castagnetto,
   Deepak T. Veliath
Wrox Press
ISBN: 1861002963

Java and XML (O'Reilly Java Tools)

by Brett McLaughlin, Mike Loukides
O'Reilly & Associates
SBN: 0596000162

Professional WAP

by Charles Arehart, Nirmal Chidambaram, Shashirikan Guruprasad,
    and more.
Wrox Press, Inc.
ISBN: 1861004044

POINTS TO REMEMBER

- Generator requires a multidisciplinary skill set and an awareness of many technologies.

- Macromedia provides some of the best community resources and events for Flash and Generator developers.

- The DashBoard provides a window into the Flash and Generator community, all within the familiar Flash Interface.

- The Flash and Generator development community offers many resource sites, training opportunities, and events that developers can use to keep abreast of the latest bugs, updates, and award-winning sites.

- Designers and developers are often asked to provide FAQs, white papers, and product comparisons to team members and/or clients. This chapter points you where to get that information.

- Because Generator is Java based, the links and resources included here are very Java-centric.

APPENDIXES

APPENDIX A

DATA-SOURCE SUMMARY FOR GENERATOR OBJECTS

The following table summarizes the data-source information for all of the Generator objects (including both the required and optional columns for each object):

Optional object	Required columns	Generator columns
Line Chart	Value: the relative height of a point in a chart	Hlabel: the label on the horizontal axis Color: the color of the line Note: To specify multiple data sources for line or scatter charts, create a semicolon-delimited list of the data sources.
Area Chart	Value: the relative height of a point in a chart	Hlabel: the label on the horizontal axis
Bar Chart	Value: the relative height of a bar in the chart	Color: the color of the bar chart URL: any valid URL Window: choose one: _self, _blank, _parent, _top Hlabel: text for label on horizontal axis Goto: frame number in parent timeline Gotolabel: label in parent timeline Note: Adding URL, Goto, or Gotolabel makes the bar a button that takes the user to a specified location when it is clicked.

Optional object	Required columns	Generator columns
Stacked Bar Chart, Stacked Area Chart, or **Stacked Line Chart**	Color: the color of a bar in the chart Value: a series of columns, Value1, Value2, Value3, and so on	
Scatter Chart and **Scatter Line Chart**	X: the X position of a point on the chart Y: the Y position of a point on the chart Clip: required if using the Plot command	Symbol: a symbol containing formatting for the plotted points (if a symbol is not specified, the points are plotted with dots) Color: used for the system default shape Hlabel: defines the text for the label on the horizontal axis. Optional for Plot command: X-scale: the X-scale of the movie clip Y-scale: the Y-scale of the movie clip Rotate: rotation of the movie clip
Stock Chart	Open: the open value Close: the close value High: the high value Low: the low value	Hlabel: the text for labels on the horizontal axis
Pie Chart	Value: the size of the pie slice in the chart Color: the color of the pie slice	URL: any valid URL Window: choose one: _self, _blank, _parent, _top Goto: frame number in the parent timeline Gotolabel: frame label in the parent timeline Note: Adding URL, Goto, or Gotolabel makes the pie slice a button that takes the user to a specified location when it is clicked.

Optional object	Required columns	Generator columns
Plot	Clip: the name of the symbol to insert from the library	X-scale: a decimal scale factor to be applied to the horizontal scale of the symbol
	X: an integer value representing the horizontal position of the symbol's center point relative to the upper left corner of the Plot area (bounding box)	Y-scale: a decimal scale factor to be applied to the vertical scale of the symbol
		Valid values for both X- and Y- scale are 0.0 to 10.0, where 1.0 represents no change in scaling
	Y: an integer value representing the vertical position of the symbol's center point relative to the upper left corner of the Plot area (bounding box)	Rotation: a decimal value specifying the angle of rotation applied to the symbol; rotation is around the center point; negative numbers rotate the symbol to the left, positive numbers, to the right
List, Scrolling List, and *Ticker*	Clip: the name of the symbol to be inserted into the list; the list contains as many items as there are rows in the data source	
List, Scrolling List, and *Ticker*	Clip: the name of the symbol to be inserted into the list; the list contains as many items as there are rows in the data source	
Multipage List	Text: the text for the list element	Symbol: a symbol containing a graphic for a list element, or special text formatting for list elements
		URL: any valid URL
		Window: choose one: _self, _blank, _parent, _top. Default value is _self
		Note: Adding URL makes the list element a link that takes the user to a specified location when it is clicked.

Optional object	Required columns	Generator columns
Radio Button	Text: the text to appear next to each radio button; one radio button is created for each row in the data source	Variable: columns having the same name as variables inside symbol files; there should be one column for each variable to replace
Table	Clip: the name of the symbol to be inserted in the table; this must be the first column in the data source.	Variable: columns having the same name as variables inside symbol files; there should be one column for each variable to replace.

APPENDIX B

GENERATE OPTIONS

Offline Generator has several options (command-line switches) that modify the default operation of the program. See chapter 9 for detailed information on most of these:

-help: displays usage text.

-swf <filename.swf>: outputs a Flash movie.

-gif <filename.gif>: outputs a GIF movie.

-png <filename.png>: outputs a PNG image.

-qtm <filename.mov>: outputs a QuickTime 4.0 movie.

-jpg <filename.jpg>: outputs a JPEG image.

-txt <filename.txt>: outputs text within the movie.

-smap <filename.map>: outputs a server-side image map.

-cmap <filename.map>: outputs a client-side image map.

-cmapname <name>: sets client-side image map tag name.

-xwin32 <filename.exe>: outputs a Win32 projector.

-xmacppc <filename.hqx>: outputs a Mac PPC projector.

-debug <1|2|3>: specifies the debug log level.

-log <filename.txt>: specifies the debug log file.

-param <name> <value>: specifies a named parameter.

-pngBitDepth <8|24|32>:specifies the bit depth with which a PNG image should be rendered.

-defaultsize <w> <h>: specifies the default width and height of outputted images.

-bgcolor <color>: specifies the background color of the output.

-exactfit: on image output, scales contents to fit exactly within movie bounds.

-font <path>: specifies the location to search for Generator external font files.

APPENDIX C

HEX VALUES FOR URL ENCODING

Hex values for the following commonly used characters:

Tab	09	<	3C	|	7C		
Space	20	>	3E	}	7D		
"	22	@	40	~	7E		
(	28	[	5B	?	3F		
)	29	\	5C	&	26		
,	2C	]	5D	/	2F		
.	2E	^	5E	=	3D		
;	3B	`	60	#	23		
:	3A	{	7B	%	25		

A % sign tells the decoding routines that encoding has begun. The next two characters are HEX numbers that correspond to the ASCII equivalent value of space. So to encode : (a colon) you would encode as %3A; / would encode as %2F; and ? would encode as %3F.

Always URL encode your query strings. The way this is handled is not just a Flash thing. It's also a browser and server thing. To keep things as reliable as possible, always URL encode.

Here's a poor man's tool for URL encoding:

1. **Create an empty HTML page with this code:**

```
<FORM METHOD=GET>
<INPUT NAME=name>
<INPUT TYPE=SUBMIT>
</FORM>
```

2. *Open the page in a browser.*

3. *Type in the value that you need encoded.*

4. *Click Submit.*

5. *Look at the resulting location in your browser.*

The value you typed in follows ?name=

Note that both name and value in a Name/Value pair should be URL encoded. Most software tools provide methods for URL encoding strings (Perl, ASP, Java). The reason you did not need to encode values when testing your FLA is you have given the test environment Name/Value pairs for testing. The test interface doesn't require URL encoded string because you are not providing the values as part of a query string.

INDEX

How to Use the CD-ROM

1. Insert the CD-ROM into your computer's CD-ROM drive.

2. For Windows 95/98/NT/2000: Double-click the My Computer icon, find the CD-ROM icon (usually drive D), and double-click it.

   For Macintosh: Double-click the icon that appears on the desktop.

   For Linux/Solaris: If your CD-ROM drive does not auto-mount, then mount the drive and access the CD-ROM via the name you specified when mounting the drive.

3. Look in the individual chapter folders for files associated with each chapter. Look in the DEMOS folder for shareware and other types of products you can try out.

DATE DUE